THE STRANGE JOURNEY OF THE CONFEDERATE CONSTITUTION

MERCER
UNIVERSITY

MERCER UNIVERSITY PRESS

Endowed by

TOM WATSON BROWN
and
THE WATSON-BROWN FOUNDATION, INC.

THE STRANGE JOURNEY OF THE CONFEDERATE CONSTITUTION *and* OTHER STORIES FROM GEORGIA'S HISTORICAL PAST

WILLIAM RAWLINGS

MERCER UNIVERSITY PRESS
MACON, GEORGIA
2017

MUP/ H939

Published by Mercer University Press
1501 Mercer University Drive
Macon, Georgia 31207

9 8 7 6 5 4 3 2 1

Books published by Mercer University Press are printed on acid-free paper that meets the requirements of the American National Standard for Information Sciences—Permanence of Paper for Printed Library Materials.

ISBN 978-0-88146-626-3
Cataloging-in-Publication Data is available from the Library of Congress

For Laura Ashley

CONTENTS

Introduction: A Sense of Place ix

Part I: The Early Days 1783–1815 1

Overview 3

Chapter 1: The (Re)Invention of the Cotton Gin 7

Chapter 2: The Great Yazoo Fraud 17

Chapter 3: The Pine Barrens Speculation 29

Part II: The Civil War Era 1861–1865 41

Overview 43

Chapter 4: The Saga of the Lost Confederate Treasure 47

Chapter 5: The Capture of Jefferson Davis from Both a Southern and Northern Perspective 55

Chapter 6: The Strange Journey of the Confederate Constitution 75

Part III: The Reconstruction Era 1865–1877 85

Overview 87

Chapter 7: Conflict and Compromise: The Political Nature of Reconstruction 91

Chapter 8: The Freedman's Land Insurrection of 1875 107

Part IV: The Lost Cause Years 1865–1939 123

Overview 125

Chapter 9: Gutzon Borglum and the Lost Stone Mountain Confederate Memorial 131

Chapter 10: The Drum Returns Home 151

Chapter 11: The Lost Cause on the Silver Screen 157

Part V: The Golden Age of Cotton and Its Aftermath 1915–1925 167

Overview 169

Chapter 12: A Vast Pool of Oil 173
Chapter 13: A Killing on Ring Jaw Bluff 185
Chapter 14: The Myth of the Boll Weevil 205
Part VI: The Ku Klux Klan 1915–1930 215
Overview 217
Chapter 15: The Second Coming of the Invisible Empire 219
Chapter 16: Reign of Terror: The Ku Klux Klan of the 1920s in Macon, Georgia 239
Epilogue 255
The Jaybird Wray Episode 257
Appendix 261
Exploring Our Past: A Short Practical Guide to Historical Research for Writers 261
Chapter Notes 275
Acknowledgements 279
Sources and Further Reading 281
Index 285

INTRODUCTION

A SENSE OF PLACE

I do most of my writing in what was at one time the meeting room of the local Masonic Lodge. It's the ideal spot for such, a bright sunny space overlooking Sandersville's city square, whose east-facing windows light up my mornings while shielding me from the harsh rays of the afternoon sun. The Masonic Building, which I purchased a number of years ago, is one of the more prominent structures on the square. It was built in 1924 to replace the lodge on this site that burned in 1921, which itself was built in 1856 to replace the lodge that burned in the Great Fire of 1855. As nearly as I can figure, there has been a Masonic lodge on this very spot since 1847.

As small towns go, the square itself is a thing of beauty. It was laid out in a symmetrical fashion after the 1855 fire, designed to be the hub of business and government for the young, yet growing, county. The dominant structure is an imposing red brick Victorian-style courthouse, set somewhat off-center toward the north and facing what was at one time a large village green. The open area in front of the courthouse, which for most of the nineteenth century was the site of the public cotton scale, has since been encroached upon by parking, leaving a sliver of greenery shaded under an ancient elm tree. There are benches and an open-air bandstand, another relic of a bygone era now used most often for impromptu weddings performed by the county probate judge. It is here that I sometimes take a break from writing, sitting in the shade as I observe the comings and goings of the rural county seat.

From my perspective, there in the shade of the elm in the middle of the city square, one cannot help but have a deep sense of the historic past. For more than 200 years, an observer seated in this one single spot would have witnessed a pageant of events great and small that shaped the history of this community, this state, and, indeed, the South. It's different today; times have changed. With the exception of the courthouse, not a single building that surrounds me is used for its original purpose. Yet, within a radius of a hundred yards of where I sit facing the courthouse, there are traces of the past, some tangible, others unseen.

Just behind me, at the southeast corner of the square, is the site of Saunders's Store, an eighteenth-century frontier trading post. Immediately in front of where I sit stands a white marble obelisk erected by the state of Georgia in 1856 in praise of Gov. Jared Irwin. The time-worn letters carved on its base commemorate Irwin's bravery as an Indian fighter, his service to the new Republic during the Revolution, and his signing of the Rescinding Act, the undoing of the Great Yazoo Fraud. It was in 1796 during Irwin's administration that Sandersville was designated as the county seat, taking its name from a misspelling of Saunders. To my right is a plaque honoring Thomas Hardwick, another governor with local ties who served the state more than a century later. Though not recorded in the inscription, it was Hardwick's opposition to the Ku Klux Klan that brought his political career to an early end.

Looking about, there are remnants of lesser, more personal, tales as well. Toward the north side of the square I can see the elegant Holt Building, its Italianate design the work of the famous architect Charles E. Choate. Constructed in 1898 and former home to the Holt Banking Company, its glory days came to an abrupt end during the economic collapse of the late 1920s, sending its once-wealthy owner to federal prison for bank fraud. Just to the east of me, my great-uncle and a close friend killed one another in 1893 in a senseless shoot-out involving family pride.

On a grander scale, it was on this spot in the early morning fog of November 26, 1864, that Confederate troops under the command of Gen. Joseph Wheeler fought a rearguard skirmish with Sherman's regiments, resulting in the deaths of several soldiers on both sides. There was a courthouse here then, as well, a grandiloquent brick structure with arches, columns, and a staircase that would benefit a Greek temple. The Yankees were said to have taken fire from the building, one of Sherman's justifications in ordering it torched. A bit more than a decade later, in August 1875, the courthouse green served as a stockade to imprison the dozens of freed slaves who had plotted to commit mass murder in order to form an independent nation known as Freedman's Land.

For more than two centuries, this one small patch of ground has borne witness to the community's successes and failures, to its joys and sorrows, to war and to peace. Each of these events is part of the greater story of the South, flowing like small tributaries into history's stream. Many writers have spoken of the Southerner's "sense of place," an ill-defined term often interpreted as meaning a physical locality that defines one's heritage, ethos, and view of the world at large. To me, it is possible that this location, in the middle of a small town in a sparsely populated community on the edge of the Coastal Plain halfway between the sea and the mountains, is one of those special places. I would like to think so, anyway.

This work is a collection of what I refer to as "stories," written accounts of some of the people, places, and things that are part of the history of Georgia and, often, the history of the South. Somewhat more than half have previously appeared in print in *Georgia Backroads* magazine.[1] Having a longstanding interest in our shared past, I find that many of the riveting tales of the past two-plus centuries can be told in a shorter format, to be read independently and at leisure. To facilitate the enjoyment of reading and to encourage further investigation by those wishing to know more, I have adopted a somewhat less formal format than the usual work of history. Major sources that served as references for individual articles are listed in an annotated bibliography at the end of each chapter. Footnotes have been kept to a minimum.

The book is divided into sections based on era, with each comprised of chapters whose events occurred during that timeframe. I begin the sections with a brief overview and descriptions of the articles that follow. Each chapter is written as a stand-alone piece. It is not necessary to read what precedes or follows it to enjoy the "story." I anticipate readers will have a varying degree of interest in the individual topics and can thus read the book in whatever order they choose. Because of the independent format of each chapter, there may be some redundancy between the introductory overview and/or the content of some of the chapters. This is deliberate.

The chapters themselves have varying formats. Most center on an interesting and important episode, person, or period in Georgia or Southern history. Three are essays expressing my opinion as an author and are offered, in part, to stimulate thought and discussion among readers. At the end of each chapter, there is an annotated bibliography titled "Sources and Resources." This section lists the primary sources consulted in the writing of the article as well as other sources that can offer additional information on the topic for readers wishing to learn more.

---

[1] See chapter notes regarding previous sites of publication and related comments.

In addition to appealing to readers interested in Georgia and Southern history, I would like to think this book would serve well as a supplemental reading source in college and Advanced Placement high school history courses. To facilitate the process of historical research for those interested in such, the appendix includes an instructional essay titled "Exploring Our Past: A Short Practical Guide to Historical Research for Writers." In it, I outline what I think are the basics of doing research when writing on historical subjects and provide information on a number of resource sites to speed the process.

Each locality, each state, and each region of America has its own history, its own stories to be passed down from generation to generation. I trust that readers will find the ones presented here both interesting and memorable.

PART I

THE EARLY DAYS: 1783–1815

OVERVIEW

THE EARLY DAYS 1783–1815

We often think of early America as a land of bold men in powdered wigs championing the primacy of life, liberty, and the pursuit of happiness while forever enshrining the concept of individual rights in the documents that created our nation. In certain situations, that scenario might have been accurate. To many, however, America represented a vast wildness to be tamed, with the lure of personal freedom tempered by the risks of life at the far reaches of civilization. Such was the case in Georgia. In 1780, during the latter years of the Revolution, the state's estimated population was a mere 56,000, the majority of whom lived within a few miles of the coast or on navigable portions of the lower Savannah River. In contrast to its modest number of inhabitants, Georgia's lands were seemingly limitless, stretching from the Atlantic coast to the Mississippi River, ancestral home to a number of Amerindian tribes. While life in the more established settlements might offer some degree of comfort, existence on the frontier could have been aptly described by the words of one seventeenth-century philosopher: "No arts; no letters; no society; and which is worst of all, continual fear, and danger of violent death; and the life of man, solitary, poor, nasty, brutish and short."[1]

During the early years of its existence as a state, the most important thing Georgia had to offer would-be citizens was land. Often ignoring issues of tenuous title and competing claims of ownership, settlers pushed steadily westward, attracted by an uncomplicated route to citizenship and a policy of liberal land grants. While settlers sought the chance to create a new life, land speculators saw the opportunity of quick profits in the buying and selling of vast tracts of raw territory. Unfortunately for the state's history, it is these scandals for which this era is most often remembered.

---

[1] From Thomas Hobbs's *Leviathan* (Chapter XIII), a 1651 treatise on social contract and governance.

Between the end of the Revolution and the formal adoption of the United States Constitution of 1789, Georgia existed as a semi-independent state under the Articles of Confederation. The state's governing body, initially a single governing assembly and later a bicameral legislature, functioned in the early days like a modern city council, addressing not only the great issues but what most might consider mundane minutiae. The right of citizenship was granted freely based on minimal residency requirements or the demonstration that the applicant had not fought on the side of the British during the Revolution. Many actions pertaining to local concerns, routine business practice, and personal issues required legislative action. These included, for example, the appointment of local sheriffs and tax collectors, the charting of corporations, and the granting of divorces. In fact, obtaining a divorce in Georgia required an act of the legislature until 1833, after which time the matter became an issue to be decided by the courts.

To become a successful state, Georgia needed to grow in population. The only practical way to increase population in the short term was through an influx of new settlers. Perhaps more so than anything else, the greatest attraction the state had to offer were her western lands. As these were settled, tax revenues would increase, allowing the funding of the many necessities of state government. During the first decades after the Revolution, the issuing of grants from the vast reserves of state-owned territory became of necessity a major concern in state policy. This task fell to the legislature or to special agencies created under its auspices.

In early America, land was one of the few things that had real economic value, and, as such, represented a mighty temptation to those willing to bend or break existing moral and legal codes. If the Yazoo land scandals were representative of the normality of the day, corruption among the legislators appears to have been rampant. The so-called Pine Barrens Speculation would suggest that this extended to much of the land-grant system of the state and the executive branch of government as well.

One of the most important events of the early postcolonial period was Eli Whitney's perfection of a new type of cotton gin, an event that would change the future of the South, of America, and of the world. While the fact is often relegated to a single paragraph in history books, the far-reaching economic, social, and demographic changes wrought by this single accomplishment are astounding. On the positive side, the production and export of cotton became the economic salvation of the early American Republic. On the negative side, the economics of cotton production were an essential factor in the persistence of American slavery and the Civil War that ended it.

This section, The Early Days 1783–1815, includes three chapters. The first, "The (Re)invention of the Cotton Gin," details Eli Whitney's pivotal genius and the initial growth of the cotton culture in the state. The second, "The Great Yazoo Fraud," is an account of this sordid affair made possible only through extensive legislative corruption. While often mentioned only in passing in many works of Georgia or Southern history, the Yazoo lands scandal forever changed the geography of the South, spawned the first of many government bail-outs, and led to several precedent-setting court decisions while reverberating in the legal system for the next three-quarters of a century.

The third chapter, "The Pine Barrens Speculation," might be considered the evil twin of the Great Yazoo Fraud. While the latter involved primarily the legislature, the Pine Barrens scandal found its corrupt roots in the system of local land courts and surveyors. As land grants required the signature of Georgia's governor, it seems inconceivable that the events could not have occurred without executive complicity, or, at the very least, incompetence. Less well known but no less extensive than the Yazoo lands scandal, relatively little has been written about this series of fraudulent transactions that involved millions of acres granted under the state's Head Right system. The extent of the fraud can be seen in one simple statistic: Georgia's land area measures approximately 35.5 million acres. Based on deeds recorded for land grants issued during the period of the Pine Barrens Speculation, the state's acreage would approximate some 55 million acres. In other words, presumably fraudulent deeds were issued for 19 million-plus nonexistent acres. The ramifications of this episode, like that of the Yazoo Fraud, continued for years. Even in the early twentieth century, unwary land buyers were still trying to find and lay claim to land whose deeds of title were originally issued in the 1790s.

CHAPTER 1

THE (RE)INVENTION OF THE COTTON GIN

History, by definition, is viewed in retrospect. Events that occurred in the past are often assumed to have been somehow ordained by the flow of time, falling into their rightful place in the creation of the world we currently know. In truth, we suppose this to be the case as we often have never considered the alternative worlds that might exist had fate put the course of history on a different path. In this light, it becomes interesting to consider the invention—or better, the reinvention—of the cotton gin by Eli Whitney in the last decade of the eighteenth century. This seemingly simple act by a single individual became a pivotal point in American, and, indeed, world history, changing the future in ways that no one could have imagined at the time. The fruits of Whitney's ingenuity contributed heavily to America's economic survival during the early years of the Republic, helped create and perpetuate the American system of slavery, nearly tore the nation apart in a devastating civil war, shaped the differing regional cultures of the North and South, and were in large part responsible for the system of global trade that we know today.

"Dixie," the minstrel tune of the 1850s, begins with the phrase, "Oh, I wish I was in the land of cotton...." It was an accurate description, because by that time, more than half a century after Whitney's invention, the entire South had, in fact, become the "land of cotton." Domains that were once forest were now a vast agricultural belt stretching from South Carolina to Georgia to Texas and beyond, an area whose culture and economy were inextricably intertwined with the production of a single crop. To be fair, it was not the cotton gin alone that brought on this change. There were other events and other forces, both locally and in distant parts of the world, that contributed, all coming together near the dawn of the nineteenth century in a way that would alter the course of world history.

In the world of the twenty-first century, cotton has become a ubiquitous commodity, the most basic of fabrics, an integral part of our daily lives.

Yet in the latter half of the eighteenth century, cloth woven from cotton was a relative rarity, oftentimes more expensive than silk. The use of cotton fibers in textiles dates from the dawn of recorded history. The plant is a member of the swamp mallow family, related to hibiscus, okra, and cacao, producing its fine fibers inside of a seedpod known as a boll. Of the more than thirty varieties found throughout the world, only four have practical use in the production of cloth. The value of any given variety of cotton is related to the climate in which it can be grown, the length and durability of its fibers, and the ease with which the fibers themselves can be separated from the seeds.

Dating from the earliest days of British settlement in North America, black-seeded, long-staple sea island cotton (*Gossypium barbadense*) was grown in limited quantities on the southern coastal islands and for a few miles inland. Its fibers were prized for their length; separating them from the seeds was easily accomplished by a roller-type gin similar to those used in Asia for centuries. However, the overall economic value of sea island cotton was limited by the relatively small area in which it could be successfully grown. In colonial days and during the early years of the American Republic, most cotton was produced and consumed locally, contributing little to the overall economy.

The other variety of cotton known to the early settlers was green-seeded upland cotton (*Gossypium hirsutum*), a wonderfully hardy variety that could be made to thrive in various types of soil far inland from the limited range of sea island cotton. Though its fibers were somewhat shorter than those of its coastal cousin, it was potentially ideal for the production of cloth. There was one major problem: the fibers of upland cotton are bound tightly to its seed, which must be removed prior to spinning the lint into thread. The roller-type gins that worked so well deseeding the sea island variety were of little use with upland cotton. The harvesting of fibers was of necessity done by hand, an arduous job that might yield a single pound of cotton fiber as the product of a full day's labor. By the year 1790, upland cotton's potential as a profitable crop was recognized, but the lack of an effective way of removing its seeds stood in the way of significant cultivation.

It is here that the young Eli Whitney enters the story. Born in 1765 into a Connecticut family of modest means, but determined to improve his lot in life, Whitney spent the initial years of his adulthood working to save money for his education. He entered Yale in 1789, graduating three years later at the relatively advanced age of twenty-seven. Whitney had apparently hoped to study law, but lacking the necessary funds, he accepted a job offer from fellow Yale graduate, Phineas Miller of Mulberry Grove Plantation, in Georgia near the city of Savannah. Despite only being a year older than Whitney, Miller was firmly established as the manager of the affairs of Catharine Greene, the owner of Mulberry Grove and widow of the noted Revolutionary War general Nathaniel Greene. Miller had been searching for a tutor to be employed on a neighboring plantation in South Carolina. Even though Whitney had never ventured south of New England, the salary offered seemed a generous one, perhaps allowing him to accumulate enough to continue his education.

Sailing south from the port of New York, Whitney arrived at Mulberry Grove in October 1792. Almost immediately it became evident that there had been some miscommunication as to what he would be paid as a tutor. The salary he was offered was only half of what he had expected to earn when he left Connecticut. For reasons that are not clear from the historical record, Whitney elected to stay at Mulberry Grove. The plantation, the confiscated property of a former loyalist who had abandoned it, had been awarded to General Greene in March 1785 for his service to the new nation during the Revolution. In June 1786, Greene died suddenly of what was said to be sunstroke, leaving his vast plantation and his extensive debts to his then-thirty-one year-old widow, the vivacious and charming "Caty" Greene. Soon after acquiring Mulberry Grove, the Greenes had hired Phineas Miller. After General Greene's death, Miller's role morphed into that of manager of Caty Greene's affairs. Some historians suggest that it was Whitney's infatuation with the young widow that led to his prolonged stay at her home.

It is fair to assume that Eli Whitney had never seen a cotton plant prior to his arrival in Georgia. His notes and letters are replete with his amazement over the varieties of fruit and other flora growing in the temperate climate of the South. It was an agrarian society in which he found himself; the conversation over dinner often revolved around subjects related to crops. In a letter to his father, Whitney reported, "During this time I heard much said of the extreme difficulty in ginning Cotton, that is, separating it from its seed. There were a number of very respectable Gentlemen at Mrs. Greene's who all agreed that if a machine could be invented which would clean the

Cotton with expedition, it would be a great thing both to the Country and to the inventor."

Whitney, with a mechanical mind and time on his hands, set out to do just that. In the letter to his father, Whitney continued, "I involuntarily happened to be thinking on the subject and struck out a plan of a Machine in my mind, which I communicated to [Phineas] Miller, (who is the agent of the Executors of Genl. Greene and resides in the family, a man of respectability and property) he was pleased with the Plan and said if I would pursue it and try and experiment to see if it would answer, he would be at the whole expense, I should loose nothing but my time, and if I succeeded we would share the profits."

Within a matter of days, Whitney had crafted a small functional model, using hooked wire to reach out through a slotted opening to pull the cotton lint from its seed. One version, perhaps apocryphal, relates that the idea came to Whitney as he observed a cat clawing at a caged chicken and snagging only feathers. By the time he left Mulberry Grove in the late spring of 1793, the young Connecticut inventor had produced a small but effective cotton gin with which one man could produce some fifty pounds of cleaned cotton fiber in a single day.

It would be inappropriate to say that Eli Whitney "invented" the cotton gin. The separation of cotton fibers from their seeds is a fundamental first step in the making of thread, rope, or cloth. In the earliest days, the fibers were pulled from the seed by hand, a slow and laborious process that might have been used by individual family units. As technology advanced, the most common type of gins were variants on the charkha roller gin, known to be in use in India and Asia as early as the thirteenth century. Two rollers mounted closely parallel to each other and rotating in opposite directions drew the cotton toward a narrow slot. The fibers were pulled from the seed and passed through the rollers while the seed itself, too large to pass through the slot, fell away. This process worked well for sea island cotton, whose seeds were not tightly bound to the lint, but was not practical for the more prolific green-seeded upland cotton. Various iterations of this basic mechanism were still used in the United States well into the nineteenth century but for the most part had been replaced by gins based on Whitney's basic idea. Whitney did not invent the cotton gin, he reimagined it. His mechanism was new and innovative. Perhaps his own ignorance of what had come before allowed him to visualize and create a new process.

While innovative, the importance of Whitney's gin was not related to its fundamental design, but rather to the timing of its invention, and that, in turn, was dependent on events taking place half a world away. For all its high hopes and bright future, America of the late eighteenth century was still an agrarian backwater, separated by thousands of miles of ocean from its primary trading partners. The vast majority of goods and commodities produced locally were consumed locally, or, if not, shipped to other parts of the new nation. There were some exports—tobacco, sea island cotton, naval stores, etc.—but in context, foreign trade was not a great part of the fledging economy. England, meanwhile, was undergoing an industrial revolution that had begun in the mid-eighteenth century. The production of textiles, formerly a cottage industry, was in a period of rapid transition. Thread production became more efficient thanks to Wyatt's spinning machine and Kay's flying shuttle, John Hargreaves's spinning jenny, Richard Arkwright's water frame spinning machine, and Samuel Compton's "mule." When coupled with mechanical looms such as those of Edmund Cartwright's, and powered by water (and later steam), a new system of centralized textile factories emerged rapidly over a few short decades. For the most part, these factories produced cloth of wool or linen; relatively speaking, cotton imports were limited in both quantity and quality. Whitney's gin, fortuitously created at just the right moment in time, was about to change all that.

Besides its new design, Whitney's gin was scalable. What worked on a small scale could be made to work on a larger, even vast, scale, able to supply raw material for England's (and the world's) nascent cotton textile industry. Prior to the 1790s, even if the mills of England had wanted to produce more cotton cloth, they could not. The supply was simply not there. The limited range in which sea island cotton grew in the Americas, the variable and often inferior quality of cotton imported from Asia and Africa, and the cost of shipping presented problems both logistic and economic. Suddenly, the potential for an immense new form of trade had been created. Planters in America could produce and gin cotton that could be sold in the export market for a significant profit. Mills in England had a new and seemingly unlimited source of raw materials to feed their expanding factory system of excellent quality and obtainable at a reasonable price. Whitney, like many others in the years that followed, should have become wealthy because of cotton. Things did not work out that way.

Eli Whitney departed Mulberry Grove in late May 1793, determined to return to Connecticut and prefect his new invention. His decision to return north was based on the more ready availability of tools and resources for the necessary work ahead. His small model had worked well, but before him lay the difficult task of building a larger version as a necessary requirement for obtaining a patent. Whitney took with him a letter of introduction written by Phineas Miller to Thomas Jefferson, then secretary of state and the person to whom patent applications were to be submitted. Miller described Whitney as a man of "strong inventive genius deserv[ing] the encouragement of the Public." By October, Whitney had made sufficient progress to submit working drawings to Jefferson as part of his patent application. By late winter 1794 he had worked through the final problems and traveled to Philadelphia to deliver his working model to the patent office. The patent was granted on March 14, 1794. In a letter to his father a few days later, Whitney, the proud inventor, averred, "My machine is the most perfect & the most valuable invention that has ever appeared in this Country." Valuable or not, it would serve to change the course of history.

Whitney may have been the creator of the new gin, but half of its patent rights were owned jointly by Phineas Miller, formally conveyed to him on June 21, 1794. Beginning several days before the formal granting of the patent and continuing through December of 1794, an advertisement appeared in the newspapers of Savannah and Augusta, the new state's largest cities. It read:

COTTON GINNING

> *The subscriber will engage to gin, in a manner equal to picking by hand, any quantity of the green seed cotton, on following terms, viz. For every five pounds delivered him in the seed, he will return one pound of clean cotton fitted for market.*
>
> *For the encouragement of cotton planters he will also mention, that GINNING MACHINES to clean the green seed cotton on the above terms will actually be erected in different parts of the country, before the harvest of the ensuing crop.*
>
> *PHINEAS MILLER*
>
> *Mulberry Grove, near Savannah*
> *March 1, 1794*

The business plan of the new firm of Miller & Whitney did not anticipate selling gins to farmers and plantation owners. Rather, they intended to use what would be described in twenty-first century terms as company-owned franchises, setting up working gins in strategic locations and allowing cotton producers to pay for their use by retaining part of the finished product. It was a potentially lucrative enterprise. According to one estimate, five pounds of raw cotton should yield approximately one and two-thirds pounds of cleaned lint suitable for spinning and weaving. Miller & Whitney's 40 percent commission was to be used to pay for the production of the gins, which were being manufactured by Whitney in Connecticut, plus a relatively smaller sum for labor and maintenance. Given the efficiency of the process, the profit potential was significant.

Whitney and the first gin of the new enterprise arrived in Georgia in May 1794. With Miller in Georgia as the businessman and Whitney in New England as the manufacturer, the business appeared to be off to a successful start. By mid-1796, five gins were operating at Mulberry Grove, ten at Augusta, and four near Washington, Georgia. There was a ginnery near Petersburg, two gins at Galphinton on the Ogeechee River, four at Waynesborough, plus others planned for Beaufort and Edisto, South Carolina.[2]

Despite Whitney's patent and the optimistic predictions for success, there were problems from the outset. The design of the gin was relatively simple and easily copied by skilled local craftsmen. And, as is often the case with new ideas, there were others who saw opportunities for improvement. Between 1794 and 1803, a total of nine new patents were granted for improvements on Whitney's original design. The most significant of these was the so-called "saw gin," which substituted a dulled serrated blade for Whitney's wire hooks in removing the lint from the seed.[3] Not only did these new patents challenge that of Whitney, the improvements increased efficiency, in the process drawing away business. Almost immediately, many of the resources of Miller & Whitney were devoted to attempts to defend their patent. Juries, often made up of farmers and men of the land, were reluctant to

---

[2] Petersburg was a thriving community on the Savannah River upstream from Augusta. The site is now submerged under Clark Hill Lake. "Waynesborough" is the former spelling of Waynesboro, Georgia.

[3] Whitney said later he had considered this option but decided to use wire hooks instead.

uphold the patent rights for what had rapidly become a fundamental and indispensable piece of machinery for the processing of raw cotton.

And there were problems for Miller & Whitney unrelated to cotton. The new American Republic was near the height of a land boom that had begun in the 1780s. As settlers and other adventurers flooded south, Georgia's western lands—later to become the states of Alabama and Mississippi—beckoned. There were huge profits to be made in land speculation, and the Georgia legislature was willing to sell millions of acres in the area at nominal costs. Phineas Miller, the financial manager of the business, invested his (and Catharine Greene's) resources heavily in the so-called Yazoo lands, only to suffer major losses when a subsequent legislature renounced the validity of the sales.[4] Beginning around 1796, the land bubble burst, sowing panic and bankruptcy among many speculators. The firm of Miller & Whitney had, on a practical basis, ceased to function by the latter years of the decade. Despite their dreams of fortune, neither partner had realized any meaningful profit. Miller, who married Caty Greene in the late spring of 1796, faced insurmountable debt, not only of his own, but also that still owed by the estate of the late General Greene. Mulberry Grove was put on the market in 1798 and finally sold at a public debtors' auction in 1800.

Whitney abandoned his gin to go on to greater things, achieving personal and financial success as a manufacturer of arms for the American government. His true legacy, however, lies in the social, demographic, political, and economic changes that trace their roots to his invention. With the potential to produce a single highly profitable crop, labor was necessary. This fell to slaves. Over the next decades, the slave population of the cotton-producing states exploded. In Georgia, for example, the number of slaves more than tripled, from 29,000 in 1790 to 105,000 in 1810. During the same period, the yearly number of bales of cotton produced in Georgia rose from 3,158 to 177,824. Slavery was as abhorrent in the latter eighteenth century as it is in the current day. It had been allowed during the formation of the Republic under a constitutional compromise, but many believed it would likely have disappeared as a permitted institution in the early nineteenth century. The profits to be realized by cotton changed all that. By 1860, on

---

[4] For a more complete review of the so-called "Great Yazoo Fraud" and the concomitant Pine Barrens Speculation, see the chapters that follow.

the cusp of the American Civil War, three-and-a-half million slaves inhabited the cotton-producing states of the South.

The justification for slavery, moral considerations aside, was an economic one. In 1790, American cotton exports to Britain were negligible. By 1800, British textile mills imported more than 16 million pounds of American cotton, some 28 percent of their total cotton imports. The figures grew steadily; by 1860, some 88 percent of Britain's total cotton imports (in excess of 1.23 *trillion* pounds) were American slave-produced raw cotton. The effect of cotton imports on the British economy was dramatic. By 1861 the price of cotton cloth had fallen to a mere 1 percent of its cost in 1784, prior to the gin and the ever-increasing efficiencies of the Industrial Revolution. Between 1815 and 1840, cotton textiles produced by her mills accounted for roughly half of all British exports. The system of trans-Atlantic cotton trade laid the groundwork for the system of international trade that exists today. The positive balance of trade funded by cotton exports kept America from becoming a debtor nation during the nineteenth and early twentieth centuries. Likewise, the export of finished cotton textiles from Britain funded her role as major world power during much of this period.

Because of the cotton culture, the societies that developed in America's North and South were fundamentally different. By its very nature, agriculture requires great amounts of land; hence, during the nineteenth century, the South became an expanse of small towns and diffuse populations while the strength (and wealth) of the North was concentrated in its cities. In the North, European immigrants made up much of the laboring class. In the South, this role was occupied by black slaves. These sharp demographic differences persisted after the Civil War and well into the twentieth century.

Cotton meant money and money meant power. By the mid-nineteenth century, America's economic engine was cotton. In the South, wealthy planters made up much of the ruling class. In the North, it was the bankers, ship owners, and brokers whose fortunes were inextricably tied to the cotton trade. In many ways, the American Civil War was a struggle over power and economics, much of which could trace its roots to the plantation-based cotton culture and its necessary evil, slavery. Even in the present day, more than two centuries after young Eli Whitney arrived at Mulberry Grove plantation, the North and South have distinctly different social and political cultures, much of which can be traced back to the days of cotton's dominance.

Phineas Miller, Eli Whitney's business partner, died in 1803 at Dungeness Plantation on Georgia's Cumberland Island, where he and Caty Greene had moved after losing Mulberry Grove. In an ironic twist, it was Miller's investment in the Georgia Yazoo lands that eventually yielded a profit for Whitney. In 1802, the state of Georgia ceded her western territory to the United States government in exchange for assuming all liabilities related to the ill-fated Yazoo land fraud. In 1814, the federal government voted to pay a total of $5 million to those who had suffered financial losses based on the actions of the state of Georgia that nullified the land sales. It was Miller's speculation in the Yazoo lands that drained capital and good will from the gin enterprise in Georgia. As a result of the bailout, Miller's estate profited handsomely. Four years later, in a negotiated settlement, Whitney was awarded $15,000 as part of the final settlement of the affairs of Miller & Whitney.

Sources and Resources

Beckert, Sven. *Empire of Cotton—A Global History*. New York: Alfred A. Knopf, 2014. As implied by the title, the author focuses on the role of cotton in world trade, stating, "[It is] the story of the making and remaking of global capitalism and with it of the modern world."

"Correspondence of Eli Whitney Relative to the Invention of the Cotton Gin." *The American Historical Review*. 3 (1897): 90–127. http://www.jstor.org/stable/1832812. Accessed 15 October 2015. This article, dating from 1897 but available online, is a valuable primary source based on Whitney's correspondence relative to the cotton gin, accompanied by interesting contextual commentary.

Dattel, Gene. *Cotton and Race in the Making of America*. Chicago: Ivan R. Dee, 2009. Dattel's well-researched and well-written narrative focuses on the economic and social aspects of the cotton trade, especially as these factors shaped modern America.

Mirsky, Jeannette and Allan Nevins. *The World of Eli Whitney*. New York: The MacMillan Company, 1952. This is far and away the best single biography of Eli Whitney, with significant details regarding the cotton gin and his later life. It is based in large part on Whitney's letters and papers, accompanied by insightful commentary and context.

Porcher, Richard D. and Sarah Fick. *The Story of Sea Island Cotton*. Layton, UT: Gibbs Smith, 2005. Even though the focus of this work is sea island cotton, it includes an excellent history of cotton production in general, with extensive details on the Southern cotton culture that accompanied it.

Yafa, Stephen. *Cotton*. New York: Penguin Books, 2005. A good general history of cotton from the earliest days to the present.

An 1822 portrait of Eli Whitney by Samuel Morse, depicting the inventor nearly three decades after his re-creation of the cotton gin. By this time, Whitney had become a successful manufacturer.

Yale University Art Gallery

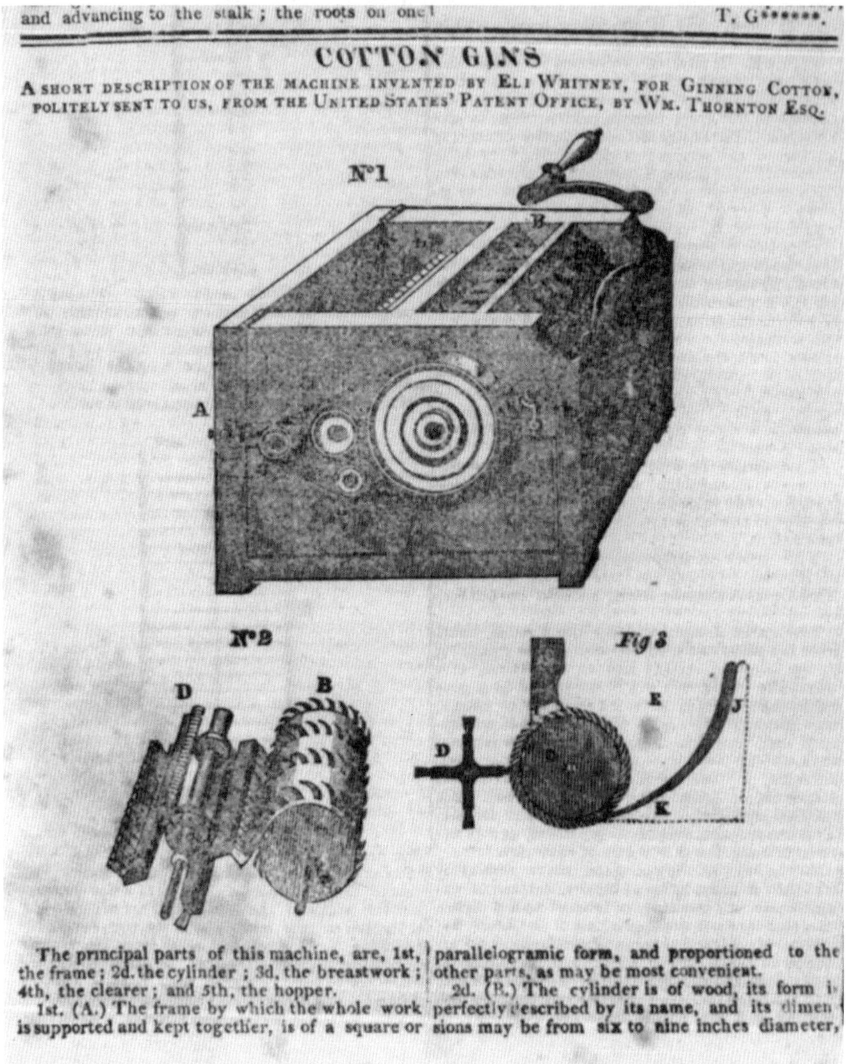
and advancing to the stalk ; the roots on one l T. G*******.

COTTON GINS

A SHORT DESCRIPTION OF THE MACHINE INVENTED BY ELI WHITNEY, FOR GINNING COTTON, POLITELY SENT TO US, FROM THE UNITED STATES' PATENT OFFICE, BY WM. THORNTON ESQ.

The principal parts of this machine, are, 1st, the frame; 2d. the cylinder ; 3d, the breastwork ; 4th, the clearer ; and 5th, the hopper.

1st. (A.) The frame by which the whole work is supported and kept together, is of a square or parallelogramic form, and proportioned to the other parts, as may be most convenient.

2d. (B.) The cylinder is of wood, its form is perfectly described by its name, and its dimensions may be from six to nine inches diameter,

This early illustration Whitney's cotton gin was supplied by the US Patent Office and published in the *American Farmer* in 1823. This simple machine would dramatically change the course of American history.

Library of Congress

More than a century after the invention of the cotton gin, much of the South remained a vast plantation devoted to the production of this single crop. It was a labor-intensive enterprise, most of which was supplied by African-Americans, who remained second-class citizens for decades after the end of the Civil War.

Library of Congress

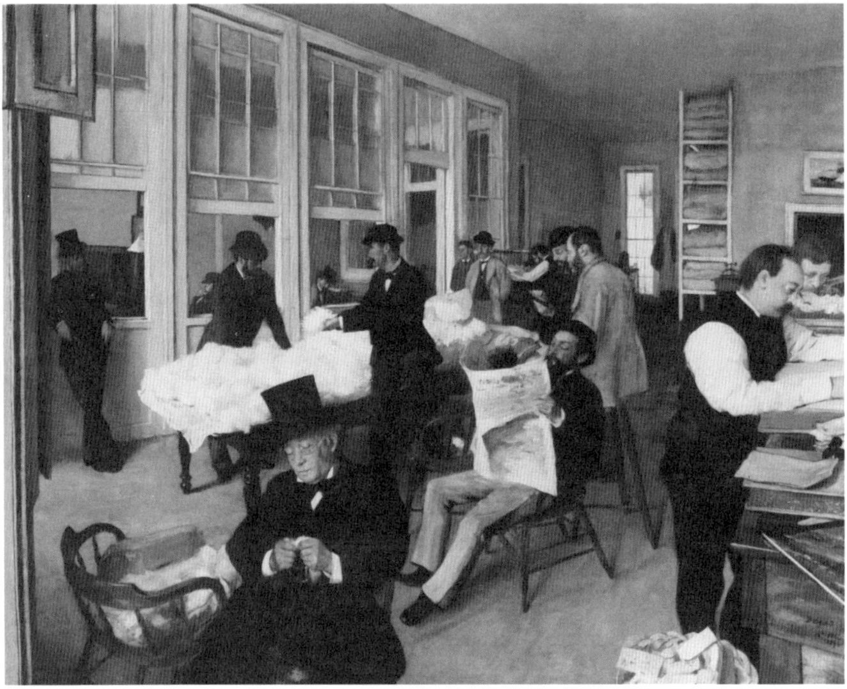

By the mid-nineteenth century, cotton had become the United States' prime export, providing a positive balance-of-trade and helping to establish the modern system of international commerce. This painting of a New Orleans cotton exchange was created by Edgar Degas on visit the city in 1873. Cotton had become a world commodity, traded as eagerly in New York or London as it was in the Deep South.

Musée des Beaux-Arts, Pau, France

CHAPTER 2

THE GREAT YAZOO FRAUD

Real estate speculation, aggressive lobbyists closely allied with crooked and self-serving politicians, insider deals tacked on as riders to popular legislation, intense scrutiny by the press, public outrage, political downfall, and the inevitable government bailout. While this might sound like a tale ripped from current headlines, it actually happened more than 200 years ago during a series of events that came to be known as the Great Yazoo Fraud. One historian described the episode as "an ugly and notorious drama, marked by corruption and base passions," another as "a conspiracy of the darkest character and of deliberate villainy."

Simply put, the Yazoo Fraud was an almost-successful attempt by a group of well-connected speculators to purchase millions of acres from the state of Georgia for scarcely more than a cent an acre. The resulting public outrage forever changed the boundaries of the state and continued to echo through the political and legal landscape of postcolonial America for decades to follow.

To understand the Yazoo Fraud, it is first necessary to understand the land use and population patterns of the new American Republic in the eighteenth century. North America at the time was a vast and sparsely inhabited region. England had extensive claims, as did both France and Spain. Most European settlements were on or within a few miles of the seacoast or, alternatively, inland on navigable waterways. The fields, forests, and mountains were ruled, for the most part, by various Amerindian tribes, some friendly to the new settlers, others less so. The *entire* population of the United States in 1791 was slightly fewer than 3.9 million inhabitants, including slaves. By comparison, this figure is nearly 2 million less than the estimated population of metropolitan Atlanta in the first quarter of the twenty-first century. In terms of land area, Georgia was the largest of the sixteen states yet ranked thirteenth in population, with only 82,548 inhabitants, 35 percent of whom were slaves. In contrast, North Carolina had a population of 393,751 and South Carolina 249,073.

By the late 1780s, Georgia's boundaries were reasonably well established based on the former royal charter and affirmed by international agreements. To the north, the border with Tennessee and North Carolina set at the 35th parallel was accepted, if not yet fully mapped. To the south, the 31st parallel (today marking the line between Alabama and Florida) was recognized, but again, unmarked. The Mississippi River was undisputed as Georgia's western boundary, dating back to 1763 in the colonial era.

The 1783 Treaty of Paris that formally ended the American Revolution ceded Florida back to its previous owner, Spain.[5] The Spanish, based on earlier British claims, asserted ownership to a large swath of land east of the Mississippi River and north as far as the mouth of the Yazoo River, leaving ownership of this part of Georgia in international dispute. To add to the confusion, Native Americans occupied this region and claimed ownership of essentially all the land in what is now the states of Alabama and Mississippi.

At the end of the American Revolution, several states asserted their own claims to various portions of the new country's western lands. By 1787, all states except Georgia and North Carolina had relinquished whatever rights to these lands they might have possessed, contributing immense regions to the public domain.[6] In 1790, North Carolina gave up her claims as well, leaving Georgia the largest state by far, her fertile lands stretching from the Atlantic coast to the Mississippi River. Fortunes could be made from the rich soils and untapped resources in this new territory. Speculation—often based on questionable claims of title and uncertain deeds—was common. By the late 1780s, Georgia's western lands were squarely in the sights of men eager to reap quick riches from the buying and selling of these unexplored areas.

There were, however, a few technical problems. In addition to the issue of disputed ownership, Article I of the new Constitution specifically reserved to Congress the right "to regulate commerce with foreign nations, and

[5] Florida remained a Spanish possession until it was purchased by the United States in 1819.

[6] When used in reference to land, the term "public domain" implies property rights are claimed by the community at large, generally through ownership by the federal or a state government.

among the several states, and with the Indian tribes."[7] The few hardy settlers who attempted to establish themselves in Georgia's western lands were frequently harassed and sometimes killed by local Indians. In 1785 the Georgia legislature established Bourbon County, which encompassed a large area around the modern city of Natchez on the Mississippi River. This was done in part to cement the state's claim to the area, but by attempting to settle lands claimed both by Native Americans and a foreign power, Georgia's actions appeared to conflict with national governmental sovereignty.

Whatever the benefit, the costs of settlement and of suppressing warring tribes weighed heavily on the state budget. In 1788, the legislature dissolved Bourbon County and offered to sell part of Georgia's western lands to the United States for the sum of $171,428, the amount expended by the state on Indian wars. Part of the offer, however, specified that Congress confirm Georgia's claim to the remainder of the lands within its western boundaries beyond the Chattahoochee River. Congress, reluctant to do so, responded with an "all or nothing" resolution, finally rejecting the proposal primarily for this reason.

Despite the formidable issues of title and sovereignty, the western Georgia wilderness represented an opportunity that could not be ignored. Land speculators formed three separate companies with the purpose of acquiring large tracts in the state's western area, planning to divide, develop, and resell their purchases for a quick profit. The land in question was in some proximity to the Yazoo River,[8] hence the companies took the names the South Carolina Yazoo Company, the Tennessee Company, and the Virginia Yazoo Company. The shareholders of these companies were, for the most part, non-Georgians, running the gamut from swindlers to prominent patriots, including Patrick Henry, who served as head of the Virginia Yazoo Company.

In November 1789, the three companies petitioned the Georgia legislature, seeking to buy an *estimated* 15.5 million acres in what is now Mississippi and Alabama for $207,580, amounting to approximately 1.34 cents per acre. Their proposal called for the land to be sold with no money down and

---

[7] The current United States Constitution was ratified in 1788 and came into effect in 1789. The prior Articles of Confederation delegated foreign relations to the central government, though with different verbiage.

[8] "Yazoo" was reputed to mean "River of Death" in a local Indian language.

the balance due in two years, allowing purchasers ample time to resell the land at a significant profit. The territory involved in the proposed sale had never been surveyed. Later estimates would place the area as closer to 25.4 million acres, making the true offer about 0.8 cents per acre.

A number of Georgia residents, apparently seeing this attractive deal going to out-of-staters, formed the Georgia Yazoo Company, offering nearly triple the price tendered by the other three companies. The Georgia legislature ignored the higher offer, however, selling the land to the original applicants just nine days after receiving the first proposal. Gov. Edward Telfair duly signed the legislation over the strident objections of both the legislators opposed to the act and the citizens who had formed the Georgia Yazoo Company. Despite the allegations of fraud, the act became law on December 21, 1789.

Word of the sale of Georgia's western lands quickly reached President George Washington in Philadelphia. Washington had a number of concerns: The manner in which the land was sold carried the stench of corruption. The Indian claims in the region had not been settled. And however tenuous they may have been, Spain still exerted some claims to the land that the companies had purchased from the state. The Constitution reserved for the federal government the exclusive right to negotiate with foreign powers and the Indian tribes, both of whom would need to renounce their claims if the titles were to be considered valid.

Hoping to solidify the boundaries of the new Republic, President Washington and the American government were in the process of attempting to convince Spain to relinquish her claims in the Yazoo region when the three companies made their purchase from Georgia. Separately, James O'Fallon, one of the principles of the South Carolina Yazoo Company, had been in contact with Gen. James Wilkinson.[9] Wilkinson, who had served as a military officer in the Revolution, had secretly sworn allegiance to Spain, hoping to establish an independent republic in the Kentucky territory. In similar fashion, O'Fallon sought the protection and support of Spain for his company's claim in the Yazoo region should the fledgling American Republic fail. O'Fallon even planned to raise a private army, nominally for the protection of settlers but conceivably one that might be turned against American authority. Secretary of State Thomas Jefferson issued a sternly worded

[9] Georgia's Wilkinson County was named for General Wilkinson.

proclamation threatening O'Fallon's arrest, who prudently backed away from his plans.

The furor caused by the 1789 sale led to a unique countermeasure. The sums owed to the state were specified in fixed dollar amounts. In the days prior to single national currency and a central banking system, debts were often paid in state currency, warrants, or bills of credit, the equivalent of the day to paper currency. Such documents were subject to variations in the market and could often be purchased at a steep discount from the nominal face value. When the three Yazoo land companies tried to pay their debts to Georgia, the state treasurer refused to accept the tender of devalued paper currency and other similar bills of credit. The companies were unwilling or unable to pay with specie (gold or silver coins), so the state declined to deliver deeds to the land. The sale was thus effectively nullified.

Despite the negative outcome of the 1789 attempt, ingenious men in search of a profit are not easily dissuaded. As well, the passage of a few years had made the prospect (and value) of new lands all the more appealing to both investors and buyers alike. The peaceful years that followed the Revolution had brought a flood of new settlers from Virginia, the Carolinas, and the North to Georgia, all eager for their own piece of America. There were rumors of a remarkable new machine, the cotton gin, which allowed the white fiber to be successfully grown far inland, a source of potential wealth for the industrious farmer.

In November 1794, a group of four newly formed companies again petitioned the Georgia legislature for the right to purchase millions of acres in the western part of the state. The Georgia Company, the Georgia Mississippi Company, the Tennessee Company, and the Virginia Yazoo Company were composed of some of the same individuals from the abortive 1789 purchase as well as many newcomers. In a blatant conflict of interest, the Georgia Company's head was none other than Georgia's United States senator James Gunn. Wade Hampton and Robert Morris were now members of the Virginia Yazoo Company.[10] With this second offer, the companies were de-

[10] Wade Hampton was a wealthy planter and grandfather of the Confederate general of the same name. Robert Morris, often referred to as the "financier of the American Revolution," was at the time a United States senator from Pennsylvania. He figured prominently in Georgia's Pine Barrens Speculation, which occurred concomitantly.

termined not to repeat the mistakes made in the earlier attempt. Notwithstanding the objections of the federal government and titular claims by Spain and the Indians, a joint legislative committee gave a positive report to the proposal after scarcely more than a week of consideration. Once again, a late-forming group (the Georgia Union Company) offered to pay significantly more than the original four companies had offered for a portion of the lands. The legislators' committee inexplicably rejected the offer.

By December 20, 1794, both houses of the legislature had approved the offers of the four companies, sending the bill to Gov. George Mathews for his signature. On December 29, the governor vetoed the bill, citing seven primary reasons for doing so, including his assessment that the price was inadequate, that the bids were noncompetitive, and that the amount of land being purchased was so large that the companies would operate as monopolies. The House immediately appointed a committee to consult with the governor in the drafting of a new bill that would overcome his objections. Meanwhile, the Georgia Union Company, having failed in its first efforts to outbid the other four competitors, bid an astounding $300,000 more than their combined offers for all the land in question, at the same time offering to double the amount of land reserved for sale to citizens of the state. This offer, too, was rejected.

The authors of the bill authorizing the sale of land were not to be easily defeated. The provisions allowing the sale of the Yazoo lands were simply appended to a previously introduced popular bill authorizing payment to Georgia veterans of the American Revolution. Given the mendacious and wordy title of "An Act Supplementary to an Act for Appropriating a Part of the Unallocated Territory of this State for the Payment of the Late State Troops, and for Other Purposes Therein Mentioned, Declaring the Right to the Unappropriated Territory Thereof, for the Protection and Support of the Frontiers of the State, and for Other Purposes Therein Mentioned," this bill authorized the sale of 21.75 million acres to the four companies for the sum of $500,000. Once again, the putative and actual acreages were starkly different. The property involved was closer to 35 million acres, an area approximately the size of England, Scotland, and Wales combined, making the effective price 1.43 cents per acre.

To avoid the mistakes of 1789, the purchasers were to pay 20 percent down once the governor signed the bill, and the balance in specie or approved warrants by November 1795. The state was to provide the purchasers with full title. The House of Representatives and the Senate, sitting in the temporary capital of Augusta, passed the Act in early January 1795. Although he had vetoed essentially the same bill just weeks earlier, Governor Mathews signed the Act and it became law. The companies made the required down payments and promptly set about reselling their newly purchased lands to other eager investors, their titles now effectively guaranteed by the state of Georgia.[11]

Public reaction was swift and decisive when word spread of why the legislature had so readily endorsed the bill. Georgia senator James Gunn and James Wilson of Pennsylvania, a signer of the Declaration of Independence and an Associate Justice of the United States Supreme Court, both members of the Georgia Company, had persuaded many members of the legislature to lend their vote and support. Despite their public offices of trust, both men aggressively sought to win votes for the land sale, most often by illegal or unethical means. As would later be revealed in testimony before an investigative committee, twenty-eight of the twenty-nine members of the Georgia legislature who voted in favor of the bill had received bribes. Some were offered and accepted cash or other favors; most were given shares in the Yazoo land companies at little or no cost.

In the small cities and still-rural county seats of the state, public outrage led to formal condemnations from grand juries in all but two of Georgia's counties. Georgia's other United States senator, James Jackson, resigned his congressional seat to return home and lead the fight to repeal what had become known popularly as the "Yazoo Act." As a prominent and powerful legislator, Jackson had been offered generous bribes in return for his support of the proposed land sale, all of which he refused. After its passage, he stirred public opinion by authoring a series of newspaper articles written under the name of "Scillius" that "calmly and learnedly" condemned the Act and the enormity of its effects on the state. Continuing his fight for justice, Jackson accepted the nomination and was elected to represent Chatham County in the Georgia legislature. The newspapers of the day were full of signed and unsigned letters decrying the Yazoo Act as "robbery" and "ob-

[11] In its final form, the bill granted purchase rights to four companies, with the Upper Mississippi Company replacing the former Virginia Yazoo Company. The Upper Mississippi Company was headed by the former agent of the Virginia Yazoo Company, who "threw in his lot with several other persons, more favorably placed."

tained by fraud, collusion and corruption." By the time the newly elected legislature convened in the new capital city of Louisville in January 1796, there was an overwhelming sense that the land sale must be reversed.

Public indignation did little to deter the new landowners from the pursuit of their business plans. They paid the balances due on their purchases, busily reselling interests in Georgia's western lands for substantial profits. In the months that followed the passage of the Yazoo Act, events elsewhere conspired to increase the value of their claims. In October 1795, under the Treaty of San Lorenzo, Spain relinquished her claims to those lands north of the 31st parallel, clearing the Yazoo lands' titles of this impediment.

As the new class of lawmakers assembled in early 1796, Governor Mathews, now in the last days of his administration, sent them a message defending his signing of the Yazoo Act. It fell on deaf ears. In a rebuke to the outgoing government, Jared Irwin, an anti-Yazoo legislator from Washington County, was elected governor. A committee was established to investigate the validity and constitutionality of the Yazoo Act and given the right to subpoena witnesses and documents. James Jackson, now a state representative and one of the most prominent opponents of the Act, served as its chairman. At a series of hearings, witness after witness confirmed the widespread bribery and corruption that facilitated its passage.

On January 22, 1796, the legislative committee charged with investigating the Yazoo Act reported they were "compelled to declare, that the fraud, corruption, and collusion by which the said act was obtained, and the unconstitutionality of the same, evinces the utmost depravity in the majority of the late Legislature." The committee urged that the Act be declared void, and that it be expunged "from the face of the public record."

The committee then introduced the Rescinding Act, which, after discussion and some modification, passed overwhelmingly on February 13, 1796. This bill directed that the records of the Yazoo Act "be expunged from the faces and indexes of the books of record of the state, and that enrolled law or usurped act shall then be publicly burnt, in order that no trace of so unconstitutional, vile and fraudulent a transaction, other than the infamy attached to it by this law, shall remain in the public offices thereof." The state treasurer was directed to return to the purchasers any of the sales proceeds then in state coffers, at the time about $400,000.

On February 15, 1796, as ordered by the Rescinding Act, the Yazoo Act papers were ritually put to torch by the gathered legislators on the grounds of the State House in Louisville. Reports claimed that the flame that consumed the documents was kindled by "fire from Heaven" by use of a magnifying glass to focus the sun's rays. Although most historians seem to consider this an apocryphal tale, a contemporary note in the *Augusta Chronicle* appears to confirm the origin of the flame. Accurate or not, the image of the burning of the Yazoo Fraud papers has firmly entrenched itself in Georgia history.

Whatever the plans of the Georgia legislature, the speculators—now in apparent legal possession of the title to the Yazoo lands—were not deterred. By the time the Rescinding Act was signed into law, most of the shares in the land companies had been resold for a profit. In a somewhat ironic twist, on the same day the Rescinding Act was passed, the Georgia Mississippi Company closed the sale of its entire holdings for more than a million dollars, a 700 percent profit over the purchase price paid a year earlier. Although the resold shares of the companies were widely distributed, a majority were sold in Boston and New England. The slowness with which news traveled in those days shielded many buyers from knowledge of the anger of the citizens of Georgia at this "usurpation" of the state's land.

An immediate result of the attempted deception with which the Yazoo Act was passed was a provision inserted in the Georgia Constitution of 1798 requiring that the titles of proposed statutes accurately reflect the actual content contained therein. This provision, among the first such in the United States, has remained essentially unchanged in all of Georgia's subsequent constitutions and has become standard verbiage in similar documents throughout the nation.

Over the ensuing months and years, a number of lawsuits and claims were filed by Yazoo-area landowners seeking damages for the then-worthless titles to land purchased under the provisions of the Yazoo Act. A 1793 United States Supreme Court decision, *Chisholm v. Georgia,* confirmed the rights of a citizen of one state to sue the government of another state in federal court. In response, the states ratified the Eleventh Amendment to the Constitution in February 1795, effectively forbidding citizens from suing state governments. The titles to the Yazoo lands sold under the 1795 bill were guaranteed by the state of Georgia. The Rescinding Act of the following year nullified the sales, thus theoretically allowing Georgia to retrospectively deny its warranty of these titles. This situation led to the landmark case of *Fletcher v. Peck*, eventually decided by the Supreme Court in 1810.

John Peck of Massachusetts had sold 15,000 acres he acquired under the Yazoo Act to Robert Fletcher of New Hampshire. Peck gave Fletcher a warranty deed based on the original title delivered by the state of Georgia. In June 1803, Fletcher sued Peck in federal court, citing a defective title and demanding return of his money. Peck was represented by John Quincy Adams, the future president, and the Supreme Court ruled in his favor, declaring Georgia's Rescinding Act unconstitutional because it violated the Contract Clause in Article I of the Constitution.

By this time, the Supreme Court's decision carried little significance for Georgia, which ultimately might have been required to warrant the title to Peck's land. In the months that followed the passage of the Rescinding Act in 1796, the state began negotiations to sell all of its western lands to the federal government. Georgia's prime purpose was to extricate itself from the legal mess and liability claims created by the Acts of 1795 and 1796. After several years of negotiation, an agreement was reached in 1802, and Georgia transferred to the United States title to the area that later became Alabama and Mississippi. Part of the agreement specified the national government would assume the task and liability of settling the Yazoo land claims.

The issue smoldered in Congress for more than a decade until 1814, when a bill passed appropriating $5 million to settle all outstanding Yazoo Act claims. Money to fund the settlements was to come from the sale of land in the territory. These settlements were to be paid to holders of the worthless deeds from Georgia. According to one source, however, by 1814 the speculators had already made profits of more than $3.5 million. Of the $5 million appropriated by Congress, $4,282,151.12½ was ultimately paid, so few "victims" of the land fraud suffered any significant financial loss.

Congress's bailout did not stop the lawsuits. The last to be settled involved the New England Land Company, which had bought the entire holdings of the Georgia Mississippi Company. Its lawsuit against the United States government was finally dismissed in October 1864, some seventy-five years after the first attempt by speculators to buy the Yazoo lands.

Today, few of Georgia's citizens have heard of the Great Yazoo Fraud, and even fewer are familiar with the details of the sordid matter. Other scandals, some greater, some not, have relegated it to ancient history. The players and the details may change, but one factor remains constant: the combination of greed and government is a potent recipe for disaster.

Sources and Resources

Clark, Helen. *The Yazoo Land Fraud.* Louisville, GA: The Jefferson County Historical Society, 2009. This reproduction of a 1948 master's thesis submitted by Helen Clark is, without a doubt, one of the most comprehensive reviews of the Great Yazoo Fraud. Privately published by the historical society of the county where the burning of the Yazoo Fraud papers took place, it is a superb resource for those wishing to explore these events in greater depth.

Elsmere, Jane. "The Notorious Yazoo Land Fraud Case." *The Georgia Historical Quarterly* 51 (1967): 425–42. This article focuses in detail on the infamous *Fletcher v. Peck* case, decided by the United States Supreme Court in 1810. This was the first case in which the Supreme Court ruled a state law unconstitutional and helped solidify the concept of contract law in the new American Republic.

Heath, William E. "The Yazoo Land Fraud." *The Georgia Historical Quarterly* 16 (1932): 274–91. A good general review article from a scholarly journal.

Stevens, William B. *A History of Georgia.* Vol. II. Philadelphia: E. H. Butler & Co., 1859: 457–96. In his pre-Civil War history of the state, Stevens devotes a long, if wordy, chapter to the "Yazoo Speculations," stating, "Few events in the history of our country, none certainly in the annals of Georgia, involved greater principles of law and equity, or were more exciting to all classes of the community...than the Yazoo sale."

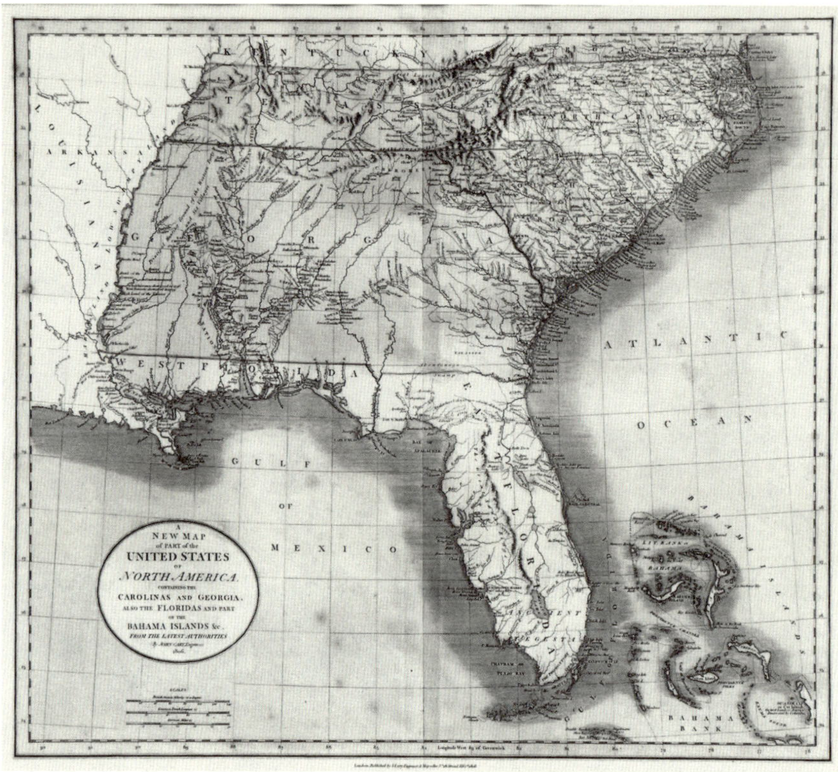

This map of the southeastern United States was already out of date by the time it was published in Great Britain in 1806. Georgia's lands, which had originally stretched from the Atlantic Ocean to the Mississippi River, were then far smaller based on an 1802 agreement with the federal government in which the United States indemnified Georgia for claims arising from the Yazoo land sales in exchange for the state ceding to the national government the land that now comprises most of Alabama and Mississippi.

Author's Collection

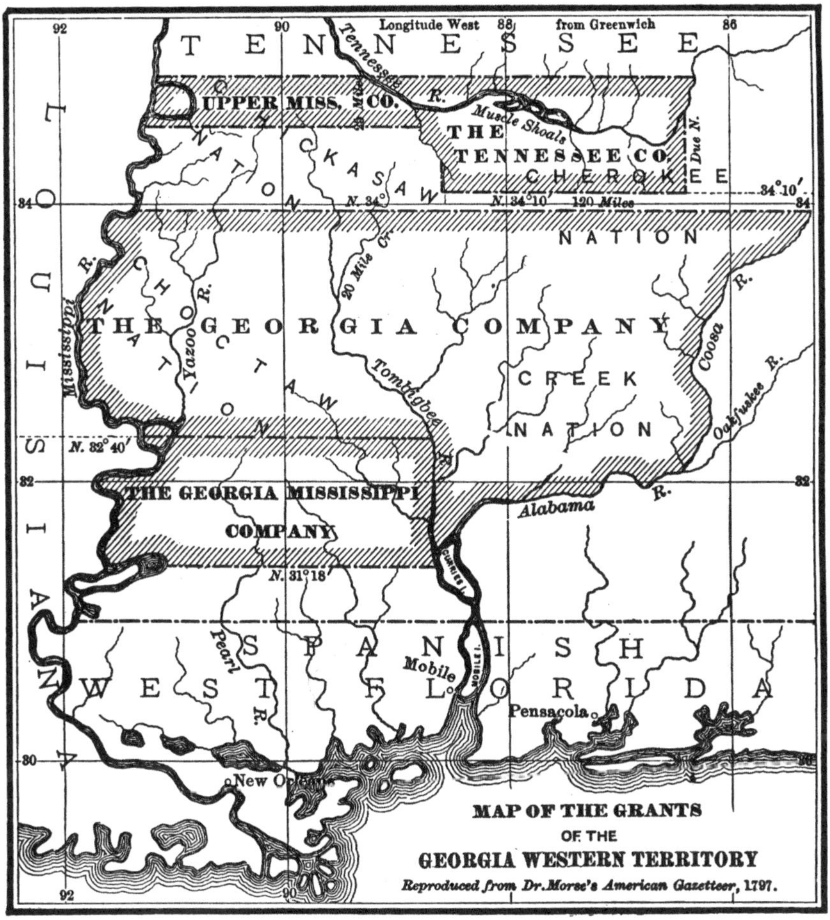

In the so-called "Great Yazoo Fraud," approximately 35 million acres were sold for less than 1.5 cents per acre to four companies composed of speculators who planned to resell their interests for a quick profit.

Public Domain

Georgia's first permanent capital was located in Louisville, on the Ogeechee River. It was here that the infamous Yazoo Fraud documents were publically burned on February 15, 1796, the flames allegedly kindled by "fire drawn from heaven" generated by a magnifying glass.

Auhtor's Collection

CHAPTER 3

THE PINE BARRENS SPECULATION

> "Land speculation and land fraud are about as American as baseball and apple pie."
>
> —F. W. Cadle in *Georgia Land Surveying History and Law*

The record vaults of Georgia's courthouses and archives hold a vast treasure trove of the state's history: records of births, deaths, crimes punished, properties bought and sold, fortunes won and lost. Recorded by hand in the flowing script of centuries past, these dusty ledgers often reveal a surprising glimpse of the great events of bygone days. A curious observer, searching the deed books of the Washington County courthouse in Sandersville, will encounter an unusual series of massive land sales involving hundreds of thousands of acres of property. These lands, bought and sold in the middle to late nineteenth century, carry chains of title that can easily be traced back to original land grants made decades earlier. If the records are to be believed, it would appear that the total number of acres transferred by these deeds exceeds the total land area of the county by a significant degree. Even stranger, among the former owners of these tracts are the names of some of the most wealthy and powerful men from the earliest days of the American Republic.

These deeds, and hundreds of others like them in various courthouses and archives across the state, are remnants of one of the more notable land frauds in American history, the so-called Pine Barrens Speculation of the 1790s. While often overshadowed by the better known Yazoo Fraud, this episode was equally corrupt, for well over a century ensnaring innumerable speculators in the purchase of land that had—at best—been misrepresented, and, at worst, did not exist. The corrupt few who masterminded the schemes profited. For most, however, the bitter reward was the realization that they had been duped.

To understand the Pine Barrens scandal, it is first necessary to understand how original land grants were made on Georgia's wild and unsettled western frontier in the late eighteenth century. From her earliest days as a colony and extending well into the nineteenth century, one of the greatest priorities of Georgia's trustees, officers of the Crown, and later state officials, was the recruitment of settlers for her vast territory. Initially abutting Spanish claims in the south and French claims in the west, settlers served not only to affirm the colony's and later the state's territory, but also to act as a citizen militia in times of conflict and a source of tax revenue in times of peace.

The settlement of the colony of Georgia began in the 1730s with the establishment of Savannah and other outposts along coastal areas to the south. From there, colonization spread up the Savannah River to the Fall Line shoals at Augusta, then westward, first to the Ogeechee River, then to the Oconee River, and subsequently beyond. Rivers and well-established Indian trails were the main routes of travel and commerce. Initially, most settlement was confined to coastal areas and along the rivers. Inland, south and east of the geologic Fall Line, much of what would later become the modern state of Georgia was covered by vast tracts of longleaf pine that thrived in the sandy, relatively infertile soil of the coastal plain. These lands were referred to as "pine barrens," perhaps suitable for subsistence farming, but far less desirable than those of the piedmont that stretched from north of the Fall Line to the foothills of the Appalachians.

In 1777, in the midst of the American Revolution, the twelve former parishes of the colony of Georgia were reconstituted as the counties of Richmond, Burke, Chatham, Effingham, Liberty, Glynn, and Camden, with Wilkes County added from lands ceded by the Creeks and Cherokees in 1773. With the formal end of hostilities with the Treaty of Paris in September 1783, Georgia held the distinction of being the largest and least populated of the American states, a mecca for those seeking a new start on the frontier. Excluding her western territory (that area that today forms most of the states of Alabama and Mississippi), more than 95 percent of Georgia's lands were held in the public domain. Land policy naturally became one of the driving forces in state government.

As had been the practice under the former colonial rule, land was granted to new settlers under a head-right grant system. The head of a household was eligible to receive 200 acres plus 50 acres for each family member and 50 acres for each slave up to a total of ten. The total amount granted could not exceed 1,000 acres. The rules and policies varied somewhat over time, with exceptions and bonus lands granted for certain types of land improvements or to reward service to the state or nation. The dispensing of public lands was delegated to so-called land courts created among the first acts of the new state assembly in 1783. These were locally based and composed of justices of the peace.

The process of obtaining a land grant was somewhat complicated. The first step was the issuance of a warrant from the land court to a potential grantee. To obtain a warrant, an applicant was required to appear before the court, swear that he was legally eligible to apply for a land grant, and describe the property that he wished to settle. If the court approved of his application—apparently most did so with little formality—a warrant was issued directing the county surveyor to survey the desired property, marking metes and bounds, and record a plat locally. A copy of this plat and warrant were then sent to the secretary of state's office to be signed by the governor, formalizing the title and ownership of the land in the name of the new grantee.

The first major expansion of lands for settlement after the Revolution was based on Native American territorial concessions in two areas. In the northeast of the state, the Cherokee ceded rights to land between the Tugaloo and Upper Oconee rivers in May 1783. In November of that year, a minority faction of the Creek nation gave up their rights to a huge swath of land between the Ogeechee and Oconee rivers, its upper border near modern-day Athens, and its lower border bounded by the Altamaha River and the northwestern boundary of Liberty County. Despite some uncertainty as to the legitimacy of the state's claim,[12] these two areas were incorporated in February 1784 as Franklin County in the north and Washington County immediately to the south, both named for heroes of the recent Revolutionary conflict. For the next two decades, this long crescent of land encompassed by the newly formed counties would be the source of the majority of Georgia's head-right land grants.[13]

---

[12] There were legitimate questions as to whether the state had the right to negotiate directly with the Indian tribes, and some question as to whether or not the Creek signatories to the treaties held the power to transfer land claims.

[13] Both Franklin and Washington counties, like the majority of the state's original counties, were divided and subdivided into new counties as the population grew in local areas. Franklin County originally encompassed all or part of Barrow, Jack-

The uncertainty of the Revolutionary conflict generated a huge pent-up demand for new lands by would-be settlers. With the war over, by the hundreds and thousands they descended on Georgia from states to the north, seeking a new start on the southern frontier. The land court given the responsibility for dispensing warrants for the newly opened Washington and Franklin counties was set up in Augusta and began receiving petitions and issuing warrants in April 1784. As described by one historian, "By late April the small river town on what was then Georgia's northwestern frontier had become overrun with recently discharged soldiers, expectant settlers, hopeful immigrants from other states, speculators, rough backwoodsmen, and an intermingling of Indians, all bent on grabbing up warrants for as much land as possible or at least sharing in the spectacle that was taking place."

There was no legal prohibition against the buying, selling, or trading of warrants, a practice that became increasingly common over the next few years. As the land courts of the counties were left to their own interpretation of the law, an individual might buy up a series of warrants and have them combined in a single warrant by the court. Despite the nominal prohibition on grants greater than 1,000 acres, by 1787, a number of warrant holders received individual grants ranging up to 50,000 acres. To put a halt to this perceived abuse, in 1788 Gov. George Handley issued an executive order that surveyors were not to issue grants for warrants greater than 1,000 acres in size. In response, the land courts circumvented this prohibition by issuing multiple warrants to a single individual in the amount of 1,000 acres each, which were then surveyed in contiguous tracts for the grantee.

There seems little doubt that the system was corrupt and that many involved at all levels were at the least aware of, if not actively participating, in the schemes. While the land sales that came to be known as the Yazoo Fraud were the product of a corrupt state assembly, the contemporaneous Pine Barrens Speculation was made possible by malfeasance on a local and county level, aided and/or abetted by members of the executive branch of state government. The records suggest that the actions of some land courts

---

son, Oconee, Clarke, Madison, Banks, Hart, Stephens, Gwinnett, Hall, and Habersham counties in addition to South Carolina's Pickens, Oconee, and Anderson counties. Washington County included all or part of Oglethorpe, Oconee, Greene, Hancock, Baldwin, Jefferson, Johnson, Laurens, Emanuel, Montgomery, and Tattnall counties.

and surveyors were influenced by bribery and collaboration with speculators whose primary purpose was acquiring land to be quickly resold for a profit.

While the acquisition of land grants by speculators was a factor from the earliest of the head-right grants, this activity seemed to reach its peak in 1793 and 1794, described as "organized corruption on a grand scale." Although land grant fraud existed in multiple counties, much of it took place in the new counties of Franklin and Washington or in counties carved from their original boundaries. At least three county surveyors were parties to the fraud: Richard Dawson, James Shorter, and Thomas Cooper received 1,412,000 acres, 1,219,000 acres, and 277,000 acres respectively, some of which they had surveyed for themselves or for each other. The physical impossibility of completing the surveys in the time they were alleged to have taken place indicates their fraudulent nature. For example, Shorter "surveyed" 52,000 acres on August 29, 1793, with Cooper "surveying" some 100,000 acres on August 6 and 118,000 acres on August 18 of the same year. During this same timeframe, some "nineteen other persons each received grants ranging from 250,000 to 500,000 acres, thirty-three persons each received 100,000 to 250,000 acres, twenty-eight persons each received 50,000 to 100,000 acres, and forty persons each received 10,000 to 50,000 acres."

As records of the day were commonly kept in the form of hand-written documents, the sheer difficulty of completing the paperwork became a daunting task. To streamline the chore, the conspirators went so far as to *pre-print* grants showing names of the grantees, surveyors, chain carriers, date of the warrant, date of the survey, etc. Writing about the episode to Georgia secretary of state Philip Cook in 1890, historian Charles C. Jones Jr. said,

> It was in this extensive domain and that comprehended within the original limits of Franklin and Washington Counties that the pine-barren speculation was inaugurated and prosecuted by its projectors. The region—sparsely populated—was little more than a vast solitude. At home, the lands were practically valueless. While aware that there was no market for them within the limits of Georgia, parties conceived the idea of making them a convenient base for manipulation and speculation at distant points, notably in Philadelphia as a focal place. Plans were accordingly laid and machinery under the semblance of law was put in practical operation to secure a paper title to immense tracts in

> this region which could be utilized in furtherance of the contemplated speculation.
>
> Individuals were selected to act as magistrates, form land courts and issue the warrants which constituted the preliminary step under the Head-right System then in vogue in Georgia. Other parties were named who, as convenient and willing tools, were to discharge the duties of surveyors, and make or profess to make, the locations and surveys contemplated by the warrants. Everything being thus arranged, these unscrupulous speculators, without hindrance, perfected their plans, put their tools to work, had such warrants issued as they pleased and placed upon paper the most extravagant surveys when, in most instances, no chain had been stretched, or a single tree had been actually marked. Land forgeries, thus encompassed, were issued and returned to the Surveyor-General's office. They involved millions of acres.[14]

As a further bogus embellishment of the speculators, Jones pointed out, "In order to enhance the character of the land, and dignity of the native forest with which they were clothed, corner and station trees were described as oak, walnut, hickory, etc., etc., when in fact the entire region was a uniform pine barren. Streams and watercourses were delineated where none existed."

Although probable land fraud existed under most of the governors of the latter years of the eighteenth century, many of the fraudulent documents appear to have been signed during the administration of Gov. George Mathews from November 1793 to January 1796.

For example, over a two-month period between November 1794 and January 1795, Mathews "examined and signed" forty-three large grants ranging in size from 2,000 to 231,000 acres, totaling some 2,929,000 acres in addition to a number of smaller grants of a thousand acres or less.

By this time, the massive and public nature of the fraud had become evident, eliciting strong protests from many honest citizens and settlers who saw their rightful land holdings overlain by the spurious plats and titles granted to the speculators. In late 1794, the same legislature that would later pass the Yazoo Act made efforts to reign in the corruption, empowering the governor to stay illegal and suspect land transactions. In 1796, a law was passed providing for the popular election of county land surveyors, freeing

[14] Charles Colcock Jones Jr. (1831–1893) was Georgia's preeminent historian of the nineteenth century. He published a number of significant works but is perhaps best known for his *History of Georgia* (1883).

them from the control of the land courts. But by this time most of the damage had been done.

Actual Land Areas of Head-Right Counties
Compared to Acres Granted in Those Counties

Head-Right County	Acres in County as of 1839	Acres Allegedly Granted Under Head-Right System
Bryan	276,480	111,091
Bulloch	605,440	358,217
Burke	665,600	619,006
Camden	720,000	1,928,688
Chatham	268,800	55,619
Columbia	320,000	145,055
Effingham	310,400	1,149,791
Elbert	327,680	121,870
Franklin	499,200	5,126,548
Glynn	253,440	1,785,375
Greene	268,800	324,278
Hancock	288,640	56,727
Jackson	337,920	175,120
Jefferson	376,320	71,593
Liberty	393,600	870,680
Lincoln	126,720	14,624
McIntosh	422,200	667,251
Montgomery	407,680	7,436,995
Oglethorpe	286,720	55,018
Richmond	201,600	443,457
Screven	345,600	242,656
Warren	274,560	95,239
Washington	416,720	5,018,048
Wilkes	323,840	2,224,920
Totals	8,717,960	29,097,866

Chart modified from Absalom Chappell's *Miscellanies of Georgia, Historical, Biographical, Descriptive, Etc.* and Samuel G. McLendon's *History of the Public Domain of Georgia.*

The massive scope of fraud was not totally evident until years later. In 1839, a special state finance commission investigating the matter received two reports from Georgia's surveyor general. One noted that the *actual* number of acres in the state totaled 35,515,526 while the other reported that *based on registered maps and records*, the state's acreage was measured 54,816,782. This discrepancy of more than 19 million acres was, for the most part, accounted for by fraudulent land grants in the twenty-four then-existing head-right counties. These contained an actual land area of 8,717,960 acres. The total grants for these counties, however, equaled some 29,097,866 acres, more than three and a third acres granted for each acre actually in existence.

The counties most affected were Montgomery, Washington, and Franklin, where land grants exceeded the counties' actual size by a factor of eighteen, twelve, and ten, respectively. This was accomplished by what was at the time termed "shingling," the layering of "successive competing head-right warrants and claims" that were duly recorded in the surveyor general's office.[15]

Prompted in large part by the public outcry against the corruption of both the Pine Barrens Speculation and the Yazoo Fraud, subsequent land grants in Georgia were conducted under an impartial lottery system formalized under the Land Lottery Act of 1803. Under this scheme, lands available for public distribution were surveyed in advance by the state, with grants made based on the random drawing of lots. This method removed, for the most part, opportunities to influence the process though bribery or other malfeasance. A series of lotteries over the next three decades distributed most of the state's land that remained in the public domain.

The transition to a fair and honest lottery system did nothing to undo past transgressions. Millions of acres of state territory, much of it mythical, continued to exist in the form of head-right grants from the 1790s. As noted by Jones, pine barren land was "practically valueless" in Georgia, yet, enhanced by legal descriptions that replaced scrub and wiregrass with oak and

---

[15] The term "shingling" finds its origin in roofing shingles, which are laid one over the other in an overlapping fashion. See discussion in Chappell. It should be appreciated that by 1839, the original counties of Franklin and Washington had been further divided into a number of other counties. Montgomery County, originally a part of Washington, was created in December 1793, near the peak of the Pine Barrens Speculation. It is notable that some of the records related to these transactions and recorded in the 1860s and 1870s in the Washington County courthouse refer to landmarks that do not (and did not at that time) lie within the boundaries of the county. This is quite consistent with the fraudulent nature of the claims.

walnut, it continued to be bought and sold for more than a century. Among the first and more prominent men to be entrapped was Robert Morris. Born in Liverpool in 1734, Morris immigrated to Maryland at age thirteen. By the start of the American Revolution, he had become one of the wealthiest men in the colonies. His belief in the American cause, backed by his skill and resources, earned him the title of "Financier of the Revolution." He was a signer of the Declaration of Independence, the Articles of Confederation, and the Constitution of 1789 and later served as one of Pennsylvania's senators. Taking an active role in the new Republic's affairs, Morris, along with George Washington, was considered one of the most powerful men in the nation.

Aside from his political involvement, Morris was a natural entrepreneur and speculator, amassing his fortune through diverse business interests. In 1795, he and two associates formed the North American Land Company, funded by the sale of stock. Its purpose was to buy up raw land in the new American states and resell it at a profit to settlers and other speculators, both in the United States and in Europe. Among the 6 million acres acquired by the company were approximately 2,300,000 acres of Georgia land grants generated during the Pine Barrens Speculation. With the collapse of the American real estate market in 1796, and warnings in French newspapers naming Morris personally and advising of the fraudulent nature of the Georgia land titles, he was forced to declare bankruptcy. Sent to debtors' prison in 1798, the once-fabulously rich businessman was jailed for three and a half years until released under the Bankruptcy Act of 1800, enacted by Congress in part to secure Morris's freedom. He died in poverty in 1806.

On a practical basis many, perhaps most, of the land grants obtained during the Pine Barrens Speculation were eventually recognized as fraudulent documents. More than two-thirds of the total acreage allegedly granted was included in more than one grant or, alternatively, simply could not be identified based on its legal description—if it existed at all. For other large tracts held by speculators for the purpose of resale, property taxes often went unpaid, resulting in the land reverting to state ownership. Despite such dubious or legally nonexistent titles, the land continued to be bought and sold well into the early twentieth century. The fate of the lands once held by Robert Morris and the North American Land Company provide a typical example.

For years, the assets of the North American Land Company were tied up in bankruptcy. In the mid-nineteenth century, New Yorker Robert L. Pell, whose Georgia land holdings in the former head-right counties eventually totaled some 4 million acres, acquired many of company's land titles from the trustees. In the immediate post-Civil War era, Pell made a concerted effort to sell his properties, going so far as to publish a pamphlet in 1865 extolling the land's qualities, pointing out how easily fortunes could be made by the would-be buyer. The vast pine barrens, with their sandy soil and swampy lowlands, had now become a potential paradise for the savvy investor: "The soil is fertile, the climate healthy, and they offer opportunities and facilities for the creation of wealth, unsurpassed by any section of equal extent in the entire South." Focusing the value of the forest resources, Pell calculated that an investor could earn between $78,500 and $87,750 *in profit* per thousand acres from sales of timber alone, not to mention the value of the residual land for agriculture, etc. Despite this exorbitant opportunity for the creation of wealth, Pell let it be known that he was willing to part with his tracts at what must have appeared to be a bargain price.[16]

Pell's adroit marketing found at least some success. Deeds recorded in the Washington County courthouse indicate that on May 30, 1867, he sold 5,000 acres to Mary C. Rand of Staten Island, New York. In September 1870, E. A. Roland of New York City bought 8,000 acres, with a sale for 2,000 acres to James Morgan of Brooklyn, New York, the following spring. In each case, the recorded transaction price was $100. There is no record that any of the buyers were later able to dispose of their purchases.

The attempt of unwary buyers to lay claim to various head-right grant tracts dating to the 1790s continued well into the twentieth century. In his

[16] Pell's pamphlet included copies of statements from county clerks in Emanuel, Montgomery, Tatnall, and Washington counties generally acknowledging the existence of deeds recorded in Pell's name and extolling the quality of the land in the county. A letter to Pell from an attorney in Laurens County states, "It is our opinion that the title to said lands are good and perfect, they having been regularly granted as appears on record in the Secretary of State's office." There was a caveat, however, as the lawyer goes on to say, "'Tis true perhaps that there may be some squatters who have illegally settled on parts of the land," adding, "They...may be easily ejected." There seems to be little doubt that nearly three-quarters of a century after the original grants were issued, the "squatters" would consider themselves the legitimate landowners, vigorously opposing a buyer's attempt to remove them.

Annual Report for 1911, Secretary of State Philip Cook reiterated, "These grants have always been regarded as fraudulent and worthless, not a single provision of law having been complied with by the grantees, or those claiming under them." Noting that during his time in office he had received more than a hundred inquiries about these Pine Barrens Speculation grants, Cook called on the legislature to take action to protect legitimate landowners from the holders of false claims. The problem had become so recurrent and vexsome that he prepared a form letter to be sent out in response, hoping "to protect innocent people from designing and unscrupulous land-sharks who are offering them for sale all over the United States by showing the utter worthlessness of all such fraudulent grants, which are not worth the paper upon which they are written."

There is no evidence that those who masterminded or perpetuated the fraudulent land deeds that later became known as the Pine Barrens Speculation suffered any significant adverse consequences. Like the many other land sale scams that have existed over the years, greed and desire for a quick profit were the main motivators for both sellers and buyers. Oftentimes—as in the case of the Georgia lands of Robert Pell—decades elapsed between the creation of the deeds and their eventual sale (or resale) to gullible and naïve buyers. The documents and deeds appeared to be legitimate and had been duly recorded in the public records of the state. While this might impart an air of legitimacy to the claims, in fact, it carried no endorsement. The sellers would allege that they were merely transferring whatever interest they might hold in the property; it was up to the buyer to affirm the exact nature of what he or she was purchasing. *Caveat emptor.*

Sources and Resources

The best single account of the Pine Barrens Speculation is found in *Georgia Land Surveying History and Law* by Farris W. Cadle (University of Georgia Press, 1991). Using both original and secondary sources, Cadle gives an excellent historical overview of the various methods used to transfer land from the public domain to new settlers from the earliest days of the colony to the mid-nineteenth century.

Other primary and/or contemporary sources include:

Chappell, Absalom H. *Miscellanies of Georgia, Historical, Biographical, Descriptive, Etc.*, Part II. Atlanta: James F. Meegan, 1874: 43–56.

McLendon, Samuel G. *History of the Public Domain of Georgia.* Atlanta: Foote & Davies Co., 1924.

Pell, Robert L., *The Lands Belonging to Robert L. Pell in the State of Georgia.* New York: Privately printed pamphlet, 1865.

Chappell and McLendon were both members of state government, with their accounts reflecting their knowledge and perspective of the Pine Barrens Speculation. The full texts of both works are available electronically from several sources. A complete copy of Pell's sales pamphlet is in the collection of the Hargrett Library of the University of Georgia in Athens.

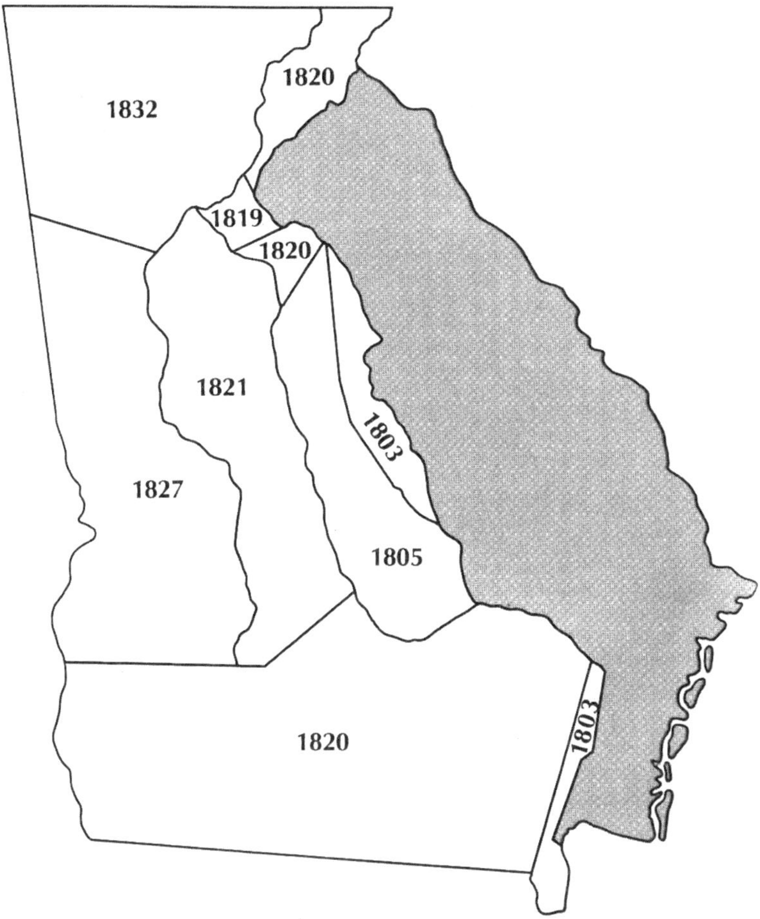

For two decades between 1783 and 1803, Georgia's vast uncolonized lands were deeded to individuals via on a headright system based on family size and other considerations. Fraud was rampant, leading to a new lottery system for the awarding of land grants in 1803 and thereafter. The area in which property was deeded to owners under the headright system is shown as the shaded area on this map.

State of Georgia.

By His Excellency GEORGE MATHEWS, Captain-General, Governor, and Commander in Chief in and over the said State, and of the Militia thereof.

To all to whom these Presents shall come, GREETING:

KNOW YE, That, in Pursuance of the Act for opening the LAND-OFFICE, and by Virtue of the Powers in me vested, I HAVE given and granted, and, by these Presents, in the Name and Behalf of the said State, DO give and grant unto William Pollard his Heirs and Assigns forever, ALL that Tract or Parcel of Land, containing Nine hundred & Seventy Acres, situate, lying and being in the County of Washington in the said State, and butting and bounding North East by Rayless lands, North West by ... said Pollards Land

having such Shape, Form, and Marks, as appear by a Plat of the same hereunto annexed; together with all and singular the Rights, Members, and Appurtenances thereof, whatsoever, to the said Tract or Parcel of Land belonging, or in any wise appertaining; and also all the Estate, Right, Title, Interest, Claim and Demand of the State aforesaid, of, in, to, or out of, the same; TO HAVE AND TO HOLD the said Tract or Parcel of Land, and all and singular the Premises aforesaid, with their and every of their Rights, Members, and Appurtenances, unto the said William Pollard his Heirs and Assigns, to his and their own proper Use and Behoof forever, in Fee simple.

GIVEN under my Hand, and the Great Seal of the said State, this Eighteenth Day of November in the Year of our LORD One Thousand Seven Hundred and Ninety four, and in the Nineteenth Year of American Independence.

SIGNED by his EXCELLENCY the GOVERNOR, the 18th Day of Nov. 1794.

Geo Mathews

This land grant for 979 acres in Washington County, Georgia, was signed by Governor George Mathews at the peak of the Pine Barrens Speculation in November 1794. It was among family papers passed down to the author.

Author's Collection

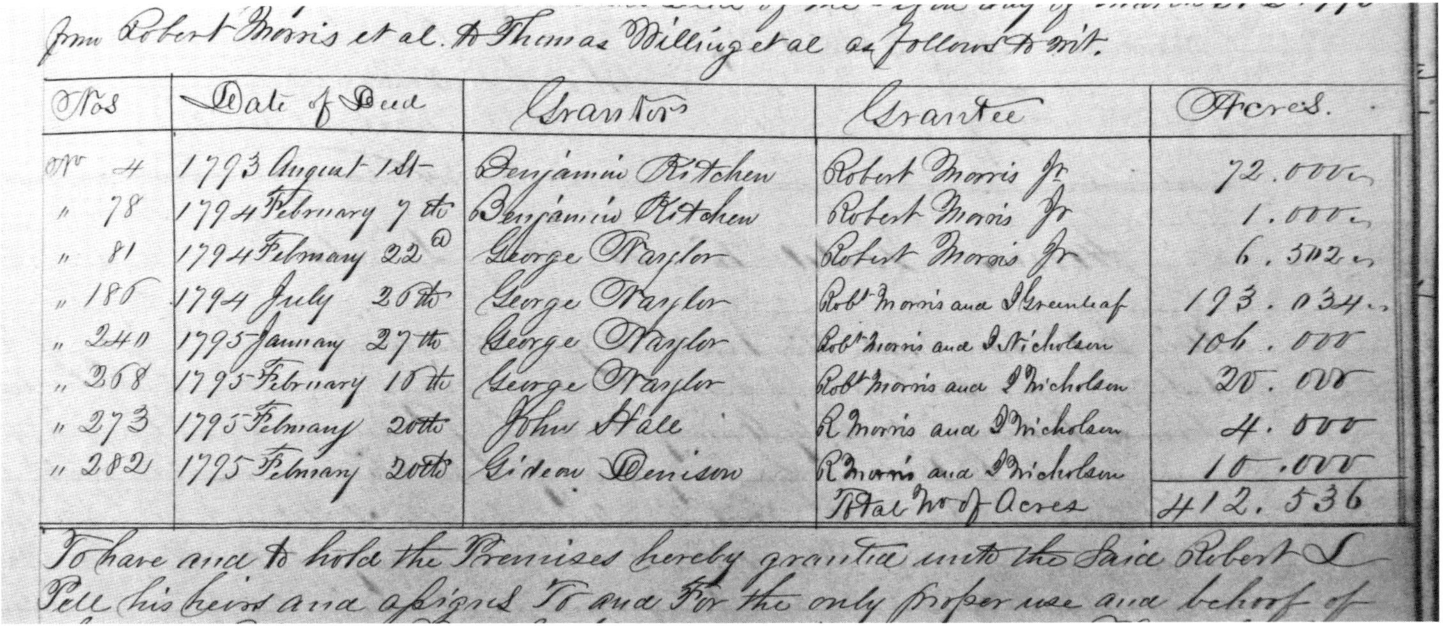

from Robert Morris et al. to Thomas Willing et al as follows to wit.

Nos	Date of Deed	Grantor	Grantee	Acres.
No 4	1793 August 1st	Benjamin Kitchen	Robert Morris Jr	72.000
" 78	1794 February 7th	Benjamin Kitchen	Robert Morris Jr	1.000
" 81	1794 February 22d	George Taylor	Robert Morris Jr	6.502
" 186	1794 July 26th	George Taylor	Robt Morris and J Greenleaf	193.034
" 240	1795 January 27th	George Taylor	Robt Morris and J Nicholson	106.000
" 268	1795 February 10th	George Taylor	Robt Morris and J Nicholson	20.000
" 273	1795 February 20th	John Hall	R Morris and J Nicholson	4.000
" 282	1795 February 20th	Gideon Denison	R Morris and J Nicholson	10.000
			Total No of Acres	412.536

To have and to hold the Premises hereby granted unto the said Robert L Pell his heirs and assigns To and For the only proper use and behoof of

Deed records from the late 1860s recorded in the Washington County Courthouse in Sandersville, Georgia, include several large land transactions involving Robert Pell, a New York land speculator. The eight tracts recorded here trace their original titles to the 1790s, and were previously owned by Robert Morris, one of the prominent figures of the American Revolution. The total 412,536 acres cited in these transactions alone equals nearly the entire area of the county. There is little doubt that these transactions refer to land that does not exist, or are otherwise fraudulent.

Author's Collection

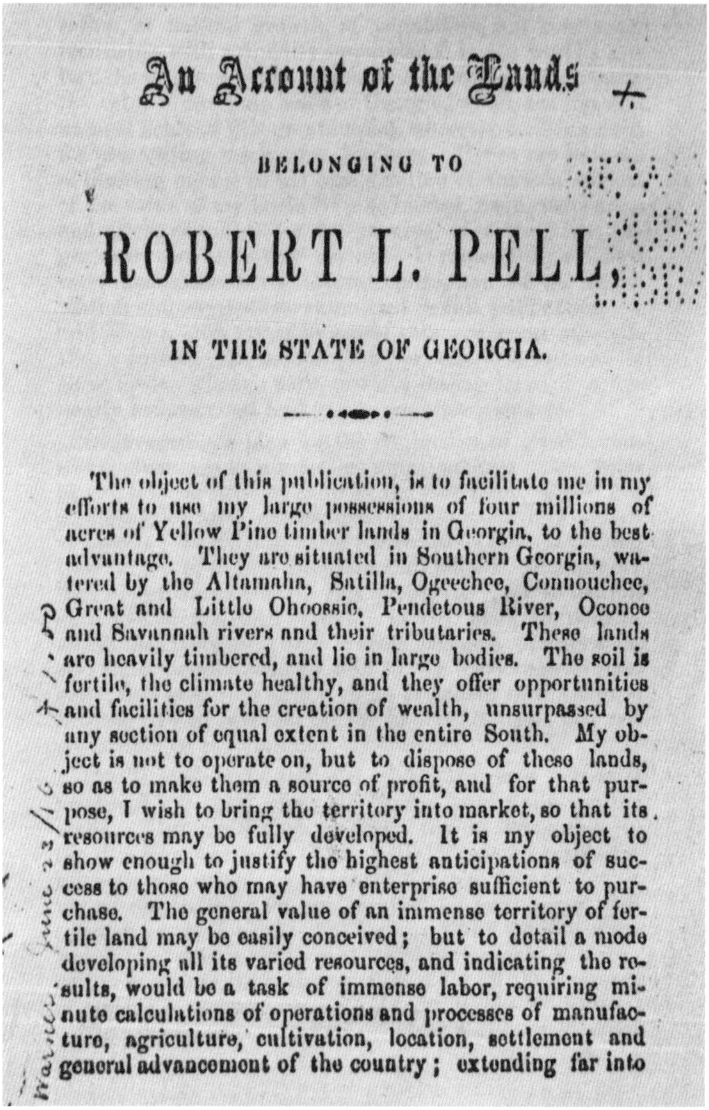

An Account of the Lands

BELONGING TO

ROBERT L. PELL,

IN THE STATE OF GEORGIA.

The object of this publication, is to facilitate me in my efforts to use my large possessions of four millions of acres of Yellow Pine timber lands in Georgia, to the best advantage. They are situated in Southern Georgia, watered by the Altamaha, Satilla, Ogeechee, Connouchee, Great and Little Ohoossie, Pendetous River, Oconee and Savannah rivers and their tributaries. These lands are heavily timbered, and lie in large bodies. The soil is fertile, the climate healthy, and they offer opportunities and facilities for the creation of wealth, unsurpassed by any section of equal extent in the entire South. My object is not to operate on, but to dispose of these lands, so as to make them a source of profit, and for that purpose, I wish to bring the territory into market, so that its resources may be fully developed. It is my object to show enough to justify the highest anticipations of success to those who may have enterprise sufficient to purchase. The general value of an immense territory of fertile land may be easily conceived; but to detail a mode developing all its varied resources, and indicating the results, would be a task of immense labor, requiring minute calculations of operations and processes of manufacture, agriculture, cultivation, location, settlement and general advancement of the country; extending far into

Robert Pell, a New York land speculator, acquired an alleged four million acres in Georgia, a portion of it with ownership titles dating back to the Pine Barrens Speculation of the 1790s. In this 1865 pamphlet, he offers his holdings for sale, extoling the quality of the land and its economic potential. How much of the land offered for sale actually existed is another matter, however.

Hargrett Rare Book and Manuscript Library, University of Georgia

PART II

THE CIVIL WAR ERA 1861–1865

OVERVIEW

THE CIVIL WAR ERA 1861–1865

The Civil War is remembered as one of the defining moments in the history of the American Republic. It was a horrific conflict, splitting the relatively young nation asunder, and responsible for more American deaths than all of the major wars of the twentieth century combined.[17] In some respects, it was the inevitable outcome of divisions that had plagued America since the country's formation.

Although occasionally presented in terms of states' rights or economic issues, the root cause of the Civil War was the issue of slavery. Allowed under the Constitution of 1789, slavery was considered by many from the outset to be an abomination, a rejection of one of the fundamental issues of human rights addressed by that very document. Many historians have speculated that slavery as a permitted institution would have died a quiet death early in the nineteenth century had it not been for one remarkable occurrence that the framers of the Constitution could not have predicted: the invention of the cotton gin.

In the first decade or so following the American Revolution, the United States was a relatively homogenous country in many ways. There were differences in the ethnic background of the population, land use patterns, and commerce based on geography and climate, but nothing so major as to bring the individual states to consider secession and the formation of a new nation. With Eli Whitney's gin (and the subsequent improvements that made it even more efficient), cotton production soon became America's prime economic engine. From the late 1790s through the 1850s, vast swaths of land from the Carolinas to Texas were devoted to cotton. It was a labor-

[17] Exact estimates vary, but the total number of deaths attributed to the Civil War exceeds the number of America lives lost as a result of World War I, World War II, the Korean War, and the war in Viet Nam.

intensive crop, and, as such, required human capital. This took the form of slaves.

Because of cotton, made possible by slavery, many became wealthy. This wealth was by no means limited to the South. It extended as well to the principals of the banking houses of New York, the owners of the shipping fleets of New England, and a long chain of traders, merchants, and suppliers who facilitated cotton's flow to market both in America and abroad. Britain's textile barons and Boston's Brahmins often saw returns that equaled or exceeded those of the Southern plantation owner. Abomination or not, slavery made the production of cotton possible, leading many to turn a moral blind eye. By 1860, America's nearly 4 million slaves made up 12.6 percent of the nation's total population. Of that number, however, some 89 percent resided in the eleven Southern states that would form the Confederacy. As such, slavery became defined as a geographic institution.

Democracies are built on compromise. The issue of slavery had threatened the United States for decades prior to the Civil War. The Missouri Compromise of 1820 and the Compromise of 1850, both of which addressed the issue of slavery in new states and territories as America expanded westward, had temporarily dampened the political fires that would lead to secession.

It was not to last. At the start of the second half of the nineteenth century, the South and her export of cotton had become the prime source of America's export income. Not surprisingly, the wealthy planter class controlled the region's reins of power. The increasingly real threats to the continuation of slavery as a permitted institution became an existential peril to the South's wealth and political power. In his infamous "Cotton is King" speech, delivered to the Senate on March 4, 1858, Sen. James Henry Hammond of South Carolina gave a vigorous moral and economic defense of slavery, at the same time noting that the South could exist and thrive as a nation independent of the rest of the United States.[18]

In what was perhaps an inevitable clash of opposing moral, political, and economic viewpoints, eleven Southern states voted to secede and form a new nation, the Confederate States of America, and in the process changing

---

[18] Senator Hammond's address to the Senate is readily available in both complete and excerpted formats from a number of sources accessed via an Internet search.

the course of history. Many books, both fiction and nonfiction, have been written about the Civil War era. Even though the events they recount occurred more than a century and a half ago, the topic fascinates Americans interested in our shared national history. In fact, printed titles on Civil War-related topics consistently represent one of the largest categories in American literary output year after year. Readers seeking to learn more about the era are often overwhelmed by the sheer volume of titles, having no idea where to begin. On a personal basis, I consider Pulitzer Prize-winning author James M. McPherson's *Ordeal by Fire: The Civil War and Reconstruction* an excellent and most readable overview. Originally published in 1982, it is available in updated editions in both print and electronic formats.

In this section on the Civil War I have chosen to focus on a single episode, the flight of the Confederate government south after the fall of Richmond, Virginia, in April 1865. The first of the three chapters, "The Saga of the Lost Confederate Treasure," examines the events that produced the legends of hidden gold. The second, "The Capture of Jefferson Davis from Both a Southern and Northern Perspective," is an account of the final act in the saga of the attempted escape of the president and his party from pursuing federal troops. The third, "The Strange Journey of the Confederate Constitution," is the intriguing and complicated tale of how the original Confederate Constitution ended up in the Hargrett Rare Book and Manuscript Library at the University of Georgia in Athens.

CHAPTER 4

THE SAGA OF THE LOST CONFEDERATE TREASURE

The basic facts of the story seem simple enough. In early April 1865, President Jefferson Davis and other high-ranking members of the Confederate government fled the capital of Richmond, Virginia, under pressure from rapidly advancing Federal troops. Accompanying them were all of the cash reserves held in the Richmond treasury of the beleaguered Confederacy, as well as the gold reserves of the Richmond banks, the total value of which was estimated by some to be in the millions of dollars. When Jefferson Davis and his ragged group were finally captured by members of the Fourth Michigan Calvary in south Georgia near Irwinville on May 10th, they had only a few dollars in their possession. What became of this precious cargo?

Over the years, tales of the "lost Confederate treasure" have become ingrained in American culture and folklore. From movies to books to the Internet, speculation and stories abound as to "what really happened." Dozens of cities and counties across the South and even further afield each have their own unique account as to where the treasure might be hidden—accompanied by, of course, logical reasons as to why it hasn't yet been found. The Clint Eastwood classic *The Good, the Bad, and the Ugly* revolves around a search for missing Confederate gold. The 2005 film *Sahara*, based on a book of the same name by Clive Cussler, finds gold from the Confederate treasury in the middle of the African desert. What actually became of the gold, silver, and other valuables carried South by the fleeing government? Did the leaders of the Confederacy steal it, as some have alleged? Was it buried in some secret location to be dug up by future generations, or did the treasure suffer a more mundane fate? Why do rumors of "lost Confederate gold" persist even today, spurring on generation after generation of treasure hunters? The facts, sketchy as they may be at times, present a somewhat more prosaic account than that bandied about in popular imagination.

On Sunday, April 2, 1865, the advancing Union army faced tattered and battle-weary Confederate soldiers defending Richmond, Virginia, under the overall command of Gen. Robert E. Lee. Realizing that his lines could not hold and that the fall of the Confederate capital was imminent, General Lee sent an urgent message to President Jefferson Davis warning him that the government must evacuate the capital or face certain capture. For weeks, members of the government had been preparing for the possibility of the fall of Richmond. Lee's telegram was delivered to President Davis during morning services at St. Paul's Episcopal Church. Davis received the news, then quietly arose and left the sanctuary. Others, members of the Confederate military and government, soon followed. Plans for an emergency evacuation were rapidly put into action. Shortly before midnight, a special train carrying the president, members of his cabinet, and the essential documents and archives of the government departed Richmond for Danville, Virginia. In spite of the bleak news, there was hope, perhaps unrealistic, that this would be a temporary setback and that the struggle for the survival of the Confederacy would continue.

A few hours later, a second train departed the Richmond station, following the fleeing government south. On board were all the hard currency reserves of the Confederate States of America under the guard of a group of young midshipmen from the Confederate Navy who had scuttled their vessel in the James River. Aboard this train were boxes and kegs containing "gold and silver, double-eagles, Mexican dollars, some ingots, and even a fair quantity of copper pennies, totaling more than $327,000 in Confederate treasure specie, and perhaps $450,000 or more from the Richmond banks.[19] Some boxes contained five sacks of $5,000 each in gold coin, weighing over seventy-five pounds per box."[20] There were some five tons of Mexican silver coins alone, bringing the total weight of the treasure to more than nine tons. In addition to the precious metals, there was a significant quantity of valuable jewelry donated to the cause by Confederate women. The commander in charge of the midshipmen guards referred to it all as "a very troublesome elephant."[21]

---

[19] "Specie" refers to money in the form of coins, as opposed to paper currency. Mexican silver coins in this context are more properly termed "pesos" but were commonly referred to as "dollars."

[20] William C. Davis, *An Honorable Defeat: The Last Days of the Confederate Government*, 85.

[21] Ibid, 86.

Rumors and speculation aside, the truth is that the exact value of the gold and silver carried south by the fleeing government can only be estimated. The destruction and disorder that accompanied the fall of the Confederacy led to the loss of most of the records that could have been used to establish a more exact estimate. The figure of $327,000 as the total amount of the hard reserves held in the central Confederate treasury would appear to be a paltry sum for any government. However, as many officials testified after the war when accused of having knowledge of the treasure's disappearance, the Confederacy was nearly broke. The reverses of the last two years of the war combined with the effective federal blockade of Southern ports had nearly drained the Treasury dry. Assuming that this estimate is in the range of accuracy, the combined worth of the Treasury, together with the Richmond bank gold, jewelry, and other valuables, would suggest that the value of the fabled "treasure" was in the range of $1 million.

With departure of the government, chaos reigned in Richmond. Retreating troops set fire to warehouses of military matériel, while looters robbed and burned stores and homes. By the end of the day on April 3, 1865, the city lay in ruins as federal troops moved in and fanned out across the city looking for stragglers. Although the fall of Richmond and the government's flight was a crushing blow, many—including President Davis—were unwilling to admit defeat. The plan was to withdraw to a safer area, reestablish the government, and continue the struggle. Barely avoiding federal marauders, the train carrying the president and members of his cabinet arrived safely in Danville, Virginia, hoping to establish a new capital there.

The respite was brief. As Davis and the government fled south, two events that would forever change the course of American history took place. On April 9, 1865, Gen. Robert E. Lee surrendered his Army of Northern Virginia to Gen. Ulysses S. Grant at Appomattox Courthouse. And only five days later, John Wilkes Booth, a Southern sympathizer, shot President Abraham Lincoln at Ford's Theater in Washington, DC. Many in the North, enraged by Lincoln's death and fueled by wild speculation in the Northern press, assumed that the dying Confederacy, and Davis in particular, were behind a plot that led to the president's assassination. The value of the funds carried by the fugitives was speculated to be as much as $13 million, possibly to be used to bribe Davis's way to freedom. There were calls for Davis's summary execution if and when he was captured and a $100,000 reward was placed on his head, an astronomical sum for the day.

Over the next four weeks, Davis and other members of the government pushed steadily south, pursued by troops from the North and avoiding the areas in their path under federal control. The treasure train followed a similar route, from Danville south to Charlotte, North Carolina, then on to Chester, South Carolina.[22] Transferred to wagons, then back into railcars, then back onto wagons once again, all the while under heavy guard, the precious cargo passed through Newberry and Abbeville, South Carolina, arriving in Washington, Georgia, on April 19th. When the threat of its capture became too great in Washington, the treasure was once more loaded onto wagons and moved first to Augusta and then back across the Savannah River to Abbeville before returning back to Washington by May 3rd.

It should be remembered that the majority of the assets of the so-called treasure belonged to the Richmond banks, not to the Confederacy. As such, they were considered held in trust and untouchable even by the fleeing government. During the weeks of flight, expenses for lodging and provisions as well as payment to the accompanying troops steadily drained the government's limited funds. A sample of known expenses includes $39,000 paid to soldiers in Greensboro, North Carolina, $108,000 paid to escorting troops near the Savannah River, and about $40,000 paid for soldiers' provisions in Augusta and Washington, Georgia. Approximately a month after departing Richmond, only about $100,000 remained in treasury funds, according to the calculations of one historian.[23]

By the fourth of May, the defeat of the Confederacy was clear. Meeting in Washington, Georgia, President Davis and the few remaining members of the cabinet still traveling with him made the decision to disband the government. Some $86,000 was given to a trusted officer to be smuggled abroad and held in Confederate accounts. The Richmond banks' funds were deposited for safekeeping in a local vault. Davis hoped to reach Florida and then perhaps travel west by boat to Texas where he would continue to lead the Confederacy's struggle. Now accompanied by his wife, Varina, and their children, who had initially departed Richmond separately from the presi-

[22] It was in Chester, South Carolina, where many of the important documents and archives of the Confederacy were abandoned when the fleeing party transferred from rail to wagon. For details of the chaos, and another interesting tale in this saga, see the chapter 6, "The Strange Journey of the Confederate Constitution."

[23] See Hanna in Sources and Resources.

dent, the group headed south toward Macon with a small band of guards. A second group of core supporters split off and planned to meet up with Davis near the Florida line. Between them, they carried what remained of the $35,000 in gold that had been allotted for expenses of the president and cabinet some weeks earlier. This was all that was left of the government funds.

On May 10th, just south of Irwinville, Georgia, and not far from the Florida line, the fugitives were surprised and captured in an early morning raid by troops from the Fourth Michigan Calvary. They had with them only a few dollars. The fabled "Confederate treasure" had disappeared. Or had it simply all been spent? The truth, however unexciting it may seem, is that at the end of the war what few hard monetary assets the Confederacy may have had were nearly depleted. There was no treasure to go missing, only groundless rumors. So why are there persistent legends about the "Confederate Gold"? Perhaps the answer lies in the old adage that underlying most myths is a grain of truth. And the truth—in this case—refers to the fate of the gold reserves of the Richmond banks.

In the mid-nineteenth century, long before today's highly regulated banking system, most banks were privately owned. They issued notes and paper currency backed by physical gold reserves. In fact, the link between the value of the US dollar and the price of gold was abandoned only in 1971.[24] In contrast to the estimated value of the Confederate treasury, the Richmond bank gold's value was more accurately recorded as approximately $451,000. Having been left for safekeeping in the Washington, Georgia, bank vault after the fugitive government split up, it fell into the hands of occupying Northern troops within a matter of days.

Given the conflict and the uncertain legal relationship between the Richmond banks and the Confederacy, the legal ownership of gold was potentially a subject of dispute. It was decided that the gold would be sent north pending final determination of this issue. Ownership issues aside, the gold was now in the custody of the United States government. It was to be carried by wagon to Abbeville, South Carolina, where it could be loaded into railcars for transportation to Washington. On May 24, 1865, a group of five wagons loaded with the Richmond bank gold set out on their long journey. After traveling approximately eighteen miles, the wagon train made camp

[24] Although on a practical basis, the United States and other major world economies had moved away from the gold standard decades earlier.

for the night near Danburg Crossroads in Lincoln County, Georgia, about three miles short of a pontoon bridge across the Savannah River.

Around midnight, the camp was invaded by approximately twenty armed horsemen. Their identity was unknown, but rumors held that the raiders were paroled soldiers, or perhaps others with military training. Taken by surprise, the wagon train's guards offered no resistance as the raiders helped themselves to the gold, apparently limited only by the amount they could fit into their saddle bags and pouches. The bandits were said to have left trails of gold coins that spilled from their overfilled bags as they fled. The next day, "local people, black and white, helped themselves to coins still laying (*sic*) about the camp site."[25] When the bank agents were finally able to total their losses, the amount missing was determined to be $251,029.90.

The theft of the gold brought immediate responses by both federal soldiers and local vigilantes who scoured the countryside, each for opposite reasons, but each hoping to recover some of the loot. There were reports that some ex-slaves were threatened with lynching during the search. Federal Gen. Edward A. Wild took over command of the military search operation, going so far as to have his men torture family members of a prominent plantation owner, but learning little in the process. In the end, the authorities recovered approximately $111,000, suggesting that some $140,000 had been absorbed into the local economy. Today, more than a century and half later, it is rumored that some local fortunes were founded on the basis of gold stolen from the Richmond banks' assets.

Stories founded on a bit of truth often change and grow with the passing years as they are passed down from generation to generation. The stories of lost Confederate riches might seem plausible at first glance, but under close examination one finds they are based more on fable than on fact. Like other myths of the South that have sprung up around the history of the Civil War, the legends of the lost Confederate treasure have taken on a life of their own. Sometimes we believe what we want to believe.[26]

---

[25] Davis, Robert S., "The Georgia Odyssey of the Confederate Gold," 580.

[26] See chapter notes for an interesting commentary on the author's personal experience with the "lost Confederate treasure."

SOURCES AND RESOURCES

The gold and silver held by the Confederate government in Richmond were certainly not the sole monetary assets of the breakaway nation. There were a number of other Confederate depositories, and many other nonmonetary governmental assets, cotton being an important example. Generally speaking, these assets, monetary and otherwise, fell into the hands of federal troops as the Union army steadily whittled away the area of the Confederacy under the control of its government. With this said, it is the gold and silver carried south with Jefferson Davis after the fall of Richmond that has attracted the most attention.

There are many sources of information that mention the alleged "Confederate treasure" but few that offer in-depth facts and analysis. The true paucity of facts is a hindrance to all such accounts. The works of A. J. Hanna and William C. Davis, cited below, are among the most complete and, equally importantly, are written in a most readable style. The interested reader should be aware that while much attention has been devoted to the "treasure," there are other equally fascinating personal and historical tales that can be gleaned from the accounts below.

Davis, Robert S. "The Georgia Odyssey of the Confederate Gold." *Georgia Historical Quarterly* 86 (2002): 569–86. A limited overview of the "Confederate gold" in Georgia that is useful for its description of the robbery of the Richmond banks' gold from the wagon train in May 1865.

Davis, William C. *An Honorable Defeat: The Last Days of the Confederate Government.* New York: Harcourt, 2001. Davis, one of the preeminent historians of the Civil War, has written a more detailed account of the fall of the Confederate government and Jefferson Davis's attempted escape. He draws heavily on Hanna's earlier account in some areas but overall presents a far more detailed record of the weeks and months that preceded and followed the fall of Richmond, Virginia, in the spring of 1865.

Hanna, Alfred J. *Fight into Oblivion.* Baton Rouge: Louisiana State University Press, 1999. Hanna's original 1938 book was reprinted in 1999 by LSU Press, together with its original illustrations and a foreword by William C. Davis. More than simply a history book, Hanna's work is a well-researched adventure tale of the flight of the Confederate government after the fall of Richmond. While part of the book is devoted to Davis's abortive escape attempt, even more focus is given to John C. Breckinridge, the senator from Kentucky and former vice president of the United States who resigned his office and joined the Confederate military, later becoming secretary of war under President Davis. Breckinridge's escape to Cuba, and subsequently to Great Britain and Canada, is an intriguing saga in and of itself.

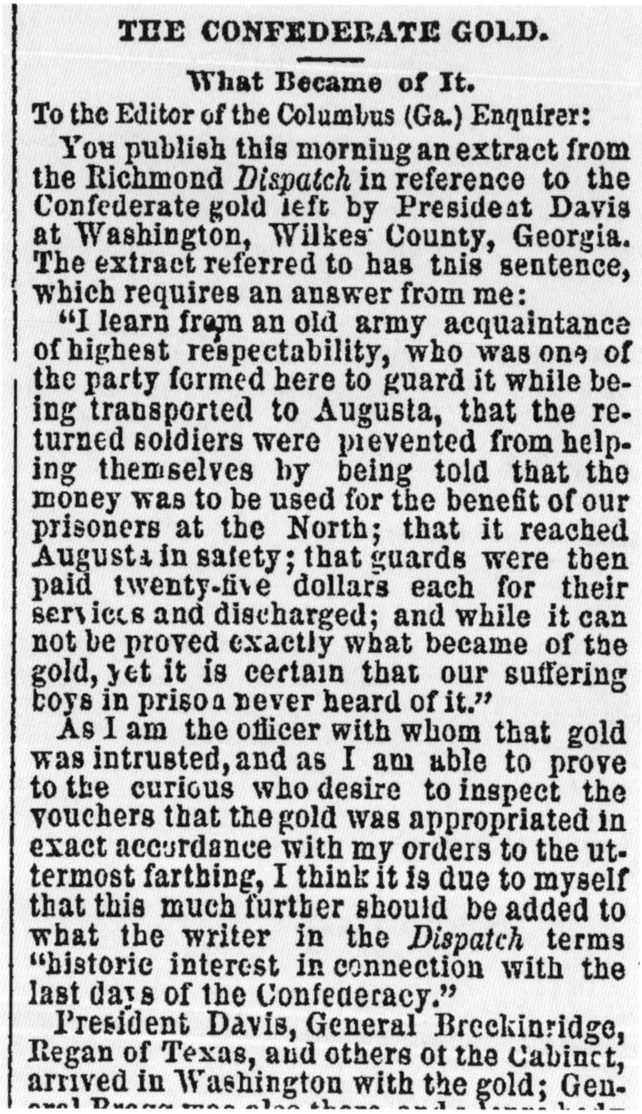

THE CONFEDERATE GOLD.

What Became of It.

To the Editor of the Columbus (Ga.) Enquirer:

You publish this morning an extract from the Richmond *Dispatch* in reference to the Confederate gold left by President Davis at Washington, Wilkes County, Georgia. The extract referred to has this sentence, which requires an answer from me:

"I learn from an old army acquaintance of highest respectability, who was one of the party formed here to guard it while being transported to Augusta, that the returned soldiers were prevented from helping themselves by being told that the money was to be used for the benefit of our prisoners at the North; that it reached Augusta in safety; that guards were then paid twenty-five dollars each for their services and discharged; and while it can not be proved exactly what became of the gold, yet it is certain that our suffering boys in prison never heard of it."

As I am the officer with whom that gold was intrusted, and as I am able to prove to the curious who desire to inspect the vouchers that the gold was appropriated in exact accordance with my orders to the uttermost farthing, I think it is due to myself that this much further should be added to what the writer in the *Dispatch* terms "historic interest in connection with the last days of the Confederacy."

President Davis, General Breckinridge, Regan of Texas, and others of the Cabinet, arrived in Washington with the gold; General

The rumors and legends that surrounded the so-called "Confederate Treasure" that allegedly accompanied the CSA's leaders' flight south provided the source of endless speculation for years after the end of the Civil War. Here is an excerpt of a typical newspaper exchange from 1872 referring to "The Confederate Gold: What Became of It."

Cincinnati Daily Enquirer, 11 March 1872

CHAPTER 5

THE CAPTURE OF JEFFERSON DAVIS FROM BOTH A SOUTHERN AND NORTHERN PERSPECTIVE

In the late 1950s, Lawrence Durrell, one of the most distinguished British authors of the twentieth century, penned a series of four novels known collectively as *The Alexandria Quartet*. The stories takes place in Alexandria, Egypt, in the period immediately before and during World War II. The first three books relate the same complex tale from the perspective of three characters; the fourth looks at the same events from a perspective of several years later. The beauty of Durrell's opus lies in the fact that even though the basic facts are the same for each character, their interpretation of the meaning and significance diverges based on their own mindset and emotional involvement.

In many ways, this same analogy can be applied to historical events surrounding the American Civil War and its aftermath, the Reconstruction era. While all may essentially agree on the facts, the interpretation thereof is often influenced by outlooks and beliefs that relate to heritage, education, and geographic home. The Lost Cause movement colored Southern thought for more than a century after the end of the conflict and remains alive and well in many parts of the former Confederacy today. In the North, the South is still often viewed as somewhat backwards; even today a Southern regional accent, for example, can be a liability in the urban world of business.

In this light, it becomes interesting to examine a single major event that occurred in the spring of 1865, the capture of Jefferson Davis, the then-fugitive president of the Confederate States of America. For the most part, the basic facts are undisputed: Davis and other high-ranking members of the Confederate government fled Richmond on April 2, 1865. Traveling south by rail and road, the besieged officials held their last formal meeting in Washington, Georgia, on May 4, 1865. Davis traveled on with a small party, hoping to reach the Gulf Coast where he might find passage to Texas and continue the struggle against the North. Instead, he was captured near Irwinville, Georgia, on May 10, 1865, by members of the Fourth Michigan Regiment, assisted by troops of the First Wisconsin Regiment.

By the second decade of the twentieth century, some half century after Lee's surrender at Appomattox, interest in events of the Civil War was at a peak. Similar to the adulation afforded members of "The Greatest Generation" fifty years or so after the end of World War II, the dwindling numbers of Confederate and Northern veterans were honored for their service and sacrifice. Their first-hand accounts of their roles in the conflict were heard with reverence and admiration by the generations that followed. In the South particularly, this timeframe represented the high point of the Lost Cause era, the informal movement that sought to "correct," and in many situations rewrite, the history of the Civil War years to reflect positively on the Confederate cause and Southern way of life.[27]

In 1917 and 1918, respectively, two articles recounting the capture of Jefferson Davis appeared in local newspapers in Sandersville, Georgia, and Portland, Oregon. The former, in the January 31, 1917, issue of the *Sandersville Georgian*, was titled, "The First Complete Story of [the] Capture of Jefferson Davis Near Irwinville, Ga." The latter, in the June 2, 1918, edition of the *Portland Oregonian* appeared under the headline, "Portland Veteran Tells of Capture of Jefferson Davis." Both recount the same events, albeit from the perspective of opposing forces. Like the accounts of the characters in Durrell's *Alexandria Quartet*, each story is slightly different even though they describe the same events.

The *Georgian* article was written by Alex W. Bealer (1860–1921), a former reporter for the *Atlanta Journal* who gave up journalism in 1896 to become a Baptist minister. News reports at the time described him as "one of Atlanta's brightest newspaper men." He subsequently went on to a distinguished career as a minister, often contributing news pieces on church-related topics to periodicals of the day. He was known to have an active interest in Civil War history, participating, for example, in the 1919 state convention of the United Daughters of the Confederacy in Valdosta, where he was pastor at the time. The *Oregonian* article was unsigned but apparently written by a staff reporter for the paper. A brief paragraph at the head of the piece states it was drawn from "the personal recollections of Theodore M.

[27] Please see the section on the Lost Cause years (1865–1939) for additional articles on this topic.

Kellogg, who was a member of [the First Wisconsin Cavalry], now living at 270 Graham Avenue, Portland."[28] Bealer's article is reproduced in its entirety. Several introductory paragraphs from the *Oregonian* article relating a brief history of the First Wisconsin Cavalry have been omitted; beyond this, the complete article has been reproduced here. Minor spelling and formatting corrections have been made to both pieces for the purpose of this account.

In comparing the two articles, there are minor differences that can be accounted for by memory and the passage of time. For example, the *Georgian* piece refers to "Judge F. H. Rowe" whereas the *Oregonian* names "Judge Rose." Both individuals are undoubtedly one in the same. For the most part, however, the basic facts are undisputed. Bealer's account picks up on the story earlier, whereas the account of the Northern veteran begins when the troops get word that the fleeing Davis party was in the area. Both articles debunk the story, widely circulated at the time, that Jefferson Davis had dressed in female disguise in trying to escape his captors.[29]

The differences in the two accounts are in the subtleties. In the Southern version, Davis is presented as "a gentleman, a soldier, and a patriot." Particular attention is paid to his concern over his wife's welfare. In the Northern account, he "berate[s]" his wife, blaming her for his capture. The Southern account makes special mention of John Davis, "a young mulatto about twenty-five, who had been a house servant to the [Jefferson Davis] family." A later paragraph refers to the young man acting "in the free and easy way of the southern Negro," a paternalistic statement that reflected the attitude toward persons of color held by many Americans of the day. This is also consistent with the myths of the Lost Cause movement, one of which held that the Southern way of life, including the social position of slaves and subsequently ex-slaves, was superior to that of the North. Reflecting differing views on the legitimacy of the secession that precipitated the conflict, Bealer's article speaks of "the War Between the States," in sharp contrast to the *Oregonian* account, which refers to "rebel officers," "rebeldom," and "rebellion" while detailing the destruction visited upon matériel and infrastruc-

[28] Please see "Sources and Resources" at the end of the chapter for additional information regarding the uncertain authorship of the *Oregonian* article.

[29] Inflamed by the recent assassination of President Lincoln, Northern newspapers were full of vengeful editorials referring to Davis as a "traitor" captured in petticoats. P. T. Barnum, the great American showman and founder of the Barnum & Bailey Circus, was said to have offered a $500 reward for "Jeff Davis' petticoats."

ture of military importance. The account of the "friendly fire" incident that resulted in the death of two Michigan troops and the wounding of several others is not found in Bealer's article. Despite their differences, both articles present an interesting window on an important episode in American history.

The Southern Account

The First Complete Story of the Capture of Jefferson Davis
Near Irwinville, Georgia
by Alex W. Bealer

The last chapter of the War Between the States has never been fully written. It deals with the flight of Jefferson Davis, after the fall of the Confederacy, a flight that lasted for a week and that led him through the lonely pine forests of south Georgia. It began at Washington, in Wilkes County, the home of General Robert Toombs,[30] known as "the fire-eating Bob Toombs," and ended in the woods near Irwinville, about 175 miles in a southwesterly direction from the starting point.

John Davis, the Negro who drove Mrs. Davis out of Richmond and who was driving the carriage in which Mr. Davis was riding with his wife when arrested, is still living on a farm near Eastman, in Dodge County, Georgia. In Dublin, the county seat of Laurens, lives Captain J. A. Thomas, an ex-Confederate soldier who might have changed the history of the South had he known that the closed carriage, which passed through Dublin on Sunday morning, the 7th of May 1865, contained the President and his wife.

When it was seen that the fall of Richmond was inevitable, the first thought of Mr. Davis was to know that his wife was protected and to make an effort to reach some point on the Gulf from which she could take passage for England. A closed carriage was secured for Mrs. Davis, and John Davis, a young mulatto about twenty-five, who had been a house servant in the family, was secured as the driver. A suitable escort was provided and the party started for the South.

[30]Robert A. Toombs (1810–1885) was an ardent secessionist and one of Georgia's United States senators at the start of the Civil War in 1861.

Mr. Davis, Judge Reagan[31] of Texas, and others followed making their way to the home of General Toombs, in Washington, one of the most aristocratic towns in the State. On the night of Wednesday, May 3rd, 1865, the last cabinet meeting of the Confederacy was held in the upper room of the old Heard home, also known as the state banking building. The only lingering hope for the success of the Confederacy at that time seemed to center about the plains of Texas upon which some of the leaders of the failing cause thought that a final stand might be made. It was known that a price had been set upon the head of Mr. Davis and the members of his cabinet. The present and pressing need was a place of safety. It was decided Mr. Davis should reach a southern port and embark for England with his family as soon as Mrs. Davis and the children could be located.

Knowing that the whole country was filled with spies, Mr. Davis thought it best to travel with as little display as possible. On the morning of Thursday, May 4th, with a single companion, he rode out of Washington, Georgia, bound for the south. It had been agreed that Judge Reagan and others should follow him some hours later. About twelve miles out from Washington, Mr. Davis and his companion, without disclosing their identity, secured lodgings and had their horses cared for.

Just after dark Thursday night, Judge Reagan and a small party left Washington and sometime during Friday morning overtook Mr. Davis. Others who had left Washington in small parties joined them until they had quite a company made up of some of the most distinguished men in the South, men whose names had been on the lips of the whole country.

At sunset on Friday, May 5th, the party having traveled fifty miles from Washington, came to a prosperous looking farm house and there they decided to camp for the night if suitable arrangements could be made. It was the home of Mr. Lee Warthen who had had been in the army and who had just returned to rebuild his shattered fortune. He and his brother lived on quite an extensive plantation at what is now known as Warthen, in Washington County. Just before his death in 1915, Mr. Lee Warthen told the story of the visit of Mr. Davis to his home.

---

[31]John H. Reagan (1818–1905) was postmaster general in Jefferson Davis's cabinet. At the time of secession, he was member of the United States House of Representatives from the state of Texas.

"A few days after my return from Appomattox," said he, "I rode over the place on a tour of inspection. Just before dark I returned to the house and was surprised to see the road in front of the dwelling full of soldiers. I thought they were Yankees as I knew the country was being scoured for Mr. Davis and members of his cabinet. I estimated that there were not less than fifty men in the party. I hitched my horse and walked over to where my brother was negotiating with a member of the party for food and horses and men. To my surprise the man proposed to pay for what we let him have in gold. This was very unusual as Yankee soldiers had been taking what they wanted without paying for it. A wagonload of provisions drawn by a yoke of oxen was sent out to the men and the leader asked for a suitable place where they could camp for the night. They were directed to a woody dale, two miles south of Warthen, known as the Griffin Pond. Two hundred yards back from the road the camp was pitched. There the tents and men were out of sight and sound of any one who might pass along the main road.

"It began to dawn on me before the soldiers left the house that they were Confederates and not Yankees. It was evident from their behavior that they were concealing something. I told the man with whom we had been talking what I thought and he replied in an evasive manner that they had to be careful as they had with them some members of the Confederate Senate. The moon was shining brightly when they left and I thought one of the men resembled Jefferson Davis as I had last seen him.

"When the leader paid for the supplies with gold, I asked 'Where did you get all that gold? It's the first I have seen in four years.' He turned on his heel and walked away saying in a low tone, 'I reckon we stole it.' At dark the man with whom we had traded, and whose name we did not learn, sent the party to the camping ground while he remained behind and took supper with us. We conversed on general topics and when the meal was finished he mounted his horse and galloped away toward the camp. Soon afterwards he sent the oxen home but kept the wagon until the next day.

"About 7 o'clock the next morning I rode over to the camp. A Negro was standing near the wagon and men were standing about in small groups talking. A distinguished looking man passed by and gazed at me as if he expected to be recognized. He had gray beard about two weeks old on his face and as he mounted his horse I recognized him as the same man who had attracted my attention the night before, and I was satisfied that he was Jefferson Davis. Senator Reagan rode off by his side and the whole party fell in behind and in a few moments the camp was deserted. I rode by the side of two of them in the rear, but they showed that they did not care to talk. Then I rode toward the head of the column but the leader galloped up and I knew that they did not want me to go ahead of them.

"In a brief conversation he asked what I thought of enlisting men to join the Confederate army in Texas, which he said had not surrendered. It was evident to me that some ill-advised persons wished to prolong the war and I told him I thought this would be folly, as the country was utterly exhausted and had neither men nor means to prolong the struggle.

"I rode away from the company and stopped at my plantation. I called my overseer and pointed out to him Jefferson Davis. I thought the leaders were acting unwisely. While they were seeking to conceal their identity, their actions were such as to provoke inquiry from everyone with whom they came in contact. The outfit was very different from that of ordinary returning soldiers. The stock was in splendid condition and the men were not bedraggled and weary looking, as was the case with most of the soldiers coming back to their homes.

"It was Saturday morning when Mr. Davis resumed his journey. That afternoon a small party, escorting Mrs. Davis passed, going in the same direction. Sunday afternoon General John C. Breckenridge[32] passed, accompanied by a single soldier. They were both travel-stained and weary. Colonel Jack Lane, of Sandersville, was guiding them through the country. The general rode up to my gate and after making himself known, said, 'The Yankees are scouring the country for us and I want all the information I can get.' I directed him how to travel with safety and he went on his way. I learned soon afterwards that he came near running into soldiers who captured Mr. Davis. He happened to see them in a distance and, riding into the woods, remained concealed until they had passed."

---

[32]John C. Breckinridge (1821–1875) was the vice president of the United States from 1857 to 1861 under President James Buchanan. He subsequently served as senator from Kentucky until the outbreak of the war, at which time he joined the Confederate army and was convicted of treason by the Senate. Commissioned a brigadier general, he served with distinction in a number of battles before being appointed as Davis's secretary of war during the final months of the conflict. Fleeing south at the same time as the Confederate cabinet, he eventually escaped to Cuba and subsequently to Europe, where he remained until issued amnesty by President Andrew Johnson in 1868.

Learning from returning soldiers that special efforts were being made to arrest him, Mr. Davis decided to break the company in which he was traveling into small parties. This was done to keep from attracting too much attention. They all took different roads but pushed on toward the south. The roads were filled with returning soldiers and small parties attracted no attention. Just being nightfall on Saturday Mr. Davis, Judge Reagan, and a small escort reached the east bank of the Oconee River, one of the muddy streams of the state. The road ran down to Blackshear's Ferry, which is still in operation five miles from the little city of Dublin. Here they decided to camp for the night. On going down to the ferry to talk with the ferryman and get what information they could, they found several men who lived not far away and who were discussing a very important bit of news. A wagon train was passing through the country, and from the appearance of stock, which was sleek and well fed, it was decided that the travelers must have money and it would prove profitable to rob the train.

When Mr. Davis heard this news he was considerably agitated, concluding that the wagon was the one in which his wife and children were traveling. He had not heard from them since they left Richmond, but he knew it was about time for them to be in this vicinity. He felt it was his duty to go to the assistance of his wife, and his friends decided to accompany him. Upon inquiry, they learned that the road on which the train was traveling was ten miles to the east. Saddling their horses, they were soon on their way to render what protection they could to Mrs. Davis.

Just after passing through Warthen where Mr. Davis and his party had camped, Mrs. Davis reached Sandersville, a town then untouched by a railroad. Here it was afterwards learned, the plot to rob the wagon had been hatched. Wash Renfroe, who afterwards became prominent in the politics of the state, heard of the plan, and knowing that Mrs. Davis was in the party, persuaded the men to abandon the robbery. Ignorant of her danger, Mrs. Davis passed along through the big woods until she came about dark on Saturday night to the home of Mr. E. L. Blackshear, ten miles from Dublin. Here she was entertained for the night with true Georgia hospitality.

It was a long and lonely ride that Mr. Davis and his men took that night. It was not more than ten miles, but, having no guide, they found it difficult to make their way. Much of the time they were in the pine woods. The value of the timber had not become apparent and most of it was untouched by the ax. The great trees, some of them a hundred feet tall, loomed above them and made mournful music in the breezes of the night. Now and then a sluggish stream, with a swamp on either side, was encountered, and with great difficulty the horses floundered through to the solid ground on the other side. It was nearly daylight when the road they had been seeking was reached. It happened that Mr. Davis came out of the woods only a short distance from the home of Mr. Blackshear, and his joy may be better imagined than described when he learned that his family were there and that they had not been harmed during the night.

After an early breakfast, his party secured all the information they could as to the roads and location of the federal troops and set out for the south. Mr. Davis was riding in the carriage with his wife. It was driven by the Negro, John Davis. About 11 o'clock Sunday morning the party drove into the town of Dublin, and here made a brief stop. Judge F. H. Rowe, who owned the store there, when informed that a party of travelers desired to buy some provisions, went down to his place of business. Learning that the party was led by Mr. Davis, he gave them all a cordial invitation to his home for dinner. The invitation was deemed prudent to decline, and after securing the needed provisions, the journey was resumed.

While the carriage was waiting in front of the store, quite a number of people gathered about it to ask questions. Among them were many Negroes, one of them a comely young woman, attracted the attention of the driver, John Davis. In the free and easy way of the southern Negro, he entered into a conversation with her and learned that her name was Della Conaway. During the brief time of waiting he managed to talk love to her. She had really made a deep impression upon him, and he had in like manner impressed her as a young man of more than usual importance since he was driving such fine folks behind such splendid looking horses.

The horses and mules were unusually fine and showed that they had been given the best attention. Among those who came to see the party was Captain J. A. Thomas, a young man who had just returned from the war, and who is still living in Dublin, where he is an active practitioner at the bar. This young man was a great lover of fine horse flesh, and he lingered long about the carriage, casting admiring glances at the splendid saddle horses that were tied not far away. He watched the party as they moved off along the road leading toward the Ocmulgee River, about forty miles to the southwest. That afternoon he went out for a horseback ride. When a few miles out of Dublin, on the Hawkinsville road, he met a company of Michigan cavalry going to town. On his return he learned that the company had decided to camp there for the night and that they were seeking Jefferson Davis. He also learned that similar companies were scouting the country for the Confederate leader and the members of his cabinet. This Michigan cavalry overtook Mr. Davis and arrested him at Irwinville on the next Wednesday morning.

In speaking of the arrival of this company, Captain Thomas said, "I did not know until later that Mr. and Mrs. Davis were in the carriage I had seen that morning in Dublin. If I had known it I could have secured a good horse and in two or three hours could have overtaken them. The great pine forests at that time were untouched by the ax of the turpentine man or by the saw of the lumber mill. The country was sparsely settled and I was familiar with almost every foot of it. It would have been an easy matter to turn into the forest with Mr. Davis. Without doubt I could have kept him hidden for six months or more, and then, when the excitement had died away, he could have made his way to the coast and from there to England. If this had been done he would have been spared the anguish and humiliation of Fortress Monroe."[33]

To show how feasible it would have been to keep Mr. Davis hidden I need but state that General Breckenridge went to a farm in the piney woods of Montgomery County and there remained unmolested for a number of weeks. When he was leaving he paid for his board by giving up a handsome gold watch. It is now the property of Judge E. D. Graham of McRae, who inherited it from his grandfather, the man who kept the general concealed from the soldiers who were searching for him.

Unconscious of the fact that the enemy was so close behind them, the President and his wife enjoyed that Sunday's drive through the heart of the big pine woods of the wiregrass country. The new buds on the young trees were giving out their spicy springtime odor and on every side the wild azaleas, called honeysuckles in Georgia, were filling the air with their fragrance. Everywhere mocking birds were mating. The new leaves on the trees they

[33] After his capture, Jefferson Davis was imprisoned at Fortress Monroe, Virginia, between May 1865 and December 1868. His initial treatment was harsh, being held in leg irons in an unheated casement of the fort. In late fall of 1865, he was moved to better quarters and was eventually released on bail after two years of imprisonment. Although indicted for treason, Davis was never tried. With others, he was granted amnesty in late 1868.

passed were fresh and beautiful, and the bright tints contrasted harmoniously with the darker color of the murmuring pines. All this, with the magnolias and bays, which were beginning to bloom along the watercourses must have reminded them of their beloved Beauvoir.

Late in the afternoon the clouds began to gather, and they decided to camp before the night came on. Passing through what is now known as Gum Swamp, they forded the Little Ocmulgee River, a small stream of black-looking water, and climbed a long hill on the other side. On the top of the hill they found an ideal camping place, and there they spent the night. The site of the old camp is now occupied by a farm house in which live Mr. Bill Flanders and his wife. It is four miles from Eastman, the capital of Dodge County. Neither the town nor the county was then in existence. The exact spot on which the camp stood is occupied today by an old cabin which is rapidly falling into decay. In front of it is a splendid pomegranate tree which is laden every year with beautiful fruit. The road up the hill now goes into Eastman, but at that time it turned to the left and went winding through the woods toward the Ocmulgee River. Since then the road has been changed, the original highway having been fenced in and another cut at right angles to the Eastman road. A few of the old pines beneath which the Davis party passed are still standing, gnarled and weather beaten. The opening in the trees can still be seen. Although more than half a century has passed, the wiregrass had not obliterated all traces of the road. Here and there white streaks, the old wagon ruts, are plainly visible.

After conferring together, it was decided that it would be safer for Mr. Davis to push on faster, as he needed to make better time than could be made if he remained with his wife. With a small body guard, he rode from the camp early Monday morning leaving Mrs. Davis to follow with the carriage. It was raining when the day dawned, and it continued to rain until night. The travelers were unacquainted with the roads, and several times they missed their course, and much time was lost. Just before night after one of these detours, they came back to the main road and overtook Mrs. Davis and her party. They reached Poor Robin ferry across the Ocmulgee River, before dark, and were ferried across by Mr. Alex Wilcox. They stopped for a short time at Poor Robin spring, but decided to camp in the village of Abbeville. They pitched their tent under an old oak tree which now stands in the front yard of John M. Warren, Judge of the Court of Ordinary for the County of Wilcox. The United States Daughters of the Confederacy have taken the old tree under their care and are doing all they can to prolong its life.

Tuesday morning Mr. Davis resumed his journey with his wife. They halted for the night in a pine grove on the outskirts of the little village of Irwinville. Here, in the early morning hours of Wednesday, May 10th, they were surrounded by the company of Michigan cavalry which had camped in Dublin just after they left the place. Without any resistance on the part of the Confederates, Mr. Davis was arrested. The captors turned the carriage about and started with their prisoner back to Macon. The driver on this trip was John Davis, the young Negro who had brought Mrs. Davis down from Richmond.

Wednesday night the party camped under the same tree in Abbeville where they had camped on Monday night. That old tree has about it more than the usual amount of historical interest, as under its branches Mr. Davis spent two nights, one as a free man and another as a prisoner of the United States.

The news of the arrest of Mr. Davis spread rapidly through the village of Abbeville and the surrounding country. The whole population turned out to look upon the distinguished prisoner. Many who were loyal to him in the hour of his downfall called to pay their respects and tender their sympathies. Among them was a patriotic fire-eating old rebel, Major Reid. He had an impediment in his speech, stuttering so badly he could hardly be understood. This was especially true when he was excited. After seeing Mr. Davis, he approached the leader of the soldiers and asked what would be done with the prisoner.

"We intend to hang him," replied the solder, at which the old gentleman flew into a rage and in broken sentences, cursed the whole army and dared them to try the hanging game. He grew red in the face and stuttered out that it would be a d—m shame and a stain on the civilized world to hang Jeff Davis, for being a gentleman, a soldier, and a patriot.

At Macon the party was broken up and Mr. Davis was sent to Fortress Monroe. John Davis, the young Negro, while traveling back to Macon, was thinking about the young girl he had seen in Dublin. As soon as he was relieved in Macon, he made his way back to hunt her up. He found her, courted her, married her and settled down as a farm hand in Laurens County. There they lived until ten years ago, when they moved over to the adjoining county, Dodge, near Eastman, with his family. They had thirteen children, three of whom died in infancy. The youngest was named Jeff. The old driver is still vigorous in body for his old age, being about eighty. His mind is not very clear as to the past. He remembers very little about the details of the journey from Richmond to Irwinville. He says that he was a servant in the Davis home in Mississippi and went with them to Richmond.

I asked him about the story of Mr. Davis being dressed like a woman, and he gave me one particular which was doubtless the foundation on which the fabrication was erected. When Mr. Davis was arrested he wore about his shoulders a long cape, part of an overcoat, and on his head was a black felt hat. He was a spare built man, and as he walked out toward the soldiers one of them said: "Look at that woman, she's got on boots!" John says there was a bonnet in the carriage belonging to Mrs. Davis, and as her husband desired to escape arrest, he put it on while passing through the towns along the way. No attempt to resist the soldiers was made, although there were several "six-shooters" in the carriage.

This story of the flight of Mr. Davis, which has never before been told in full, fills up a gap in history of the closing days of the War Between the States and gives some important details that will prove interesting to the younger generations in the North as well as in the South.

The Northern Account

Portland Veteran Tells of Capture of Jefferson Davis

General Wilson with the first, second, and third divisions of the Cavalry Corps and three batteries of artillery crossed the Tennessee River on the eleventh day of March 1865 at Chickasaw, Alabama, and began his memorable expedition through the heart of "rebeldom," which had not yet been touched by any Union forces, destroying millions of army property, such as arms, military stores, arsenals, and gun works, railroads and powder works, subsisting off the country, but respecting private buildings. Fighting nearly every day, and arriving at Macon, Georgia, on April 20, 1865.

After the surrender of the city and fortifications, we went into camp about two miles north of the city to rest awhile, the war then being over.

While resting quietly in camp on the evening of May 6 our Lieutenant-Colonel, Henry Harnden, received orders to report at once to division headquarters. General J. G. Croxton was in command in the absence of General

McCook, our division commander. Colonel Harnden was informed that it was reported that Jeff Davis, president of the Southern Confederacy, was in South Carolina, making his way south and west into Georgia, that a portion of his cabinet was with him, and that they were accompanied by 600 or 700 men; that he, Colonel Harnden had been selected to command a detachment of a part of the First Wisconsin Cavalry to endeavor to cut him off and capture him if possible; that the march must be made immediately and not wait for rations.

The General was asked if he thought the number of men with the regiment in camp would be sufficient to take on the expedition. He replied, "that in the opinion of General Wilson, it was." He said that the escort of Davis might not show much fight, but if they did, he would risk our being able to take care of them, and that if Jeff Davis should get hurt in the fight, General Wilson would not feel very bad over it.

It was about sunset when we left Macon, crossed the bridge over the Ocmulgee River and took a line of march eastward toward Savannah. The country was very poor, and we had to look out sharp for forage, etc., but during the night we came to a plantation where there was forage, so we halted and fed our horses. Up to this time no one but the Colonel had any idea as to where we were going, or for what purpose we had been ordered out, but when we were ready to mount our horses again, he made known to us the object of our expedition. We were also told that if we encountered Davis and his escort they perhaps would greatly outnumber us, and were probably the pick of the Confederate army; that they would no doubt fight desperately; that it would be a battle to the death, and that Jeff Davis must not be allowed to escape in any event, but as we had never been whipped, he had no fear of being whipped now. This was all greeted with cheers, and all were impatient to go forward.

We continued our march all night and the next day, May 7, until near Dublin, a town on the west bank of the Oconee River. Scouting parties were sent out during the night and day endeavoring to get information regarding parties who were continually crossing our road, but those men invariably proved to be from General Johnston's army, who having surrendered to Sherman were on their way home on parole.

Upon arriving at Dublin we noticed the people appeared to be considerably excited at our presences, but the Colonel caused it to be given out that we were establishing a courier post between Macon and Savannah. The town was full of Confederate officers in uniform, standing around in groups, talking by themselves, with looks that boded no good to us, but at the same time our Colonel was receiving invitations to take up his quarters for the night, or longer, in houses of several gentleman, who seemed quite anxious for him to do so, which was indeed very unusual.

The invitations being declined, he remained with the men, who were bivouacked on a flat between the town and the river. We were very tired that night, having been on duty 35 hours, 24 of which had been spent in the saddle, and we were asleep as soon as we touched the ground.

We had, however, hardly settled down to rest when the Colonel received word through some lookouts and a colored servant of the Colonel, who had been investigating a little on his own hook, that Davis and party, with wagons, had been in town and left in a hurry down the river when it was known that we were approaching, and that a larger party went down on the other side of the river. The ferryman at the river would tell us nothing about the party who crossed that day.

After it was definitely known that it was Davis and party who had skipped off down the river road, we were ordered to saddle up and moved off in pursuit. We learned that the party, or especially Davis and his wife, had accepted an invitation to dine with Judge Rose, but had to leave before dinner was ready. Judge Rose was one of the men who urged our Colonel to stop at his house the same evening a short time after Davis had left.

It was dark and the roads in the pine woods were not much more than trails. We became confused and after a little time found ourselves coming into Dublin again. With daylight coming we soon found the trail and wagon tracks and left. Five miles out we found the bridge at Turkey Creek torn up, which caused some delay, but learned at a house that we were really on the track of the Davis party. The wagon tracks could be plainly seen for a while, when it commenced to rain and soon obliterated all semblance of a track.

We were then in the great pine woods of the South, with scarcely an inhabitant, but we still pushed blindly on. Parties were sent circling around to find the road, but without success. They, however, found a horseman and brought him in, who in reply to questions said he knew nothing of any party, that he was a poor man looking for some lost sheep. It was noticed that he was riding a very fine horse and was told that we would take his horse unless he quit lying. He soon confessed that he knew, but it was eleven miles away and in another direction. He was placed between two guards and ordered to guide us there which he did. We found Davis's camp, but they were gone. After dismissing the guide we found a poor plantation near where there was some forage which we appropriated. The owner said he did not know where the party we were looking for had gone, but he thought they had crossed Gum Swamp, but that the rains had so raised the water that it would be impossible for us to cross. He was ordered to get his horses and lead us through the swamp or we would stay and eat him out of house and home. He got his horse quickly and led the way through the swamp where the water for miles was up to the saddle.

Dismissing the man we pushed on through the dense woods over a fairly good road until we reached Alligator Creek Swamp. Darkness coming on we camped in the swamp, and during the night there came a terrible thunder storm and high wind, blowing down many trees around us. As soon as it was light enough to see on the morning of May 9, we started out in a southwestern direction, until we struck the Ocmulgee River, and continuing down the river until we came to a ferry, where we crossed in a small boat which delayed us two hours or more, and materially affected the events of the next day, and the history of the expedition.

A few miles further on we came to the little town called Abbeville, where on inquiry we learned that the party with wagons had passed through town during the night and gone on toward Irwinville.

We halted a short time near the forks of the road leading down from Hawkinsville to feed our horses. Just as we were moving out again we saw four men riding down from the north from Hawkinsville having the United States uniform on. Colonel Harnden and an orderly rode out to meet them and found they belonged to the Fourth Michigan Cavalry, Lieutenant-Colonel Pritchard commanding. The regiment soon came up, when Colonel Harnden inquired of Colonel Pritchard if he had any news of Jeff Davis. He said he had not, but he had been ordered to go to Abbeville and to patrol the river and prevent Davis from crossing. He also said that he had orders to camp his regiment at Abbeville and guard the crossings of the Ocmulgee, and gave no intimation that he intended any other course. He had left Macon since our departure, but up to that time had heard nothing of Davis.

Colonel Harnden then informed Colonel Pritchard that Davis had already crossed the river and was now on the road toward Irwinville, and that we had been on his trail for several days and expected to come upon him that night or early in the morning and invited him to join us. He replied that he must comply with his orders to patrol the river. We asked him if he had any rations to spare as our party had next to nothing to eat. He said they had started off in a hurry and had no rations. Bidding him goodbye we moved on and shortly came to the place where the Davis party had stopped for lunch, and their fires were still burning. Continuing on we came to a place where there was some water and grass, where we halted to rest and graze our horses. All we had to eat was a little cornmeal.

It was thought that Davis would cross the river ahead, a small branch of the Ocmulgee, before stopping to camp. It was so late that it was thought best not to attempt to cross the ford in the dark, as Davis would take the alarm and escape. Before the break of day we were in the saddle again. This was May 10. Putting forward an advance guard of Sergeant George Hussey and six men, with instructions to keep a little ahead and keep a sharp lookout for the enemy, we moved on. We expected to meet Davis's escort and a strong rear guard.

We had made but a mile or so when we came to a swale where a trail branched off to a field where the Davis camp was located. Our advance guard was fired upon suddenly, by what we judged to be 20 or 30 muskets. The Colonel galloped forward and met the sergeant and his men coming back, several of them being wounded. The sergeant said he had been fired upon by the enemy's pickets. Several men were ordered forward then, and, dashing up toward the enemy, we were fired into again. It was just light enough to distinguish the forms of men in front of us, and as they seemed to be in considerable force and determined to stand, a part of our men dismounted, advanced, and opened fire on them. They broke and retreated into the swamp. It was getting light when the Colonel's attention was called to about 100 mounted men coming down on our flank.

Never mind, said the Colonel, we will whip them yet, and, directing Sergeant Horr, with a number of men, to pursue the party who had fired on us first and not let them rally, then forming a line facing the newcomers, who fired on us as they approached, we opened on them with Spencer carbines. They were soon thrown into confusion, and, following up our fire with a mounted saber charge, we captured a few of them and found that they were the Fourth Michigan Cavalry. The Colonel ordered "Cease firing," which stopped on both sides. We were greatly surprised on finding out who had fired on us.

Colonel Pritchard tried to explain how it happened, but our Colonel called him down in strong terms and they rode into the Davis camp together. The first men who fired on us were driven into the camp and all went in together. Pritchard said he had not been in the Davis camp yet. Two men of the Fourth Michigan were killed and several wounded, three of our regiment were wounded, but none killed.

The first person the Colonel saw on going into the camp was John H. Reagen, the Postmaster-General of the late Confederacy, lately the United States Senator from Texas.[34] He said: "Well, you have got the old gentleman at last." Colonel Harnden asked who he referred to. He said, "I mean President Davis." Harnden said, "Please point him out to me." "There he stands," he said pointing to a tall elderly and rather dignified-looking gentleman standing a short distance away in front of a tent.

We rode up and Colonel Harnden dismounted and saluted and asked if this was Mr. Davis. "Yes," he replied, "I am President Davis." At this the soldiers set up a shout that Jeff Davis was captured and the soldiers began to sing, "We will hang Jeff Davis on a sour apple tree," to the tune of "John Brown."

In the camp were two tents and eight ambulances, each drawn by four mules. There were also several fine saddle horses. Besides Jeff Davis, there were Mr. Reagan, Colonel Harrison, Mrs. Davis, her sister, Miss Howell, and a number of rebel officers from Johnston's army and a lot of teamsters, servants, and others, but no fighting men, as we had supposed.

It appears that when the firing began Mr. Davis, being alarmed at the noise, hastily arose, threw a shawl around him and started out with his wife on one side and a colored woman on the other. Before reaching the woods they were asked by a soldier as to where they were going. The colored woman replied, "Down to de creek to tote a pail of watah." They were told to go back to the camp and stay there, the soldier not knowing who they were. The first one to recognize and speak to Davis was Colonel Harnden, who entered into conversation with him, but with poor satisfaction to either

The Colonel would not call him Mr. President, but Mr. Davis, when he would be corrected with the statement, "I am President Davis," and speaking of "your Government" with greatest contempt. Harnden said to him that if he had fulfilled his engagement to dine with Judge Rose we

[34] Reagan had been a United States representative, not a senator, from Texas.

should probably have made his acquaintance back in Dublin. Upon this he turned and said, "Well, sir, I can assure you that if you had met me then I had those with me who would not have allowed this great indignity to have been put upon me, and it is well for you that you were not in time to see me then." Harnden replied that it would have afforded him the greatest of pleasure to have met his friends and tried the question with them. He began to berate his wife and blamed her for his capture, for it seemed that he had intended joining the other party before, but his wife persuaded him to accompany her a little farther. He had planned to go to the home of Mrs. Davis in Mississippi, then he would cross the Mississippi River and join Kirby Smith and continue the war some longer, so in the capture of Jeff Davis the final period was put upon the rebellion.

After a short rest and caring for the wounded and burying the dead, we all began our return march to Macon, arriving on May 12.

Now a word regarding the movements of Colonel Pritchard and the Fourth Michigan Regiment in connection with the capture of Jeff Davis. After meeting us on the afternoon of the 9th, being informed of the whereabouts of Davis, and declaring that he must obey orders to camp at Abbeville and watch the river, declining to join us in the pursuit, he started immediately around on an all-night march traveling about forty miles to Irwinville and beyond Davis's camp and sent a large detachment to get in between us and the camp, with orders to fire on all comers.

Colonel Pritchard was liable to a court martial for his actions and would have been tried for murder if it had not occurred just at the close of the war, when everybody was rejoicing over the salvation of the Union.

Many stories have been told about Jeff Davis being disguised or camouflaged in female attire, on attempting to make his escape on the morning of his capture, but such was not the case; he only had a shawl or dressing gown thrown around his head and shoulders and dressed as usual.

Sources and Resources

Numerous accounts of the capture of Jefferson Davis are readily available in both print and electronic form. For example, the Colonel Harnden mentioned in the Wisconsin trooper's narrative published a short book in 1898 titled *The Capture of Jefferson Davis*. The story is quite similar to that which appeared in the *Oregonian* but goes into greater detail. Although attributed to "the personal recollections of Theodore M. Kellogg," it would appear that this article was in large part drawn from Harnden's book. The interested reader is invited to draw his or her own conclusions. An electronic copy the work can be accessed via the Internet archive: https://archive.org/details/captureofdavisjeff00harnrich.

The site of the Davis party's capture in Irwin County, Georgia, has been memorialized by the creation of the Jefferson Davis Memorial Historic Site, which includes a museum and 13-acre tract. The two general histories provide details of the flight of the Confederate government and the capture of Jefferson Davis. Please see Chapter 4's "Sources and Resources" for additional commentary on these two works.

Davis, William C. An Honorable Defeat: The Last Days of the Confederate Government. New York: Harcourt, 2001.

Hanna, Alfred J. Flight Into Oblivion. Baton Rouge: Louisiana State University Press, 1999. This LSU edition is a reproduction of Hanna's original 1938 book with a new introduction by William C. Davis.

With the impending fall of the Confederate capital, Richmond, Virginia, in early April 1865, President Jefferson Davis and several of his cabinet ministers fled south, hoping to escape to more secure territory or possibly abroad. The attempt was unsuccessful, and Davis was captured near Irwinville, Georgia some six weeks later.

Library of Congress

Various stories of the capture of Jefferson Davis became popular topics in the Northern press. In this contemporary cartoon titled, "The True Story of the Capture of Jeff. Davis," the Confederate President is seen disguised as an old woman in an attempt to elude Union troops searching for him.

Library of Congress

In this 1865 Currier & Ives print, Jefferson Davis is seen fleeing Union troops clothed in a dress and bonnet. He carries a sack of gold and a knife while saying, "Leave me alone you blood thirsty villains: I thought your government was more magnanimous than to hunt down women and children!"

Library of Congress

The saga of the capture of Jefferson Davis was woven into the various myths of the Lost Cause. In June 1936, the Ocilla, Georgia Chapter of the United Daughters of the Confederacy dedicated this monument as part of an eighty-acre park commemorating the site where Union troops took Davis into custody.

Library of Congress

CHAPTER 6

THE STRANGE JOURNEY OF THE CONFEDERATE CONSTITUTION

On Pennsylvania Avenue in Washington, DC, midway between the Capitol and the White House, the National Archives of the United States occupies an imposing building behind whose Corinthian columns are the most important historic documents of the Republic. More than a million visitors a year pass through its doors, many of them stopping to view the nation's Constitution, displayed by day behind bulletproof glass while secured at night in an underground vault. Its words, handwritten on vellum, have shaped the country's direction for more than two centuries.

Some 500 miles to the southwest, another quite similar document, its words also inscribed on vellum, reposes in a lead-lined cylinder inside of a biometrically secured storage vault, rarely on public display and only then to a relatively small number of curious visitors. This opus, crafted in haste in the late winter of 1861 and now relegated to near obscurity, is the Constitution of the Confederate States of America. Its very existence and how it arrived in its current location is one of the more fascinating tales in American history.

The Confederate States of America officially came into existence in February 1861 when delegates from six seceding southern states (later joined by a seventh, Texas) met in Montgomery, Alabama, for the purpose of establishing the legal framework for a new union. Operating at first under a provisional constitution adopted after only four days of discussion, the delegates served both as a provisional congress and a constituent assembly charged with drafting a new permanent charter. There was general agreement that the constitution should follow that of the 1787 United States Constitution[35] but with changes to reflect the deep political differences that

[35] As a point of clarification, the Constitution of the United States was drafted in 1787, ratified in 1788, and came into force in 1789. Though generally referred to

had led to the states' secession from the Union. On March 11, 1861, the delegates unanimously approved a permanent constitution, sending it to the individual states for ratification.

At first blush, the new Constitution might appear quite similar to the 1787 document, but in practice, the changes were profound and fundamental. States' rights were emphasized, with words noting that in forming a new union, "each state [was] acting in its sovereign and independent character." The "favor and guidance of Almighty God" was invoked, in contrast to the old charter that simply sought the "Blessings of Liberty." Among the numerous revisions and changes in governmental and parliamentary procedure, monetary appropriations required the approval of two-thirds of both houses of Congress, and the president was provided with a line-item veto. Laws and resolutions having the force of law could "relate to but one subject, and that shall be expressed in the title." The president and vice president were both limited to a single six-year term.

The US Constitution had condoned slavery in limited form, referring to those enslaved under the euphemism of "other Persons." The Confederate Constitution directly affirmed "the right of property in negro slaves" while banning "the importation of negroes of the African race" from foreign countries and non-slave-holding states and territories of the United States.

Georgia's Alexander H. Stephens, speaking in late March 1861 to a group in support of the state's ratification of the new constitution, opined,

> It amply secures all our ancient rights, franchises, and liberties. All the great principles of the Magna Charta are retained in it. No citizen is deprived of life, liberty, or property but by the judgment of his peers under the law of the land. The great principle of religious liberty, which was the honor and pride of the old constitution, is still maintained and secured. All the essentials of the old constitution, which have endeared it to the hearts of the American people, have been preserved and perpetuated. Some changes have been made.... They form great improvements upon the old constitution.[36]

---

simply as "the Constitution," at times it is called "the Constitution of 1787" or "the Constitution of 1789." Both titles are correct but sometimes confusing.

[36] A number of full-text versions of Stephens's so-called "Cornerstone Speech" are available via the Internet. http://teachingamericanhistory.org/library/index.asp?documentprint=76 is a typical example.

By the end of the year, the Constitution had been approved by the states of Georgia, Florida, Alabama, Mississippi, Texas, South Carolina, North Carolina, Virginia, Arkansas, Tennessee, and Louisiana, as well as secessionist factions from the states of Kansas and Missouri.

In May 1861, the capital of the Confederacy was moved from Montgomery to Richmond, Virginia. Jefferson Davis, who had served as "provisional" president since February of that year, was formally elected to a six-year term in November. His inauguration took place on Richmond's Capitol Square in February 1862 amidst the bustle of a government at war. The new nation's Constitution, as well as other vital documents, were held in safekeeping there, where they would remain for the next three years.

Despite able leadership, a dedicated military, and a fervid belief in the Cause, the Confederacy's survival was perhaps doubtful from the start. Early battlefield victories were soon negated by a tide of defeat. By late 1864, nothing short of a miracle could have saved the embattled new nation. The inevitably of forthcoming events, while often not admitted publically, was not lost on those in power in Richmond. Tentative plans to evacuate the capital had been discussed for months. As the sad winter of 1865 merged into spring, actions to move the seat of government were well underway.

With the sound of cannon booming in the distance and the capital city of Richmond in flames, Jefferson Davis and the Confederate cabinet evacuated the city by train on the night of April 2, 1865. Some of the papers and documents of the government traveled with them; others were on trains that followed or had been removed from the city earlier in anticipation of its fall. Stopping first in Danville, Virginia, attempts were made to continue a functioning government. Under pressure from Union troops, Davis and the cabinet soon were forced to move further south, first to Greensboro, North Carolina, for a few days, then to Charlotte. News of Lee's surrender on April 9th, followed by Lincoln's assassination five days later, dashed whatever faint hope the few government officials might have had. By late April, they had become fugitives, fleeing in fear of their lives and freedom.

Most of the journey of the fallen government thus far had been made by rail, but south of Charlotte, the rail line led to Columbia, South Carolina, now occupied by Union troops. Traveling as far as the rail depot in Chester, South Carolina, the route of the fleeing president and cabinet then turned overland to continue by horse and wagon. It was here that apparently many of the more important records of the Confederacy were abandoned and here that the next part of the saga of the journey of the Confederate Constitution began.

The fate of many of the documents of the Confederate government was unknown for years, lost in the fog of war and the chaos that followed the fall of the short-lived nation. As the smoke cleared and the dust settled, various and varying accounts of the flight of Jefferson Davis and the Confederate cabinet from Richmond began to emerge, often with questions of the fate of the mythical "Confederate treasure" that supposedly accompanied them. Little attention was given to the whereabouts of the records of the fallen government. Over the next decade, however, governmental documents would appear from time to time, cautiously sought by museums and collectors alike.

On Monday, March 26, 1883, an unsigned news article appeared on the third page of the *Sun*, a politically conservative paper published in New York.[37] Titled "Two Relics of the War," it recounted in the chatty style of the day how a former Union general had in his possession a gold pen used by Gen. Robert E. Lee to sign the articles of surrender at Appomattox. The main thrust of the article, however, was the account of an individual described only as "an ex-Confederate who happened to be present" and who also happened to have with him what appeared to be the original parchment copies of both the provisional and permanent constitutions of the Confederate States of America.

After displaying the documents to those present, the "ex-Confederate" began his account of how the constitutions had come into his possession:

> The month of April 1865...found everything and everybody in South Carolina in a state of demoralization. Charleston had been occupied by the Union troops. Columbia burned and all of the smaller towns and hamlets of the state were filled with refugees from the coast. People who once lived in luxury were content to sleep in stables, and a pound of salt or a handful of tea or coffee were of more avail in securing food for a meal or two than a $100 Confederate note. My own wife, child, and servant were sleeping on empty boxes in the attic of a country store in the town of Chester, S.C., and yet it was here that the Governor of

[37] *The Sun* (New York), 26 March 1883. Minor corrections have been made in punctuation. This and other issues may be accessed via the Library of Congress/Chronicling America website: http://chroniclingamerica.loc.gov.

the State and Lieut. Gen. Hood, the Texan, came one day to take "pot luck" with us from a table consisting of a plank resting on the end of two flour barrels.

The news from the front was disheartening. The evacuation of Richmond, the surrender of Lee, and the concentration of Sherman's forces in North Carolina around the remnant of the Confederate army, meant serious business, of which we began to feel there could be but one result. Our own little town, on the line of the railroad between Columbia, S.C., and Charlotte, N.C., suddenly became the resort for all the tramps, stragglers, and deserters who could make their way thither. Leather, salt, cotton and army provisions had been stored in one place and another, and to a lot of hungry and ragged men, without discipline or organization, the prizes were tempting. Even the aged countrymen—the out-in-the-cold people—were eager to join in a general raid, and scoop up the remnants of the Confederacy.

On one of these exciting days a dusty looking quartermaster galloped up to the piazza where I was smoking a pipe, and, recognizing me as an old army acquaintance, hurriedly exclaimed, "Major [General] Kilpatrick[38] is within a mile and a half of the town, and the whole command will be here in less than half an hour. Down at the depot is a large amount of freight I've brought down from Richmond. Don't know what it is. Ain't gonna stay to find out. The boys are looting the place already and I'm off for Augusta, across the country. The game's up. If you stay here, take a look at the ruins."

Having been in a good many scares during four years of active service, the report concerning the presence of Gen. Kilpatrick gave me little concern, but I am free to confess that I was thoroughly afraid of my own people, who by this time were little better than an uncontrollable mob. Shots had been exchanged in the public square, and ill-feeling prevailed between the citizens and the guerrillas, for no other name could be applied to the disorganized bands of cavalry and infantry gathered there for plunder. Hastily mounting my horse, I galloped to a neighboring cotton warehouse, and fortunately found there a negro with a four-mule team and large cotton truck. An energetic order and a few Confederate bills made him a willing servant, and we hurried to the depot, nearly a mile distant.

---

[38] Major General Hugh Judson Kilpatrick was a Union officer who served in the Carolinas campaign under General William T. Sherman. According to one biographer, "He delighted in destroying Southern property."

> Soldiers and civilians were looting the place. Two or three men had been shot and their bodies tumbled out on the railway track, and all present, saving a few helpless officers, were intent on securing their share of the plunder. Strange to say, it consisted only of the absolute necessities of life, sole leather, sugar, bacon, salt, and a trifle of rice, and perhaps a few barrels of coffee that had run the blockade. Making my way to the opposite end of the depot, I recognized at a glance the freight that had been deposited by my frightened friend. There were some twenty or thirty iron-bound boxes that evidently had never been opened. Six of these were quickly loaded on the wagon, together with several other huge boxes fastened with iron clasps and padlocks, and a number of smaller packages. Much had to be left behind, but I have thought many times that a little more opportunity and a few more wagons would have enabled me to save some of the most valuable records of the Confederate Government. As it was, I found in the six boxes a mass of English bond paper, probably 200 reams, which proved of great value and in some of the smaller packages a lot of useless tax receipts that were subsequently destroyed. The real prizes, however, were in the heavy oak and padlocked boxes, the contents which comprised the two Constitutions of the Confederacy, Provisional and Permanent, the treaties made with the Indian tribes west of the Mississippi by Gen. Albert Pike, the Confederate Indian Commissioner, the drawings of inventions deposited in the Confederate Patent Office, a goodly portion of the Patent Office library, the decisions from the Attorney-General from 1861 to 1865, a superb eleven-barrel pistol, the private portfolio of Judah P. Benjamin with his name stamped upon it, and a large quantity of French and English writing paper such as is in use in all Governmental departments.

The speaker went on to say that "most" of the articles mentioned "have found their way into the hands of other persons who are deeply interested in their preservation." In answer to a query as to what he proposed to do with the provisional and permanent constitutions, the "ex-Confederate" replied,

> That's the question; there isn't a Southern historical society, to say nothing of the relatives of the signers, able to purchase the parchments and remove them from the personal care with which they have been sacredly guarded by a Southern woman for the last eighteen years. Considerable sums of money have been offered for them by individuals, and the probability is that eventually they will find their way to Washington, or to some public or private library, or to the British Museum.

This last paragraph belied the true nature of the "news" item. It was, in fact, a thinly disguised effort to market what the author clearly believed to be among the most valuable documents of the Confederacy. But who was this man, and why now—nearly two decades after the end of hostilities—was he seeking to sell these unique bits of American history? The "ex-Confederate" was, in fact, Felix Gregory De Fontaine, then a newspaper editor in New York, but formerly one of the best known of Southern war correspondents.

Felix De Fontaine's sympathies did indeed lie with the South, but by choice, not birth. He was born in 1834 in Boston, son of *Chevalier* Louis Antoine De Fontaine, a French nobleman who had fled Paris with King Charles X following the revolution of 1830. Settling in Boston, the elder De Fontaine soon married a Miss Allen, reputed to be a member of the family of American patriot Ethan Allen. Young Felix became a reporter and writer, making a name for himself in his chosen field before moving to South Carolina in 1860. He married a girl from Charleston, founding the *Daily South Carolinian* in the capital city of Columbia shortly thereafter. Clearly committed to the position of the seceding states, he became "one of the most ardent defenders of the South."[39]

De Fontaine established himself as a war correspondent in April 1861 when he sent the exclusive first report of the bombardment of Fort Sumter to the *New York Herald.* Reputedly, his friendship with Gen. P. G. T. Beauregard—also of French descent—gave him early access to the telegraph to transmit the story. During the following years of war, De Fontaine penned numerous articles under the *nom de plume* of "Personne." The "four years of active service" described by the "ex-Confederate" in the *Sun* article apparently referred to the years spent reporting the war.

De Fontaine's presence in Chester at the time of the arrival of Confederate records was totally fortuitous. He continued to publish his newspaper in Columbia until mid-February 1865, when much of the city was burned while occupied by Union troops under the command of Gen. William T. Sherman. Like many of the citizens of the state's capital, he fled with his family to the countryside. By late April, he had apparently resumed publication of his newspaper in Chester. One account suggests that De Fontaine's primary reason for looting the trunks from the depot was the war-driven

[39] James A. Hayt, "The Confederate Archives and Felix G. De Fontaine," *The South Carolina Historical Magazine* 57 (1956): 202.

scarcity of paper on which to print his newspaper. The search for newsprint may have led to the accidental discovery of the Confederate documents.[40]

In the 1870s De Fontaine moved to New York, serving first as editor of the *Evening Telegram* and later in various editorial positions with the *New York Herald*. In the early 1880s, he encountered financial difficulties and sought to sell items that he had collected from the Confederate archives and secretly held for nearly two decades. The article in the *Sun* soon brought him in contact with the De Renne family of Savannah, avid collectors of Civil War historical documents.

George Wymberley Jones De Renne, scion of one of Georgia's oldest and wealthiest families, was a noted bibliophile and historian, building an outstanding library collection of historic writings. Following his death in 1880, his wife, Mary Nuttall De Renne, continued and expanded his collection of books, manuscripts, and relics, focusing especially on printed works and ephemera related to the Civil War. In response to the article in the *Sun*, she contacted De Fontaine and began negotiations over the purchase of the Constitution. Offers went back and forth through intermediaries for several months, with Mrs. De Renne finally purchasing the Permanent Constitution in early July 1883 for the sum of $1,500.[41]

For the next several decades, the Confederate Constitution, as well as other unique and valuable written works pertaining to Georgia history, were part of the De Renne collections. Following Mary De Renne's death, the tradition was carried on by her son, Wymberley Jones De Renne, and subsequently her grandson, Wymberley Wormsloe De Renne. While Mary De Renne's immense collection of Georgiana[42] and Confederate memorabilia was impressive, her son's endeavors in the same field was to exceed even hers. Wymberley Jones De Renne added a large number of important historical works as well as Georgia governmental documents. To house and protect his growing collection, in 1907 and 1908, he constructed a "fireproof" library building on the grounds of his estate at Wormsloe on the Isle of

[40] Dallas D. Irvine, "The Fate of the Confederate Archives," *The American Historical Review* 44 (1939): 840.

[41] The Provisional Constitution was sold a few months later to banker and philanthropist W. W. Corcoran, eventually ending up in the Museum of the Confederacy in Richmond, Virginia.

[42] When used in this context, "Georgiana" refers to items related to the state of Georgia, usually items of historical interest.

Hope near Savannah. For the most part, the Constitution remained in safe-keeping in the vault of a Savannah bank. Between 1909 and 1914, it was on loan and displayed at the Library of Congress.

Wymberley Jones De Renne died in 1916, leaving his estate in trust to his three surviving children. With the crash of the cotton economy in the 1920s followed by the Great Depression of the 1930s, the family fell into deep financial difficulty. Properties were mortgaged, and there was the possibility of the loss of Wormsloe, which had been in the family since the mid-eighteenth century. The one thing of great value that the family had was the De Renne Library collections. In 1931, the decision was made to sell the collection to the University of Georgia. Although the Board of Regents was receptive to the idea, funds for purchase were scarce. Negotiations dragged on for years, stymied in part by the objections of then-governor Eugene Talmadge. An alternative possibility of a sale to Duke University was considered but then dismissed as the University of Georgia agreed to buy the collection in the early spring of 1938. The initial purchase price of $60,000, however, specifically excluded the crown jewel, the Confederate Constitution. This was eventually purchased by the university in late 1938 for the princely sum of $20,000, the vast majority of which went to pay De Renne family creditors.[43]

For three-quarters of a century, the original Constitution of the Confederate States of America has been part of the extensive historical collections of the University of Georgia in Athens. Written on five joined vellum sheets and measuring more than two by twelve-and-a-half feet in dimension, it is now preserved in the university's Richard B. Russell Building, which is home to the Special Collections Libraries. The fragile document is brought out once yearly for public view on (or near) April 26th, Georgia's Confederate Memorial Day. In addition to the Constitution, the Special Collections comprise a treasure trove of historical books, Civil War memorabilia, maps, and other documents pertaining to Georgia and Southern history dating back nearly 500 years. The historic importance of this document, which once defined the hopes and dreams of a breakaway nation, cannot be overstated. Even more remarkable, perhaps, is its survival and the circuitous route that led to its current home.

---

[43] William H. Bragg, *De Renne: Three Generations of a Georgia Family* (Athens: University of Georgia Press, 1999): 355.

SOURCES AND RESOURCES

The Confederate Constitution remains in the collection of Hargrett Rare Book and Manuscript Library in Athens, Georgia. Information on the University of Georgia's Special Collections Libraries, located at 300 South Hull Street in Athens, can be obtained by calling 706-542-7123 or online at http://www.libs.uga.edu/scl. The gallery space displays both permanent and rotating collections open to the public free of charge during set hours on weekdays and weekends.

The following works can provide both general and more specific information on the topics mentioned in this chapter:

Bragg, William H. *De Renne: Three Generations of a Georgia Family.* Athens: University of Georgia Press, 1999. A multigenerational history of one of Georgia's most prominent families.

Davis, William C. *An Honorable Defeat: The Last Days of the Confederate Government.* New York: Harcourt, 2001. Please see commentary on this work in the Sources and Resources section at the end of chapter 4.

Hanna, Alfred J. *Fight into Oblivion.* Baton Rouge: Louisiana State University Press, 1999. Please see commentary on this work in the Sources and Resources section at the end of chapter 4.

Hayt, James A. "The Confederate Archives and Felix G. De Fontaine." *The South Carolina Historical Magazine* 57 (1956): 199–203.

Irvine, Dallas D. "The Fate of the Confederate Archives." *The American Historical Review.* 44 (1939): 823–41.

Felix G. De Fontaine was a noted Southern war correspondent living in South Carolina. How he came into possession of the original Constitution of the CSA was the result of a totally fortuitous series of events.

Hargrett Rare Book and Manuscript Library, University of Georgia

In 1907–1908 W. J. De Renne constructed a freestanding "fireproof" library building on his estate at Wormsloe Plantation, near Savannah, to house his collection of historic books and documents. Much of his original collection is now owned by the University of Georgia.

Hargrett Rare Book and Manuscript Library, University of Georgia

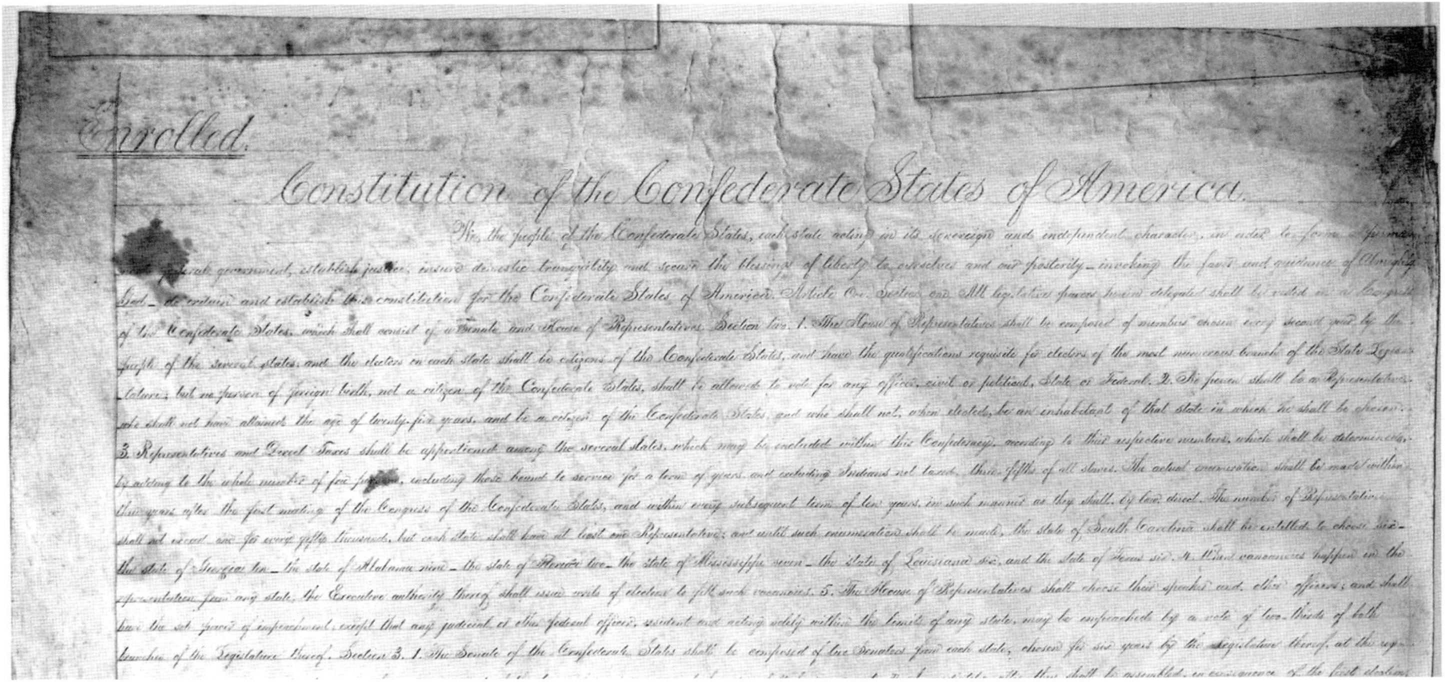
Enrolled.

Constitution of the Confederate States of America.

The Confederate Constitution, penned on five vellum sheets, was closely modeled on the 1787 United States Constitution. It is now located in a secure vault at the Hargrett Rare Book and Manuscript Library on the campus of the University of Georgia in Athens.

Hargrett Rare Book and Manuscript Library, University of Georgia

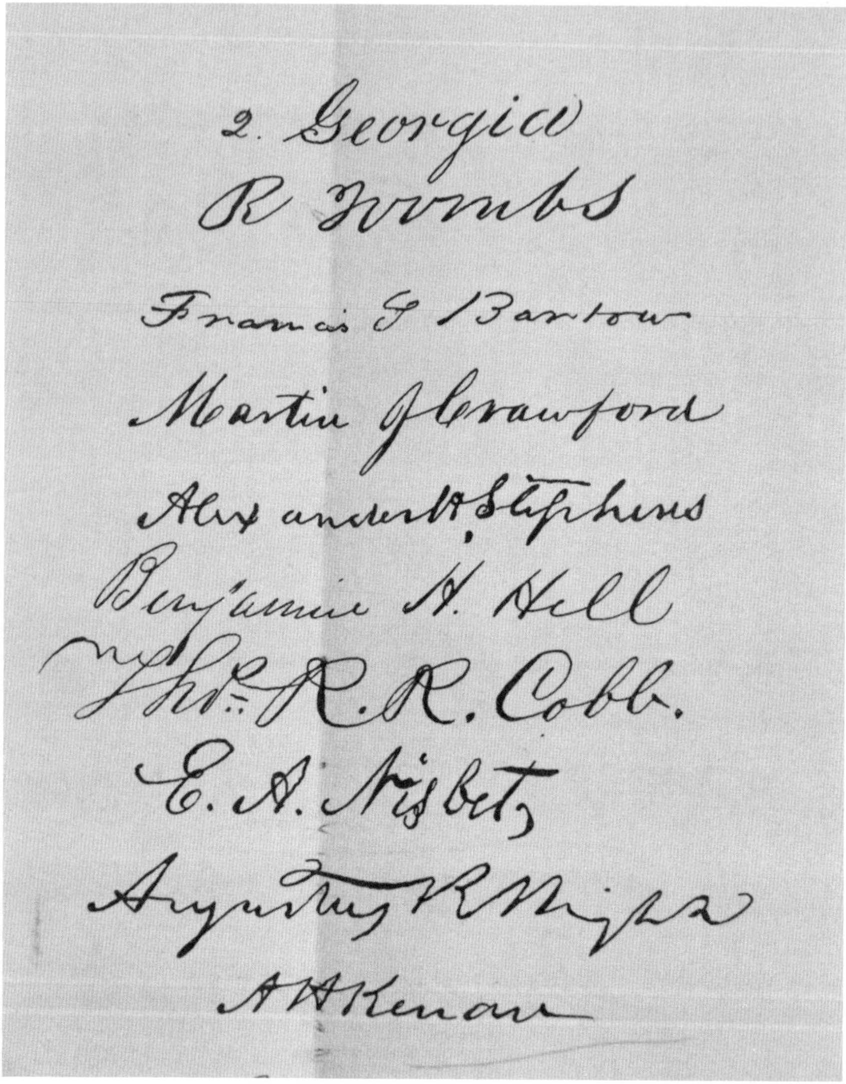

2. Georgia
R Toombs
Francis S Bartow
Martin J Crawford
Alexander H. Stephens
Benjamin H. Hill
Thos. R. R. Cobb.
E. A. Nisbet,
Augustus R Wright
A H Kenan

Signatories to the 1861 Constitution from Georgia included a number of prominent leaders of the day. This photo is from a reproduction of the Confederate Constitution produced by W. J. De Renne in 1909. The pamphlet, privately printed, had a press run of 150 copies.

Hargrett Rare Book and Manuscript Library, University of Georgia

PART III

THE RECONSTRUCTION ERA 1865–1877

OVERVIEW

THE RECONSTRUCTION ERA 1865–1877

If the Civil War was ferocious and horrific, the Reconstruction years that followed were simply ugly. The war and its aftermath had caused hundreds of thousands of deaths, deposed and discredited a way of life based on agriculture and slavery, and created an entire new class of citizens from the former slaves. Like most conflicts, the end did not arrive gracefully. Disputes and animosities that once found their solution through legislative compromise were now decided unilaterally by the victors, often enforced through the power of the sword. While both sides suffered massive casualties, it was the South on whose home ground the conflict took place. As vividly described by one historian,

> The South in 1865 presented a bleak landscape of destruction and desolation. Burned-out plantations, fields growing up in weeds, and railroads without tracks, bridges or rolling stock marked the trail of the conquering Union Armies. The collapse of Confederate authority left large areas without law and order. Roaming bands of guerillas and deserters plundered defenseless homes. Hundreds of thousands of black freedmen and white refugees suffered from disease, exposure and hunger. As just one example of the horrors left by the war, a pile of sixty-five horses and mules killed by Sherman's army lay unburied near Columbia, South Carolina, for six weeks because the troops had carried off all the spades and other implements.[44]

Even in areas untouched directly by the war, the social and economic systems that had become the accepted way of life were in disarray. The problems of rebuilding what many in the North hoped would be a more democratic and inclusive society were well recognized prior to the end of the conflict. The task was formally given to the Bureau of Refugees, Freedmen and

---

[44] James M. McPherson, *Ordeal by Fire: The Civil War and Reconstruction* (New York: Alfred M. Knopf, 1982): 493.

Abandoned Lands (commonly referred to as the Freedmen's Bureau), established within the War Department in March 1865. Assistance came from a number of private enterprises as well, including Northern missionary societies, religious organizations, and, in some cases, private individuals.

Political "reconstruction" in the South was primarily aimed at establishing a firm base for the Republican Party, often accomplished through the Union Leagues, organizations whose purpose was to garner votes for the party. Later, during the period of so-called "Radical Reconstruction," these goals were achieved through the disenfranchisement of those who had supported the Confederacy—a constituency that was essentially all white—and the granting of the vote to the freedmen, all of whom were black. These actions undoubtedly contributed to the climate of racial animosity that came to characterize the South of the late nineteenth and early twentieth centuries.

Retreating Northern troops were often replaced by Northern administrators, businessmen, and adventurers for whom the political and economic turmoil offered chances for personal advancement and/or monetary gain. These "carpetbaggers," named as such for the soft-sided luggage in which they carried their worldly goods, frequently became the target of resentment by local populations. Equally reviled were those known as "scalawags," native Southerners who, in what was deemed a betrayal of their local peers, worked with military, administrative, and political officials of the federal government in furtherance of the goals of Reconstruction.

It was this environment of imposed political will, social turmoil, and the breakdown of the traditional value system that gave spontaneous rise across the former Confederacy to various resistance and regulatory groups, such as the Knights of the White Camellia and White League in Louisiana, the Red Shirts in Mississippi, the Ku Klux Klan in Tennessee, and a number of others. Operating locally and regionally, their ends were often accomplished by violence and intimidation, justly earning their designation as terrorist organizations. Collectively known as the "Ku Klux Movement," these groups died out by the early to mid-1870s under vigorous federal prosecution and with the return of local political control.

To the average American of today, mention of the Reconstruction era often elicits a look of bewilderment. For those who recall the name from some high school history course, the common response is that the term refers to the years following the Civil War. When pressed further, some speculate—presumably based on the name—that "Reconstruction" was most likely a nineteenth century version of the Marshall Plan,[45] a beneficial effort on the part of the victorious North to rebuild the South following the destruction of the war. While this may be true in some respects, this era is compared by many to other dark episodes in American history, including the forceful relocations of Native Americans from the Southeast under the Indian Removal Act of 1830, or the internment of Japanese-Americans during World War II.

In reviewing the history of Reconstruction, one cannot help but be struck by the frequency with which major decisions affecting the lives and futures of millions were based on reasoning derived from political considerations and party loyalty. In the first of the two chapters in this section, I address this issue in an essay titled "Conflict and Compromise: The Political Nature of Reconstruction." By definition, essays often present the author's own views. I want to be clear that I am less concerned about expressing a viewpoint than I am in stimulating what may be to some an uncomfortable conversation. There are differing viewpoints on the nature and success (or failure) of Reconstruction, no doubt legitimately held. The intelligent reader should have the opportunity and facts from which to draw his or her own opinions.

The second chapter, "The Freedman's Land Insurrection of 1875," recounts an amazing incident that occurred in the east-central Georgia area of the late Reconstruction era. It details an abortive plot on the part of freed slaves to establish an independent state in a twenty-county area, the first step of which was to be the wholesale slaughter of the white population. In contrast to the well-known Nat Turner's Rebellion of 1831, in which an estimated fifty whites were killed, this plot, if carried to fruition, would have resulted in the deaths of thousands.[46] The discovery of the plot and the trials

---

[45] The Marshall Plan: Named for then-Secretary of State George Marshall, and officially known as the European Recovery Plan, the term refers to a monetary and technical assistance program designed to help rebuild Western European nations following the destruction of World War II. Passed by Congress in 1948, some $13 billion in then-current dollars were allotted to the effort. Part of the reasoning behind this program was to avoid the atmosphere in Germany and Italy in the post-World War I era that gave rise to the Nazis and Fascists, while at the same time establishing loyal allies who would resist the western spread of Soviet Communism.

[46] Nat Turner (1800–1831) was an African American slave who led an 1831 rebellion in Southhampton County, Virginia. More recently, awareness of this epi-

that followed were major events, attracting both national and international press coverage. Personally, I found the final outcomes the most curious part of the story, including the legal verdicts rendered to the plotters and the final fate of the chief conspirator.

sode was popularized by William Styron's Pulitzer Prize-winning 1967 novel, *The Confessions of Nat Turner.*

CHAPTER 7

CONFLICT AND COMPROMISE: THE POLITICAL NATURE OF RECONSTRUCTION

Among the various family papers and documents passed on to me over the years, one in particular stands out. It is a presidential pardon granted to Solomon Newsom, my great- great-grandfather, bestowing full "amnesty for all offenses by him committed, arising from participation, direct or implied" in the Civil War. For this order of executive clemency to take effect, he was required to swear an oath of loyalty to the United States, refuse to acquire slaves or "make use of slave labor," pay any judgments rendered against him, and abandon any claims he might have to property forfeited as a result of the conflict.[47] The certificate, dated September 28, 1865, bears the presidential seal, the stamped signature of President Andrew Johnson, and the personal signature of William H. Seward, then secretary of state.

In many ways, the pardon is a most curious document. Fifty-six years old when the war began, owning some 5,000 acres of land and nearly 150 slaves, Solomon Newsom was a member of the planter-elite who held power in the antebellum era. There is little doubt that he supported secession and the aims of the Confederacy. He invested in Confederate bonds and had other business dealings with the rebel government. His sons enlisted and fought on the side of the South. Yet less than six months after the end of the conflict, he was granted amnesty and full restoration of his civil rights, including the right to vote and elect a representative government of his choosing.

The postwar era of local control was brief. In March 1867, nearly two years after the end of the war and less than eighteen months after receiving his pardon, my great- great-grandfather, together with much of the electorate of the former Confederacy, was disenfranchised by congressional ac-

[47] From the standpoint of the law, slavery was still allowed under the Constitution. The Thirteenth Amendment was not formally ratified until December 1865.

tion. Georgia, together with nine other former Confederate states, was declared part of a military district controlled by federal troops. Existing locally elected governments were removed and administrations friendly to Northern political interests installed.

The Reconstruction era represents one of the uglier episodes in American history, a politically charged period when the Constitution was frequently ignored and the "rule of law" often forsaken. Decisions affecting the future of millions of Americans were at times based on party politics, disregarding the greater good in the never-ending struggle for political power. In comparison to the well-documented four years of the Civil War, the twelve years of Reconstruction that followed have become a relative backwater for historians and writers alike, its compromises and injustices often deemed a sideshow to the greater pageant of American history. The purpose of this essay is neither to praise nor condemn history's course during this era. Rather, my purpose is to point out that several of the pivotal events that occurred between the end of the Civil War in 1865 and the withdrawal of federal troops in 1877 were based primarily on political considerations. Specifically, I want to address the imposition of so-called "Radical Reconstruction" in 1867, the dilemma posed to the Republican Party by the ratification of the Thirteenth Amendment, and the backroom Compromise of 1877 that formally ended the era.

To assert that Reconstruction was a controversial period is an understatement of the first order. Although most historians mark its beginning with the practical end of the Civil War in April 1865 and its end with the withdrawal of federal troops in 1877, there are others who suggest it began in 1863 with the implementation of President Abraham Lincoln's Emancipation Proclamation. There is sharp disagreement as to the true purpose of many of the acts of Congress during this period. Were they designed primarily to assist the conquered South in rebuilding a more inclusive and egalitarian society? Alternatively, were there baser motives designed to maintain the status quo of political power? Or both? There were and are regional and personal differences among historians as well, often tinted in published works by the geographic or political viewpoint of the writer.[48]

By 1863, it was evident to many that the conflict would eventually be decided in favor of the North. The major issue to be defined was how to

---

[48] See the Source and Resources section at the end of this chapter for further comments regarding historical perspectives.

reinstate the former states of the Confederacy into the Union. President Lincoln favored leniency for the rebel states and a rapid return to national unity. As such, in December 1863 he proposed to reintegrate the Southern states via a presidential proclamation that came to be known as the Ten Percent Plan. In essence, with the exception of Confederate governmental officials and high-ranking military officers, citizens of a defeated Confederacy were to be offered a full pardon on rejecting slavery and signing a loyalty oath to the United States. Once 10 percent of the number that had voted in the 1860 presidential election in each state had done so, that state would be allowed to "reestablish a state government...recognized as the true government of the state." Many in Congress objected to the leniency of Lincoln's proclamation, leading to the passage of the Wade-Davis Bill by both houses in July 1864. Under this plan, pardons were to be granted only to those who could swear an oath that they had not supported the Confederacy. A majority (rather than 10 percent) of the electorate in each state would be required to sign such an oath before the state could be "readmitted" to the Union. It was this latter point, among others, that led to the president's pocket veto of the legislation.

Lincoln's view, supported by many, was that secession was not permitted under the Constitution and that the Southern states, while temporarily taken over by rebels, were, in fact, still part of the United States. Therefore, once the rebels were defeated, the Southern populace could restore a loyal government. Others, including the so-called Radical wing of the Republican Party, sharply disagreed. They asserted that secession was tantamount to treason, that the rebel states had reverted to the status of territories, and that those who formed and supported the Confederacy should suffer punishment, to include confiscation of their property and curtailment of their civil rights.

With Lincoln's assassination in April 1865, Vice President Andrew Johnson ascended to the presidency. A Democrat and former governor of Tennessee, Johnson opposed the Confederate cause and remained a staunch Unionist. His choice as Lincoln's vice-presidential running mate in the 1864 elections was designed to send a message of national unity. Johnson's past and his prior rhetoric regarding the conflict seemed to place his views closer to those of the Radical Republicans. He was bitterly opposed to the planter aristocracy, whom he blamed for the war. The initial impression was that restoration of the Union would be far more arduous under a Johnson administration. To the surprise of many, matters took a different direction.

With the war finally over, political options for the South seemed polarized to two extremes. Northern Democrats favored what has been termed "self-reconstruction." As described by one author, "Such a policy would have allowed the existing state governments to proclaim their loyalty to the Union, to supervise the election of new congressmen and senators, and then carry on as if the war had never occurred."[49] Such an option would have maintained the political power of the ex-Confederates and jeopardized the rights of the newly freed slaves. At the other extreme were the views of the Radical Republicans. Their idea was to destroy the power of those who had created the Confederacy through disenfranchisement and confiscation of property. In turn, the freed slaves would be both given the vote and granted the property of their former masters, creating a new Southern society more like that of the North. A tenuous middle ground existed, drawing from both ends of the spectrum but satisfying neither.

Johnson's presidency ushered in what has been termed Presidential Reconstruction. While he had previously indicated the need to punish the rebellious South, to the surprise of many his actions more closely reflected those of Lincoln. On May 29, 1865, he issued a proclamation offering amnesty to those who would reject slavery and sign an oath of loyalty. Excepted were certain members of the former Confederate government and military and those owning taxable property with an estimated worth of greater than $20,000. With the exception of the latter condition, which reflected Johnson's personal antipathy toward the planter class, the proclamation was remarkably similar to Lincoln's Ten Percent Plan.

In the following months, Johnson's stated views on the course of Reconstruction increasingly moved away from those of the Republicans and toward those of the Democrats. Despite being elected by Republican votes as the vice-presidential candidate of a Republican president, he was at heart both a Southerner and Democrat. During this early postwar period, Southern opinion warmed toward Johnson and his plans for rapid restoration of self-rule in the former Confederacy. Pardons were granted freely. Those who had been excluded from amnesty through their association with the

---

[49] James M. McPherson, *Ordeal by Fire: The Civil War and Reconstruction* (New York: Alfred M. Knopf, 1982): 497.

Confederacy or on the basis of their wealth had been given the right to appeal under Johnson's proclamation. Even for this group, special pardons were bestowed "liberally." Of approximately 15,000 applications, some 13,500 were approved. In September 1865, the month in which my great-great-grandfather received his, presidential pardons were granted at an average rate of a hundred a day.

As the months progressed, Southern state governments reconstituted themselves, heavily populated with members of the former political class. The newly freed slaves remained in legal limbo, free yet uncertain of their status in the postwar society. Lacking formal status as citizens,[50] and no longer beholden to their former masters, they became persons to be regulated under so-called Black Codes. The Codes (which varied from state to state), while granting many civil rights to the freedmen, were often designed to curtail their freedom through the use of such devices as the definition of vagrancy.

Matters degenerated when Congress refused to admit the representatives of the Southern states at the beginning of the December 1865 session, leaving the makeup of the legislative bodies in the hands of the North. In February 1866, both houses of Congress passed a bill extending the life of the Freedmen's Bureau and granting certain civil rights to the ex-slaves. Johnson vetoed it, citing the fact that the bill's provisions were primarily aimed at the eleven former Confederate states, none of which had been allowed to have representation in either the House or Senate. The following month, in seeking to overturn the Dred Scott decision and define the legal status of the freedmen, Congress passed a Civil Rights Act defining blacks as American citizens and granting them full rights under the Constitution. Once again, Johnson vetoed this bill for multiple reasons, among them lack of Southern congressional representation.

While Johnson's vetoes may have pleased some Democrats, they drove many otherwise moderate Republicans toward the camp of the Radicals. Meanwhile, political events in the South were seen by many in the North as allowing the South to escape its just punishment for starting the war and defending slavery. In April and July 1866, respectively, Congress passed re-

---

[50] At the end of the Civil War, the freedmen's status was still defined by the Supreme Court's Dred Scott decision confirming they did not have citizenship status (*Dred Scott v. Sandford*, 60 U.S. 393 [1857]).

vised Freedmen's Bureau and Civil Rights Acts over presidential vetoes. At the same time, legislators set about crafting a fourteenth constitutional amendment that would embody the principles of the Civil Rights Bill, granting full citizenship to freedmen, nullifying the Dred Scott decision, and extending equal protection under the law to all. The proposed amendment passed with the necessary two-thirds vote of both houses of Congress on June 13, 1866, and was sent to the states for ratification.[51]

The results of the fall elections of 1866 represented a fundamental shift in the political makeup of Congress. In the North, there was a widespread perception that the South was reverting to its old way of life. Former rebels were being elected to office and the newfound rights of the freedmen systematically suppressed. As a result, candidates supporting the view of the Radical wing of the Republican Party won an overwhelming congressional majority. The ex-Confederate states, meanwhile, completely lacked congressional representation. As the legislators debated what further action might be necessary to bring the South into line, some called for extreme measures. By way of example, a February 1867 editorial in the *New York Times*, responding to an announcement that efforts to raise relief funds for the South were faring poorly, read (in part),

> The "Northern people" are too busy with other Southern interests just now to give much attention to such commonplace matters as starvation and distress. We want the Southern people well under martial law; we want to make sure that all their negroes have the right to vote, and then we will inquire whether they are starving or not. Probably two hundred thousand will perish this year—blacks and whites indiscriminately—mainly in Northern Mississippi, Alabama, Georgia and in the back districts of South Carolina; but there will be a good many left, and it is very important that those who *are* left should be under martial law. It will not answer to let starving men have the benefit of the writ of *habeas corpus*. Besides, while they are starving, they can be managed more easily. If we feed them we should make them insolent, and they might think it unreasonable of us to stick bayonets in them afterward, in order to make them sincerely sorry for their rebellion. The best way is, now that we have got them down, to keep them down. Starving will help bring them to a realizing sense of their condition and character. There's

[51] Tennessee was the first state of the former Confederacy to ratify the amendment and was formally readmitted to the Union in July 1866.

> nothing injures a man's *morale* like feeding him when he is hungry. That's just the time you can do with him as you please.[52]

Responding to public sentiment and political expediency, Congress passed a series of acts that ended Presidential Reconstruction and ushered in what became known as Radical Reconstruction.

On March 2, 1867, Congress voted overwhelmingly for a first Reconstruction Act, euphemistically titled "An Act to Provide for the More Efficient Government of the Rebel States." President Johnson promptly vetoed it; Congress passed it over his veto the same day. Under this act, the ten remaining former Confederate states were divided into five military districts, each under the command of a brigadier general with "sufficient military force" to allow enforcement of its provisions. The existing elected state governments were declared "provisional" and illegal, and martial law was instituted, allowing trial by military tribunal, notwithstanding the existence of civilian courts. In order to facilitate the establishment of "loyal and republican State governments," a supplemental act was passed on March 23, 1867, again over Johnson's veto, to place the military in charge of voter registration and of determining voter eligibility. To be certain that the goals of the new order were carried out, Congress passed a third Reconstruction act over Johnson's veto on July 19, 1867. This legislation "declared Southern provisional governments subordinate in all respects to military rule, [and] confirmed the power of commanders to remove officials from office."[53] The powers of registration boards in determining voter eligibility were expanded, assuring that many former Confederate supporters would be denied suffrage.

The net result of these new directives was the disenfranchisement of many of the white populace who had overwhelmingly elected candidates of the Democrat Party and the granting of voting rights to the newly freed slaves, who were expected to vote nearly exclusively for the Republican ticket. For the most part, the blacks eagerly embraced their new freedom, including especially the right to vote. To ensure that this vote would go to Republicans, the South was flooded with representatives of the Union Leagues. The Union League and similar organizations were founded in various cities

---

[52] *New York Times*, February 16, 1867. The emphasized words were those of the editorialist.

[53] McPherson, *Ordeal by Fire*, 528. A fourth Reconstruction act referring to voting and voter eligibility was passed in March 1868.

of the North during the Civil War as patriotic organizations supporting national unity and the policies of President Lincoln. In the postwar period, they functionally became political arms of the Radical wing of the Republican Party. In the South, they took the form of primarily African American organizations whose main purpose was political education and marshaling of the vote for Republican candidates. According to one historian, "By the end of 1867,...virtually every black voter in the South had enrolled in the Union League or some equivalent local political organization."[54] Within a relatively short period of time, state and local governments across the South had been repopulated by newly elected officials who swore allegiance to the Republican party of the North. What the war could not accomplish through the use of force, Congress completed by political fiat enforced by martial law.

While the concept of granting citizenship and the right to vote to the freed slaves was admirable, one cannot help but view it with a tinge of cynicism. As had been adequately demonstrated in the nearly two years between the end of the war and the imposition of Radical Reconstruction, the former political class of the South was reemerging in leadership roles. The Reconstruction Acts and military rule were aimed squarely at stripping electoral control from these individuals, all of whom were white, and bestowing it on the black freedmen. In 1860, the vast majority of the African American population of the United States lived in the states that formed the Confederacy and the few Border States where slavery was permitted. At the end of the Civil War, "only six [Northern] states allowed blacks to vote on any terms."[55] In the fall of 1865, referenda on state constitutional amendments enfranchising black men in Connecticut, Minnesota, and Wisconsin failed by substantial margins. Three years later, even after Iowa and Minnesota had adopted black suffrage, "black men still lacked the right to vote in eleven of the twenty-one Northern states and all five of the border states."[56]

For practical purposes, in much of the South during the Reconstitution era, political affiliation became defined by race. It was only in this section of the nation that the African American population was large enough to have significant electoral impact. As much as any other single factor, this planted

---

[54] Eric Foner, *Reconstruction: American's Unfinished Revolution 1863–1877* (New York: Harper & Row, 1988): 283.

[55] McPherson, *Ordeal by Fire*, 500.

[56] Ibid., 545.

and helped nurture the seeds of racial animus that came to fruition in the decades that followed. Even today, a century and a half later, we speak of the allegedly monolithic "black vote" as casually as did those of the 1860s and 1870s. It was this era that gave rise to the Ku Klux Klan and similar terrorist organizations whose purpose—in part—was to restore political control to those disenfranchised under Radical Reconstruction. As such, the events of the era left a tragic legacy.

By 1870, all the former states of the Confederacy had met criteria decreed as necessary for their rejoining the Union. The Fourteenth Amendment, granting citizenship and ensuring the civil rights of the freedmen (as well as other citizens), was adopted in July 1868. The Fifteenth Amendment, assuring that a citizen's right to vote not be limited "on account of race, color or previous condition of servitude," became effective in February 1870. Despite these constitutional guarantees to electorates likely to vote Republican, there remained a potentially significant problem for the ruling party in its quest to remain in power. It was the first of the three so-called Reconstruction Amendments, the thirteenth. In abolishing slavery, this amendment effectively negated the Three-Fifths Compromise clause of the Constitution.[57] Article 1, Section 2, Paragraph 3 of the 1787 charter reads (in part), "Representatives and direct Taxes shall be apportioned among the several States which may be included within this Union, according to their respective Numbers, which shall be determined by adding to the whole Number of free Persons, including those bound to Service for a Term of Years, and excluding Indians not taxed, three fifths of all other Persons."

The term "all other Persons" refers to slaves. In 1860, roughly 40 percent of the population of the eleven Confederate states was accounted for by "other Persons," i.e., those enslaved. With the freeing of the slaves, population as measured for the purpose of allotting congressional representation would "increase" by nearly a fifth. South Carolina would see an increase of nearly 30 percent, with Georgia, Alabama, and Mississippi—all major cotton-producing states—seeing increases of approximately 21, 22, and 28 percent, respectively.[58] Article 1, Section 2, Paragraph 3 of the Constitution goes on to state the necessity for congressional reapportionment every ten

---

[57] This constitutional change was formalized under the Fourteenth Amendment.

[58] See chapter notes for a chart detailing these figures.

years "in such Manner as they shall by Law direct" based on a decennial census. While the founders directed proportional representation, they left its actual method up to the legislative branch.

In the post-Civil War era, as in the present day, many congressional issues were often decided by narrow voting margins. By freeing the slaves and granting them citizenship, the potential congressional representation of the former Confederate states could see a dramatic increase. Although Republicans remained in firm control of Congress at the time, political history would dictate that change was inevitable. The loss of even a few votes as a result of congressional reapportionment could be critical.

The concept of representative democracy is thousands of years old, as is the thorny problem of how to fairly allocate proportional representation in governmental assemblies. Perhaps not surprisingly, the methodology can represent a complex mathematical problem. In the case of the United States, each state is guaranteed at least one representative irrespective of population. The others are apportioned based on population numbers that are constantly in flux. There is a practical limit to the number of representatives that can make up a deliberative body, and as the number of states increased in the nineteenth century (and beyond), attempts to determine reasonable, fair, and politically acceptable compromises made the problem all the more difficult. Numerous methods were suggested; methods proposed by Alexander Hamilton and later Daniel Webster were most commonly used through mid-century. The size of the House of Representatives grew steadily from 59 members in early 1789 to 243 members in 1867, the increases based on an increasing number of states and a growing population.

The 1870 census was the first in which the former slaves were counted as full persons for the purpose of congressional apportionment. Congress addressed the issue in early 1872, with its decision to apply to elections to be held later that year. After some discussion, the figure of 283 representatives was chosen, a number that satisfied both the methods of Hamilton and Webster in achieving a fair distribution under constitutional provisions. Congress passed the act on February 2, 1872. New Hampshire and Vermont were each scheduled to lose a seat based on population shifts. The outcome seemed to satisfy no one, resulting in political squabbling and recalculation.

On May 30, 1872, between an act to increase the capital stock of the Washington Gas-Light Company and another fixing the rank of Professors of Mathematics in the United States Navy, Congress quietly passed an amendment to its earlier reappointment act. Nine additional seats were added to the House of Representatives, bringing the total to 292. The states of New Hampshire, Vermont, New York, Pennsylvania, Indiana, Tennessee, Louisiana, Alabama, and Florida were each granted an additional seat. The additions did not conform to any measure of fairness; they were simply political in origin. Each state granted an additional seat was ruled by a Republican administration at that time. In the elections for the Forty-Third Congress that followed, Republicans gained a total of sixty-two seats while Democrats lost fifteen.

At the end of the Civil War, many in the North saw the coming years as an opportunity to both rebuild and restructure the South, a chance to create an egalitarian society more in line with that of the North. A decade later these dreams had faded. The ardor of the original congressional Radical Republican firebrands had cooled. Congressman Thaddeus Stevens of Pennsylvania, one of the more uncompromising voices in the House, had died in 1868. Sen. Charles Sumner, another Radical leader, had softened his rhetoric. Despite the best efforts of the Republican Congress and the continued presence of federal troops, many of the former states of the Confederacy had slipped back under Democratic control. The administration of Republican president Ulysses S. Grant, which had so vigorously enforced the acts defining Radical Reconstruction, was damaged by a series of corruption scandals during the president's second term. A third term for Grant seemed out of the question. Given the growing strength of the Democrat Party, there was a reasonable chance that the Republicans could lose the White House in the 1876 elections.

Meanwhile, in the South, "Reconstruction" had done little to reconstruct, repair, or maintain much of the infrastructure vital to commerce and transportation. The harbors of Savannah and Mobile remained "choked by wartime obstructions that the government had neglected to remove." Failure to dredge the mouth of the Mississippi River prevented all but shallow-draft vessels from access to the port of New Orleans. Commerce that otherwise might have gone through these ports was now diverted to Philadelphia, Boston, and New York. Much of the South's rail system had been damaged during the war. A decade later, little overall progress had been made in its rebuilding and repair. "Of the $103,294,501 spent on public works from 1865 to 1873, the South (the eleven ex-Confederate states plus Kentucky) received only $9,469,363." New York received $15,688,222, Massachusetts

$6,071,197, and Maine $3,030,500, compared with $49,103 spent in Arkansas and $24,417 in Kentucky.[59]

The presidential election of 1876 would be decided by a different electorate than that of earlier years. Americans at large seemed ready to move on and fully reintegrate the South into the Union, looking to the future instead of dwelling on the events of the past. The corruption of the Grant administration and the perceived injustices of Radical Reconstruction empowered the Democrat Party, now resurgent in the South. As events would play out, the clear winner of the popular vote did not ascend to the presidency. Once again, political considerations became paramount, leading to the unwritten Compromise of 1877.

For their candidate, Republicans chose Rutherford B. Hayes, an attorney, former Union army general, and, at the time, governor of the state of Ohio. The Democratic candidate was Samuel J. Tilden, a wealthy corporate lawyer and governor of New York. Besides the usual party rhetoric, both candidates spoke of reform, raising the possibility of a formal end to Reconstruction. While a limited number of federal troops continued to be stationed in the South, most of the states had fallen back under the control of the Democrat Party. As the returns from the November 7, 1876, balloting were gathered, it became evident that Tilden had won the popular vote by a comfortable margin, 50.9 percent versus 47.9 percent for Hayes (with the remainder going to minority candidates). The popular vote notwithstanding, it would be the results of the electoral college vote that determined who would be inaugurated as president. Of the 369 electoral votes, it appeared that Hayes had received 185 and Tilden 184. But there were problems. The allocation of the electoral votes was the prerogative of local boards in each state whose job it was to validate and certify election results. In Louisiana, Florida, and South Carolina, accounting for some 19 votes of the 369, the electoral boards were controlled by Republicans. Regardless of what appeared to be Democratic presidential victories in each state, the election boards managed to disqualify enough Democratic voters to throw the results into the Republican column. For example, "The Louisiana...board converted an apparent Tilden majority of 7,500 into a Hayes majority of 4,500 and certified the election of a Republican governor and legislature by throwing

[59] See C. Vann Woodward, *Reunion and Reaction: The Compromise of 1877 and the End of Reconstruction* (Boston: Little, Brown and Company, 1951): 56–59.

out or modifying the returns from several bulldozed parishes."[60] In addition, the legitimacy of one Oregon Republican elector was called into question on constitutional grounds. To claim the presidential victory, the Republicans had to keep all twenty disputed electoral votes; the Democrats merely needed to gain one.[61]

The absence of a clear electoral victory presented a major quandary. Political activists and the public alike rapidly chose sides, with rallies, fiery rhetoric, and editorials demanding a fair resolution of the problem, each side assuming that it occupied the moral high ground. There were even rumors of a new civil war, causing President Grant to reinforce the military garrison in Washington. As the Constitution gave no guidance as to what steps to take to resolve the crisis, Congress created a special electoral commission to review and arbitrate the disputed returns. Its decision as to the outcome of the race would be final unless overturned by both houses of Congress. A resolution had to be reached by March 4, 1877, the day scheduled for the presidential inauguration. Although efforts had been carefully made to assure the political neutrality of the commission, it soon became clear that in spite of evidence of electoral fraud, the body was likely to approve the partition of votes as originally submitted by the states, leading to a victory for Republican candidate Hayes. Sensing that the chance to win the presidency was about to be jerked away, the Democrat-controlled House floated the threat of obstructionism, delaying approval or disapproval of the commission's vote beyond Inauguration Day. This would throw the election of the president into the House, which would elect Tilden.

Meanwhile, behind the scenes, certain members of Congress, politicians, and others with business and financial interests began negotiations in an attempt to resolve the dilemma. Working quietly and at first through intermediaries, the Hayes camp was approached with the possibility of a

[60] McPherson, *Ordeal by Fire*, 509.

[61] It should also be noted here that were it not for the politically structured reapportionment of 1872, the electoral college vote would have resulted in a tie, ignoring the outcome of any disputed votes. The number of electors for each state is determined by the total of its senators and representatives. Of the nine extra electoral votes based on seats in Congress granted under the amended act, five went to the Republican candidate and four to the Democratic. This would have placed the election in the Democrat-controlled House of Representatives, who presumably would have elected Tilden.

compromise that would allow the Republican Party to retain the presidency. An unwritten quid pro quo took shape over weeks of negotiation. As it appeared that the electoral commission would rule in favor of the Republicans, Democratic hopes for the presidency faded. A coalition of Southern Democrats and moderate Northern Republicans agreed to accept the commission's decision contingent on three broad conditions: First, Hayes would include in his cabinet a Southern Democrat with the power to dispense federal patronage in the former states of the Confederacy. Second, the few remaining federal troops would be withdrawn and the South allowed to pursue its own political future. This was not a new idea, as President Grant himself had been willing to consider it but had not acted. Third, the new president would support the voting of federal subsidies to rebuild the South and stimulate the Southern economy. By late February, the deal had been struck. The Democratic plan collapsed, and Rutherford B. Hayes was inaugurated president on March 4, 1877.

Hayes kept his side of the bargain. Democratic senator David M. Key of Tennessee was appointed postmaster general, a patronage-rich office that allowed him to appoint politically friendly candidates as postmasters, often replacing their Republican predecessors. In April 1877, Hayes ordered federal troops withdrawn from the South. The Republican governments of both Louisiana and South Carolina, whose claim to legitimacy was made possible only by the presence of troops, promptly collapsed and were replaced by Democratic administrations. While the South fared less well in terms of federal subsidies for public works projects and railroads, the increase as compared to the prior decade was significant.

Without a doubt, the major outcome of the Compromise of 1877 was the abandonment of the Republican hopes for becoming a viable political party in the South. In part as a reaction to the rigors of Radical Reconstruction, Southern Democrats over the ensuing years passed a series of so-called "Jim Crow laws" resulting in the systematic suppression of the voting rights of blacks and often denying them equal protection under the law. With certain exceptions, much of the vast area of the former Confederacy remained for nearly a century an agricultural region characterized by poverty, disease, and hopelessness. The events of the Reconstruction era, however well intentioned they may have been, can only be described as a series of dismal failures. In many respects, the root causes of these failures can be attributed to the triumph of party politics over considerations of the common good.

SOURCES AND RESOURCES

The following works contain general accounts of the Reconstruction era and/or specific references to topics addressed in this essay. As noted, the interpretation of the events of these postwar years is often tinged by the viewpoint of the author. In the century and a half that has elapsed, various schools of thought have waxed and waned, their ideas debated without firm consensus. Essentially all historians agree that if Reconstruction had goals, it was for the most part a failure. Its positive ideals are represented in the Thirteenth, Fourteenth, and Fifteenth Amendments, but for decades their actual implementation was another matter. In the annotated bibliography that follows, I have cited several "standard" works that were written in the mid- to late twentieth century. The choices of Coulter and Foner are deliberate. Their widely disparate opinions of many facets of the Reconstruction era serve to illustrate the role of the historian in explaining the significance of historical events.

Balinski, Michel L. and H. Peyton Young. *Fair Representation: Meeting the Ideal of One Man, One Vote.* New Haven, CT: Yale University Press, 1982. This somewhat esoteric text is an excellent and in-depth analysis of the practical problems posed by the attempt to achieve equitable distribution in representative assemblies. There are good accounts of the various methods used by the United States House of Representatives from the earliest days of the Republic to the present.

Coulter, E. Merton. *The South During Reconstruction 1865–1877.* Volume VIII of *A History of the South.* Baton Rouge: Louisiana State University Press, 1947. To quote the author, at the time a distinguished professor of history at the University of Georgia, "The point of view set forth in this work is the *South* during Reconstruction—not *Reconstruction* in the South."[62] In this regard, it is a most illuminating narrative, to be contrasted with Foner's history of Reconstruction (see below). Coulter's author's preface clearly sets out his disagreements with historians whom I believe he would describe as revisionists:

> As each generation feels constrained to rewrite the past, points of view and methods of approach necessarily change, and so revisionists arise. If they remain within the reasonable bounds of established facts, they may well make lasting contributions in fresher interpretations and in the presentation of new information; but if they depart from the old channels to attract attention in novel and unsubstantiated points of view, they themselves may soon be revised. The author of this work feels that there can be no sensible departure from the well-known facts of the Reconstruction program as it was applied

[62] Emphasis is that of Coulter.

to the South. No amount of revision can write away the grievous mistakes made in this abnormal period of American history. This writer, therefore, has not attempted it.

Foner, Eric. *Reconstruction: American's Unfinished Revolution 1863–1877*. New York: Harper & Row, 1988. The author, a professor of history at Columbia University and a Pulitzer Prize-winning author, has been described as "one of the country's most prominent historians." His opus on Reconstruction has been widely acclaimed and is considered by many to be the standard reference work on the era. His views, based in large part on the same set of facts, are quite different from that of many earlier writers on the subject, including Coulter (see above). Describing Reconstruction as "a laudable experiment in interracial democracy" and Andrew Johnson as "one of the worst presidents to occupy the White House," Foner is quick to condemn the viewpoints of many historians who preceded him, equating their views to those popularized in patently racist 1915 film *The Birth of a Nation*. His assessment of Radical Reconstruction is summarized by a quote from an essay he contributed to *The Civil War Remembered*, a publication of the United States National Park Service commemorating the sesquicentennial of the end of the conflict: "In the South, a politically mobilized black community joined with white allies to bring the Republican party to power, and with it a redefinition of the purposes and responsibilities of government."

McPherson, James M. *Ordeal by Fire: The Civil War and Reconstruction*. New York: Alfred M. Knopf, 1982. A well-written, informative overview of the American Civil War. McPherson divides his narrative into three sections. The first, "The Coming of War," covering the period from 1800 to 1860, is especially informative in delineating the forces that led to the conflict. The second and third, "The Civil War" and "Reconstruction," are concise but balanced accounts of the main events of the 1860 to 1877 years.

Polakoff, Keith I. *The Politics of Inertia: The Election of 1876 and the End of Reconstruction*. Baton Rouge: Louisiana State University Press, 1973. An account of the politics leading to the election of 1876, with particular attention to the resolution of the disputed electoral ballots and the compromise that led to the withdrawal of federal troops from the South.

Woodward, C. Vann. *Reunion and Reaction: The Compromise of 1877 and the End of Reconstruction*. Boston: Little, Brown and Company, 1951. Woodward's work is a detailed examination of the negotiations leading to the Compromise of 1877. He makes the point that American Democracy has faced many impasses since the founding of the nation, with all but one (the conflicts that led to the Civil War) resolved by "the celebrated American genius for compromise." Though some historians have disagreed with his conclusions, the informal and off-the-record tradeoffs that helped untangle the electoral stalemate shed light on the dark side of America politics.

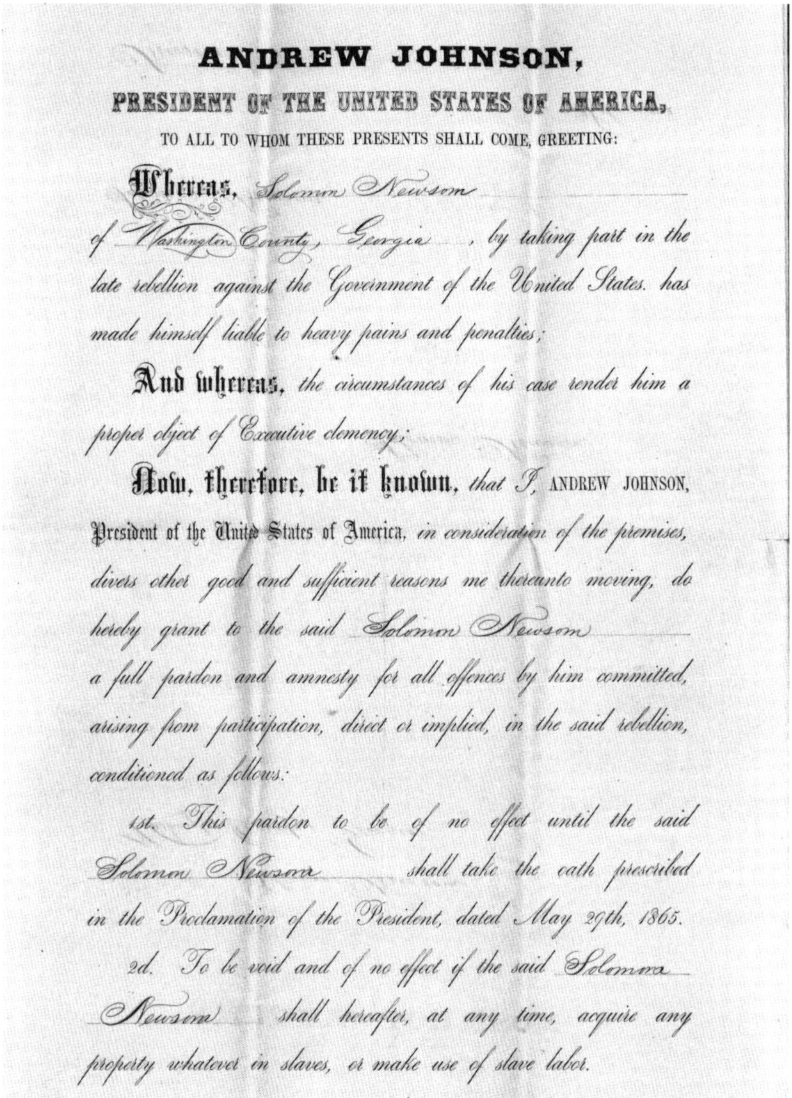

ANDREW JOHNSON,

PRESIDENT OF THE UNITED STATES OF AMERICA,

TO ALL TO WHOM THESE PRESENTS SHALL COME, GREETING:

Whereas, *Solomon Newsom* of *Washington County, Georgia*, *by taking part in the late rebellion against the Government of the United States, has made himself liable to heavy pains and penalties;*

And whereas, *the circumstances of his case render him a proper object of Executive clemency;*

Now, therefore, be it known, *that I,* ANDREW JOHNSON, President of the United States of America, *in consideration of the premises, divers other good and sufficient reasons me thereunto moving, do hereby grant to the said* *Solomon Newsom* *a full pardon and amnesty for all offences by him committed, arising from participation, direct or implied, in the said rebellion, conditioned as follows:*

1st. This pardon to be of no effect until the said *Solomon Newsom* *shall take the oath prescribed in the Proclamation of the President, dated May 29th, 1865.*

2d. To be void and of no effect if the said *Solomon Newsom* *shall hereafter, at any time, acquire any property whatever in slaves, or make use of slave labor.*

This presidential pardon granted to the author's great, great-grandfather less than five months after the end of the Civil War forgave his support of the Confederacy and restored his civil rights. Only a year and a half later, however, he and most of the former voting populace saw these rights revoked by Congress with the institution of so-called Radical Reconstruction and the declaration of martial law in ten of the eleven former Confederate states.

Author's Collection

Under a series of Congressional Acts, Radical Reconstruction was instituted in March 1867. Local and state governments were deposed, the former voting population disenfranchised, and control of the ballot effectively transferred to the newly free slaves. These acts ensured that Republican candidates would hold political power across the South.

Harper's Weekly, Vol. XI, 6 April 1867

CHAPTER 8

THE FREEDMAN'S LAND INSURRECTION OF 1875

The confessions, given freely after the arrests of dozens of conspirators, revealed horrific details of the planned insurrection. Jake Mooreman, described as "the first lieutenant of a colored company" of insurrectionists, testified,

> On last Friday or Saturday we received orders from Francis Murkerson and Cordy Harris that all our company and all the black men were to meet at No. 11, Central Railroad, to transact our business (this he explained to be the carrying out of the insurrection plans), and we were then to commence to kill all the white men and ugly white women, and take the pretty white women for ourselves. Then we were to take axes, hoes and brickbats, and take the guns and ammunition of the whites as we killed them, if the white men did not submit and give up. We were also to get all the money we could from the dead whites and divide. This movement was to commence on Friday, August 20th, 1875.

The fantastic plot had been discovered and thwarted, thus averting a spree of mass murder whose end was to be the seizure of political and economic power in a twenty-county area of east-central Georgia. Mostly forgotten in the years following its failure, the so-called Freedman's Land Insurrection remains one of the more bizarre episodes in Georgia history.

The planned insurrection was the product of the unsettled era known as Radical Reconstruction. The prime conspirators were ex-slaves and members of the Union Leagues that served as organizational nuclei for politically active freedmen in the post-Civil War South. The plot seemed to center around Joe Morris, a civil rights activist and self-styled "Messayenger" from Burke County, "General" Prince R. Rivers, a South Carolina militia leader, and Cordy Harris, a "preacher" and Union League officer from Washington County, Georgia. Theirs was not the only alleged "insurrection" in Georgia in the years following the war, but it might have been the most destructive had it been carried out. In order to understand how such an event might unfold, it is necessary to understand the period and the dynamics of political power of that day.

The Civil War ended in the spring of 1865, and with it the hopes and dreams of an aspiring nation. The period between the end of the war and the final withdrawal of federal troops from the former states of the Confederacy in 1877 is referred to as the Reconstruction era. It is generally agreed that Abraham Lincoln had favored a rapid reintegration of the rebel states with punishment and retribution on behalf of the victorious North kept to a minimum. After Lincoln's assassination in April 1865, it was initially thought that his successor, Andrew Johnson, would pursue a harder line toward the South. This turned out not to be the case, as Johnson—despite his previous harsh rhetoric—moved closer to the position held by his predecessor in office. Congress was sharply divided between Democrats, who held more moderate views, and Republicans, especially the Radical wing, who demanded reparations, confiscation of the lands of former Confederates, and disenfranchisement of those who had participated on the side of the South during the war.

One especially thorny issue was the allotment of congressional representation. The Thirteenth Amendment, which had freed the slaves, also effectively negated the so-called Three-Fifths Compromise as enumerated in Article I, Section 2, Paragraph 3 of the United States Constitution. Under this clause, slaves had counted as "three-fifths persons" for the purpose of congressional apportionment. Forty percent of the population in the eleven Confederate states—approximately 3.5 million persons—had been slaves. With freedom, the potential congressional representation of these Southern states, when readmitted to the Union, would increase dramatically at the time of the next reapportionment.

While freedmen might count in calculating congressional representation they—like most blacks of the day in both Northern and Southern states—rarely had the right to vote. Elected representatives from the South—overwhelmingly white—would presumably vote Democrat, thus forcing the Republicans from power. To counter this threatened shift in power, Congress passed a law in March 1867 euphemistically titled "An Act to Provide for the More Efficient Government of the Rebel States." This act and others that followed disenfranchised most white males and placed the South under martial law enforced by federal troops. Political power was effectively wrenched from the hands of the former ruling class and given instead to a coalition of scalawags, carpetbaggers, and former slaves voted into office by the newly enfranchised freedmen.

The Union Leagues (also referred to as Loyal Leagues) were organizations that arose in the North during the Civil War in support of the Union cause. There were several with varying degrees of central organization. During early Reconstruction, Union Leagues formed across the South, their members being Union soldiers, transplanted Northerners, Southern loyalists, missionaries, Northern teachers, and others. On a practical basis, the leagues became "a sort of bureau of the Radical Republican party, [their] chief object being to control the negro vote." In Georgia they were loosely organized under a Grand Council of the State headquartered in Atlanta.

Initially comprised of white membership, the Union League clubs opened to blacks early in the postwar period. Over a relatively short span of time, the League became a primarily black organization, though often controlled at a higher level by white Radical Republicans and their disciples. The League's overt purpose was to make certain that blacks voted the Republican ticket. But with the return of Democrat political control in Georgia in 1870, the influence of the Union Leagues waned. Over the ensuing years, the groups devolved into loosely organized black secret societies, often with a military type structure despite their nominal political nature.

The political and social environment of the Reconstruction years gave birth to the Ku Klux Klan and other similar white groups. Consisting of scattered, independent, and loosely organized bands, the Klan opposed the Union Leagues, established a way to preserve "order" that was friendly to white Southerners, and endeavored to keep blacks "in their place." The existence of antagonistic secret organizations such as the Klan on the one side and the Union Leagues on the other, was symptomatic of the virulent racial animosity present in the South during Reconstruction.

Across the South there were a number of incidents and insurrections, some major and some minor, during the Reconstruction era. Many were simply due to the freedmen attempting to exercise their newfound civil rights and freedoms, while others took on a more sinister nature. In September 1868, a dozen or more blacks marching in a political rally were killed in the so-called Camilla Massacre in Mitchell County, Georgia. In the North this incident became a *cause célèbre*, seen as yet another sign of Southern intransigence and a clear justification for the rigors of Radical Reconstruction. In the South, the specter of a crowd of marching blacks, a few of whom were armed, raised fears of race-fueled rebellion. In December of that same year, a dispute over land ownership by armed blacks in an area of former rice plantations near Savannah became known as the Ogeechee Insurrection.

In August 1870, a Union League organizer named Cudjo Fye led an armed mob of blacks in an attempt to free a black prisoner from the Jefferson County jail in Louisville, about thirty-five miles southwest of Augusta. He told his followers that he was operating under direct orders of Georgia's Republican governor, Rufus Bullock. Initially dissuaded in his efforts by local officials, Fye returned the next day with a band of "fifty or sixty armed followers," "damning the white man promiscuously," as well as threatening to burn the town "and kill every man, woman and child in it." They broke into the jail and freed the prisoner. In response, as many as a thousand armed whites from surrounding counties descended on Louisville, later assisted by federal troops. The affair ended fairly peacefully, with a number of the leaders of the mob later sentenced to prison.

By 1875, a decade after the end of the war, necessity had forced former slave and former master to peaceably coexist in a new normality. The violence, lawlessness, and "outrages" of the Ku Klux Klan and others, common during the years immediately following the conflict, became infrequent. As observers would later note, the relationship between the races in Washington County and the east-central Georgia area in general appeared on the surface to be reasonably calm, with no single issue a cause for concern. But the seeming tranquility soon ended.

Joseph ("Joe") Morris, who was to emerge as the prime ringleader of the group of insurrectionists in the 1875 affair, was born in Burke County on the plantation of Col. Robert Morrison. According to his former master, he was said to have been a "full-blooded African," average in appearance and somewhat surly. As a youth he displayed no outstanding characteristics that might belie his future infamy. A young adult when he was set free, Morris worked for a short time on a nearby plantation before dropping out of sight. Over the next few years, he was said to have traveled extensively in neighboring counties and "frequently visited" South Carolina. There he presumably met Prince Rivers, a prominent politician, leader of a local black militia, and mayor of Hamburg, South Carolina, a small town directly across the Savannah River from Augusta. In the early 1870s, Morris returned to his old home in Burke County and "at once assumed a certain air of authority over and demanded obedience from the colored population." Despite a minimal education and rudimentary literary skills, he opened a school for young blacks. A contemporary newspaper article written after the abortive insurrection stated Morris's "great ambition was to be a military hero, and to this end he devoted all his spare time. He frequently appeared in a flashy uniform, putting on the airs of a General, although without commission or command. He had a regular set of couriers who carried his orders and letters to distant negro settlements."

In May 1875, a Burke County superior court judge received a crudely worded missive citing state and federal laws and demanding that blacks be allowed to serve on local juries. It was signed by "the Hon. Joseph Morris Messayenger." Morris had become a strong advocate for the civil rights of the freedmen as black voting power waned. The return of rule in Georgia by the Democrat Party, controlled by the white population, had resulted in progressive disenfranchisement and political emasculation of the ex-slaves despite the guarantees granted under the Fourteenth and Fifteenth Amendments. A Burke County grand jury promptly indicted Morris for carrying a concealed weapon, as "some member of that body having seen a pistol protruding from under the 'Hon's' coat tails." The judge then issued a bench warrant for his arrest. Morris's petition for blacks to serve on juries was ignored.

Morris was arrested and carried before a justice of the peace, where he was arraigned prior to posting bail and being released. His trial was scheduled for a few days hence, as rumors spread of "about a hundred and fifty armed negroes" lying in wait nearby to free him if convicted. On the day of court, several witnesses were unavailable, and the matter was continued to the next session, to be held several months later. The rumors of armed gangs were never confirmed.

Over the next couple of months there was uneasiness among the white population of Burke, Jefferson, Hancock, Washington, and surrounding counties because of rumors that the blacks were "up to something." Black militia companies were said to be drilling well into the night for reasons unknown. A note was discovered referring to some future activity in Glascock and Warren counties. It was signed by "General Morris."

It was in this atmosphere of uncertainty that Ruben Mayo, sheriff of Washington County, received the following note, reproduced here without editorial correction:

Rube Mayer Sherif

You command to have cort house sweped and all cleaned for mass meeting on Saturday July 24, 1875 for Republincan party fur hon. Major General P. R. Rivers and his staf from aiken, S.C. and charmans, exicutiv committee of 19 countiys in Sandersville Washington County State of Georgia, and have you all the said rodes keep opened from No. 13 Statien [Tennille, Georgia] to the court house and the keys in your hand to put in My hands to the Mr. hon. General P. R. Rivers from S.C., and his staf and execitive commitis from 19 Counties and General Morres and his staf from S.C.

Your devoted frnds
Joseph Morris
Chairman of said company from Burke County
July 19, 1875

The note produced immediate alarm in Sandersville. In view of the blacks' recent "mid-night drills, mysterious meetings and roll calls in the still of the night" it was feared that Morris and Rivers might try to take the courthouse by force. The county Ordinary determined that the courthouse could not be *demanded* for such purposes, leading the sheriff and others to set out to defend it. The local militia was enlisted. Captain Peacock of the Washington Rifles telegraphed for an extra thousand cartridges to be sent from Macon. The Washington Dragoons were appointed as mounted police while others, both "white and colored," were deputized under the command of a Captain Weddon.

The scene on the morning of July 24, 1875, was tense. As the local newspaper described it, "The stillness of the early dawn of Saturday was broken by the war-like sound of many drums coming from the direction of Tennille [the local train depot, some three miles distant]. Between six and seven o'clock the column hove into sight, led by Cordy Harris, mounted and looking as if he was going to a funeral." The column of several hundred blacks was smaller than had been expected. Many more from around the area had planned to arrive by train, but the word had been spread that the engineers were not to stop and pick up the waiting crowds, hence hundreds more were left stranded at stations along the several rail lines that converged at Tennille.

The commercial district of Sandersville, the county seat, centered on a large symmetrical courthouse square, laid out in 1856 after a fire the preceding year had destroyed most of the previous collection of buildings. A neat new brick courthouse, built to replace the one Sherman's forces had burned in 1864 on their March to the Sea, dominated the square. The only other major structures in the grassy central portion of the square were a large platform used to weigh cotton and a monument to Gov. Jared Irwin, erected by the state in 1856 to honor his role in exposing the Great Yazoo Fraud. The county jail, a red-painted wood-frame structure, faced the square just to the north of the courthouse.

Militia and local police were present in force when the marchers arrived at the courthouse square. After the demonstrators marched back and forth for a while, Cordy Harris made a short speech on the lawn. The marchers then called for Joe Morris, their nominal leader, but he had remained at the station in Tennille. Prince Rivers was nowhere to be found, apparently having missed the train from Augusta or, alternatively, deciding to remain at the depot with Morris. Cordy Harris suggested a postponement of the meeting, which was agreed to, and the marchers soon dispersed.

Dispensing "a word of advice to the colored people of this county," the editor of the *Sandersville Herald & Georgian* wrote:

> Do you desire prosperity, peace and happiness, and the good will and confidence of the white people upon whom you are dependent for homes and employment? If yea, avoid the appearance of evil intentions. Shun such monsters as Rivers, Morris and their crowd as you would a viper in your path. Ask them for bread and they have none to give, but can preach "civil rights" until the sun goes down. Away with them! They are mischief-makers, lazy disturbers of the peace who would gladly embroil you in a disturbance, leave you to shift for yourself while they'd make off with the spoils. Bid them stay at home and attend to their own affairs and if Cordy Harris would go and live with them Washington County would not sustain any serious loss.

The editor's words, while well intentioned, echoed the viewpoint of white Democrats, who once again controlled political power in the state. He could little understand the despair experienced by many of the freedmen who had participated in the march. Their brief tastes of freedom and political clout after the war were quickly fading into an era that would be marked by tenant farming and the rule of Jim Crow, a dark epoch for Southern blacks that would last far into the next century. For these freedmen, the ill-defined concept of civil rights and the encouragement of their leaders must have offered a last hope to salvage the new and brighter future that emancipation had once seemed to promise.

Over the days that followed, rumors of trouble continued to swirl about the region. The general consensus was that the last had not been heard of Morris, Rivers, and their followers. A "faithful servant" warned a woman in Jefferson County to leave home on Friday, August 20, 1875, as she might otherwise come to some harm. Around August 17, a crudely handwritten note was found at a country store near the line between Washington and Johnson counties, "where a party of negroes had been drinking." Its contents were chilling. As reproduced "in plain English" in the *Herald & Georgian*, it read:

To Jerry Waters: You and your Company must start killing the whites on August 20. Kill every one you can find, and tell Harrison Tucker to kill all the whites he can find and go towards No. 11 Station [Bartow, Georgia] and there will meet Gen. Morris and staff and Gen. Rivers and his staff. You do as I tell you and Capt. Tucker. This must be secret. You tell brother Jake to kill every white man and get every gun he can. Make out to the white men you are very sorry they think we want to hurt them. And if you know of any man that has got money make them give it to your Treasurer and we will divide it. Have all your community needs. Kill with axes, hoes, pitchforks, and get guns, powder and shot as you kill. So I close to depend on you.

Cordy Harris, Secretary
By order of Gen. Morris and from Gen. Rivers

A courier rushed to deliver the note to Sheriff Mayo in Sandersville. The reaction was immediate. Warrants were issued; Waters, Tucker, and "Brother Jake" were arrested in short order. Cordy Harris, now a wanted man, escaped. Telegrams were dispatched to Gov. James M. Smith in Atlanta and to the sheriffs of surrounding counties. The governor authorized calling up the local militias to act as *posses comitatus* in Washington and Jefferson counties. Ex-governor Herschel V. Johnson, the presiding judge of the Middle Judicial Circuit, was instructed by Governor Smith to lead the investigation and hold a preliminary Court of Inquiry on Monday, August 23, at which time the prisoners would be arraigned.

The arrests of accused insurrectionists continued in several counties, including Washington, Johnson, Burke, Laurens, Wilkinson, and Greene. The exact number is difficult to ascertain, but judging from press reports, between two and three hundred were taken into custody. Most were held in the Washington County jail, the offense of most simply that of being a member of one of the Union League militias. A number of prisoners readily confessed, implicating Prince R. Rivers as the "arch-conspirator," with Joseph Morris under him. Cordy Harris and Francis Murkerson, both from Washington County, were local ringleaders. The killings were to begin simultaneously in Jefferson, Burke, Washington, and a portion of Richmond Counties, conducted by squads of fifteen to twenty men operating in multiple locations before linking up with their leaders.

Morris was nowhere to be found. He was rumored to be in Burke County protected by an armed group of some 500 to 1,000 men, but no such force was ever identified. There were a number of minor skirmishes with a smaller band of armed blacks resulting in more arrests, but Morris managed to make good his escape.

Feelings ran high as word of the brutal nature of the abortive insurrection spread. The *Atlanta Constitution*, with headlines screaming "War of Races!" and "Twenty Counties to be the Scene of Murder and Pillage," suggested hanging the conspirators. Meanwhile, in Sandersville a group of seven prominent local citizens posted a public letter in the local paper urging calm and adherence to the rule of law, a clear attempt to forestall any thoughts of lynching. Press coverage took on a national and international scope, with detailed articles appearing in New York and New Orleans dailies, as well as at least one British newspaper.

As news accounts disclosed the detailed confessions, Prince Rivers—now safely ensconced in his hometown of Hamburg, South Carolina—wrote to the editor of an Augusta newspaper denying that he knew either Morris or Harris, that he had never been to a political gathering of any kind in Georgia, and that "it takes all my time to give attention to my corn and cotton." Few who were familiar with the situation believed him.

On Friday, August 20, Cordy Harris surrendered to Sheriff Mayo in Sandersville. While he had been hiding amongst sympathizers he received word that he would be safer in custody and that he might be killed if he tried to flee. As arrests continued, the local jail filled to overflowing, requiring that some prisoners be held under guard in the courthouse.

Meanwhile, major newspapers around the country dispatched correspondents to assess the situation firsthand. Some accounts reported the events as merely exercises in politics. The *Portland* (Maine) *Daily Press*, a decidedly Republican newspaper, printed the account under the headline "Silly Letters Made a Pretext for a Wholesale Arrest of Negroes." The *Daily Graphic*, a New York paper, opined that the arrests were in retribution for the freedmen's attempts at exercising their civil rights. But as confessions and corroboration about the extensive nature of the plot accumulated, the voices of naysayers quieted. There seemed little doubt that there had been some plan by insurrectionists to "kill from the cradle up."

On Saturday, August 21, Governor Smith arrived in Tennille by train from Atlanta and was escorted to Sandersville in a procession of carriages accompanied by the Washington Dragoons, the mayor, aldermen, and other prominent citizens. On arrival he was briefed on the situation and examined the evidence against the plotters. The governor personally interviewed Cordy Harris in the presence of a correspondent for the *Atlanta Constitution*. Harris spoke freely, admitting the plot was an "outgrowth of the old Negro Union League organization." More recently, "Major General's Clubs" had formed for the purpose of "placing the District under the control of the colored people even if it should require the death of every white man in the country to do so." Harris claimed that "General" Morris, "General" Rivers and another man named Rev. Jerry Simmons were at the heart of the plot. Harris, described by the reporter as having a small build, thin features, and glib tongue, stated he was simply a "Baptist preacher, so-called."

Governor Smith spoke from the courthouse steps for about an hour, addressing a large mixed-race crowd. His words were calm but "earnest and emphatic." He said he had known of "Mr. Gen. Morris and his staff" prior to the recent events. Morris had tried to get arms for his private militia from the governor, threatening that "the bones of the colored people would rise up and stare him in the face" if he did not. Smith complimented the white population on their restraint in the face of the threat, while warning the blacks "against such mischief-makers as Morris, Rivers and others." To both races he said, "The law is supreme, and shall be maintained."

On August 23, the Court of Inquiry convened briefly in Sandersville, deciding to hold the prisoners while referring the matter to the grand jury for consideration. According to newspaper reports, two more notes similar in tone to the one from Cordy Harris had been discovered, as well as evidence of some outside direction, giving further evidence of the broad nature of the plot. The *Atlanta Constitution* reported, "It is positively established that the old Union League and the new secret negro military organizations are at the bottom of the fiendish and unparalleled plot. This fact is corroborated by an intercepted letter from a white radical in Atlanta cautioning Harris to be careful in his maneuvers, or his rash acts and movements would redound to the irreparable injury of the republican party and help defeat the re-election of President Grant!" The identity of the so-called "white radical" was not revealed.

The week passed peacefully, with some additional arrests being made. A sense of cautious calm prevailed, though, as the editor of the *Herald & Georgia* noted, "It has indeed seemed like war time had returned." The two companies of militia remained camped on the courthouse square, holding drills and dress parades, all dutifully watched over by guard pickets. The people of Washington County were invited to a public meeting on August 27 to honor and express appreciation for the two militia companies.

The authorities discovered an escape plot by the insurrectionists on the day of the public meeting. In order to clean the county jail, which was packed to capacity, the sheriff temporarily moved the prisoners to the courthouse yard. This led to the discovery that some of the prisoners had managed to cut away a window casing and loosen the iron bars. They had torn up blankets and bed sheets and were apparently planning a mass escape that Friday night. Until repairs could be made they were confined in a makeshift stockade.

On August 30, the grand jury assembled to hear the evidence and—if appropriate—issue indictments against the prisoners. The trials were to start immediately thereafter. The proceedings were to take place under the direction of some of the leading legal minds of the day. Judge Herschel V. Johnson, while serving as the presiding judge of the Middle Judicial Circuit, had a distinguished background. Born in Burke County, he had served briefly as a US senator in the 1840s before serving two successive terms as governor in the 1850s. In 1860, he was the vice-presidential running mate with Stephen Douglas, becoming a nationally known political figure. During the war years, he served in the Confederate Senate. Nearly sixty-three years old in the summer of 1875, he was selected to preside over the insurrection trials for his experience and insight.

Governor Smith appointed Georgia's attorney general, Nathaniel J. Hammond, to serve as lead prosecutor. To assure a fair trial for the accused, Amos T. Akerman was tapped to lead the defense. A native of New Hampshire and a graduate of Dartmouth College, Akerman had moved to Georgia in the 1850s, practicing law and farming. He enlisted in the Confederate army at the outbreak of the war, rising to the rank of colonel. In 1865, he joined the Republican Party in Georgia and was said to have become an outspoken advocate for the civil rights of the freed slaves. President Grant appointed him as United States Attorney General in 1870, in which position he led a vigorous legal attack against the Ku Klux Klan under the provisions of the Enforcement Acts. At the time of the trial, Akerman was in his mid-fifties and quietly engaged in the practice of law in Cartersville.

Judge Johnson set the tone when he opened the proceedings with his charge to the grand jury. First citing and explaining the pertinent sections of the Georgia code, he added a specific admonition to the jurymen, stating,

> The circumstances which have brought us together are well calculated to excite the indignation of the most prudent and self-possessed. It is impossible to contemplate with complacency a plot of wholesale, indiscriminate and secret murder of one race by part of the other race, which two constitute the elements of our social organization. It is difficult to suppress a feeling of vindictive revenge against those persons thus charged with plotting bloodshed and slaughter. But you and I are here in a judicial capacity, to administer justice according to law, and not according to human passions. We must not permit ourselves to be swayed in our conduct by any impulses, however natural, nor let our judgments be warped by rumors which may have been circulated in reference to the alleged insurrection. We are sworn to impartiality. We are sworn to expel from our bosoms every feeling of hatred, or malice, or revenge. We are sworn to be guided by the light of truth, and to enforce the law just as it is.

The grand jury initially issued indictments against Cordy Harris, Prince R. Rivers, Francis Murkerson, Joseph Morris, and three others. More were to follow. Rivers, denying his guilt, remained in South Carolina. Murkerson and Morris remained at large. The governor, acknowledging Morris's status as a ringleader, posted a $500 reward for his capture. As the evidence against Cordy Harris was most abundant, the state elected to try him first.

For three days the prosecution and defense presented their cases to the jury. It seemed generally agreed that Harris had made inflammatory statements, but as the trial progressed it became less clear that his actions fulfilled the narrow legal definition of "insurrection" for which he was on trial. Outside the courthouse, a crowd estimated at times to be as many as 3,000 awaited the outcome. At 8:30 P.M. on September 3, 1875, just two weeks after the planned start of the killings, the jury returned its verdict. By that time night had fallen, the parties in the courtroom "barely made visible by the presence of three or four little tallow dips placed before the judge and upon the table occupied by the reporters." Cordy Harris was found not guilty.

Later in the month, a second trial of insurrectionists was held in Wrightsville in Johnson County, once again resulting in the acquittal of the accused. By this time, the majority of those arrested had been released. With this second verdict of "not guilty," the authorities abandoned plans for further prosecution of those implicated in the plot. A Northern newspaper commented, "This trial has demonstrated the gratifying fact...that a negro can and will receive justice from the Georgia courts."

The crisis seemed to be over, but the fundamental question of "Why?" had not been answered. Perhaps the best analysis came not locally or even from the South but from the *New York Tribune*, which had followed the proceedings closely. Citing that even though "the negroes in Georgia were generally prosperous and contented," the writer noted "they seem to have had a grievance, after all, which neither we nor their white neighbors ever suspected. They believe they are kept out of their right because they have never received the 'forty acres and a mule' which every freedman was taught ten years ago to expect as his share of the confiscated estates of rebels." Perhaps those in a position to benefit from the black vote spread misinformation of this kind. Jake Mooreman, one of those implicated in the plot, told the *Tribune*, "We were all to vote for [President] Gen. Grant next year to make him king. When Grant became king, all the land would be his, and the colored people would get it on easy terms."

The *Tribune* article continued,

> After all it is no great wonder that the Southern negroes have got their heads stuffed full of such wild and mischievous notions. Carpet-bag politicians have been teaching them for ten years that the whites among whom they live are their natural enemies and oppressors, and that nothing stands between them and slavery but the power of the federal government. They have been threatened with all sorts of evils if they allowed the Republican party in the South to be overthrown, and promised all sorts of blessings if they supported Administration candidates. And they have seen abundant signs of the great ruler in Washington. They have seen his cavalry scouring the countryside at election time, and his officers arresting white politicians at pleasure for no other crime than opposing the Administration. In their eyes he has been an autocrat of almost unlimited power, and the carpet-bagger has assured them that all this power would be exerted for their benefit.

To the politically naïve freedmen, the concept of independent rule in a "Freedman's Land," as one local black man called it, might have seemed a possibility. But hope faded with the fortunes of the insurrectionists. In mid-September, this notice appeared in the local Washington County paper:

> We, the colored citizens of Washington County, call together the colored citizens of said county, on the 18th of September next, to meet at the Courthouse door in Sandersville for the purpose of choosing two upright and intelligent men to send to one or two states for the purpose of finding some suitable place for said people to emigrate to.

While Cordy Harris and other "insurrectionists" had been freed, Joe Morris remained at large, the $500 bounty for his arrest still unclaimed. This amount represented a princely sum in 1875, especially in the agrarian South.

On September 20, news broke that Morris, the "leader of the late insurrection in Middle Georgia," had been captured under most unusual circumstances in Atlanta. It was said that he had been in the city for three days, visiting US District Attorney Henry P. Farrow at night to avoid detection. Allegedly, Morris was "demanding a Ku Klux prosecution against certain citizens of Burke County." He was spotted by a detective in Farrow's office, but when he realized that he was about to be arrested, rushed into an inner office of the suite and locked the door. The detective was reluctant to arrest Morris in the court building without the permission of Farrow, which he declined to give. Farrow could not—or would not—produce a key to unlock the door.

The standoff continued. Everyone was reluctant to break down the door to capture the wanted man. The sheriff and chief of police were summoned and wrote a note to the federal judge requesting permission to arrest Morris. The judge replied that court had adjourned for the day, and he would rule on the matter later. After some consideration, an officer then climbed into the locked room through the open transom and arrested Morris without event. He was carried back to Burke County to be held for trial during the next term of court, scheduled for the spring of 1876.

News reports of the day found it strange that a federal district attorney would protect a wanted criminal, especially one accused of being one of the masterminds behind what might have been mass murder. A bit of research into Farrow's background is revealing. Prior to his political appointment as US district attorney, Farrow had been the president of the Grand Council of State in Atlanta, the head of the Union Leagues in Georgia. He was an ally of Republican governor Rufus Bullock, serving as his attorney general and at one point going to Washington "to persuade officials to a more stringent reconstruction for Georgia." Farrow was certainly aware of Morris's status as a fugitive from the law. Whether or not he had a role in the failed insurrection cannot be determined.

By early spring of 1876, most of the events of the preceding summer were fading from memory. In Burke County in late March, Joseph Morris, "the notorious colored agitator," was tried and convicted on the somewhat dubious charge, dating from a year earlier, of carrying concealed weapons. He was fined $50 and sentenced to a year of hard labor on the chain gang. As was the custom of the day, he was leased out as a convict laborer to a Mr. Henry Stephens of Stephens Pottery in Baldwin County, an enterprise making fire-brick, sewer pipe, and other terra cotta products from the local clay.

Within a few days of his arrival at the pottery, Morris was among a crew of several leased convicts, accompanied by one guard, assigned to cut wood used to fire the kilns. Between three and four in the afternoon, the group found themselves suddenly surrounded by a party of about twenty men, masked and armed. They demanded possession of the "General" and disappeared with him into the forest. It was the last that anyone ever saw or heard of the Hon. Joseph Morris, Messayenger.

Reaction to Morris's disappearance varied. Governor Smith promised to "find the guilty parties and bring them to their just punishment." The question, however, seemed to be who were the guilty parties? The *Eatonton Press and Messenger* reported that the leader of the kidnappers "spoke with the brogue of an Irishman." The *Herald & Georgian* was sure that Morris was abducted "by some of his own clan," citing a rumor that he had boasted that he wouldn't remain at Stephens Pottery long, as his followers were planning to free him. The *Augusta Chronicle* scoffed at the idea, as did most other papers, positing instead that the masked men were members of the Ku Klux Klan or others bent on Morris's permanent elimination.

Some five months later, after an exhaustive investigation, a Baldwin County grand jury admitted that Morris's disappearance "remains a mystery." The *Milledgeville Union & Recorder*, while publishing the grand jury's finding, opined, "Gov. Smith and the Democratic party we hold responsible for the outrage. They have made no real effort to secure the kidnappers of Morris."

The truth remains elusive more than a century later.

Sources and Resources

The vast majority of this tale was drawn from extensive coverage in contemporary newspapers, both regional and national. In addition, the scholarly articles listed below provide additional perspective on this turbulent time in Georgia history.

Bell, Karen B. "The Ogeechee Troubles: Federal Land Restoration and the 'Lived Realities' of Temporary Proprietors." *The Georgia Historical Quarterly* 85 (2001): 375–97.

Cason, Roberta F. "The Loyal League in Georgia." *The Georgia Historical Quarterly* 20 (1936): 125–53.

Coulter, E. Merton, "Cudjo Fye's Insurrection." *The Georgia Historical Quarterly* 38 (1954): 213–25.

Formwalt, Lee W. "The Camilla Massacre of 1868: Racial Violence as Political Propaganda." *The Georgia Historical Quarterly* 71 (1987): 399–426.

Amos T. Akerman, who served as the lead defense attorney for the insurrectionists, had a distinguished background as the United States Attorney General under President Grant. In the early 1870s he led the Federal prosecution of the Ku Klux Klan.

Mathew Brady, Library of Congress

Herschel V. Johnson, the judge appointed to hear the case of the insurrectionists, had previously served as both US Senator and Georgia governor and was the vice presidential running mate of Stephen Douglas in the 1860 presidential election. Johnson County, Georgia, is named for him.

1860 Currier and Ives print, Library of Congress

The insurrectionists were held in a make-shift stockade on the grounds of the Washington County courthouse in Sandersville. The trial of Cordy Harris took place in the courtroom inside. This image shows the courthouse as it was rebuilt in 1869 after its predecessor was burned by Sherman on his March to the Sea in 1864.

Washington County Historical Society

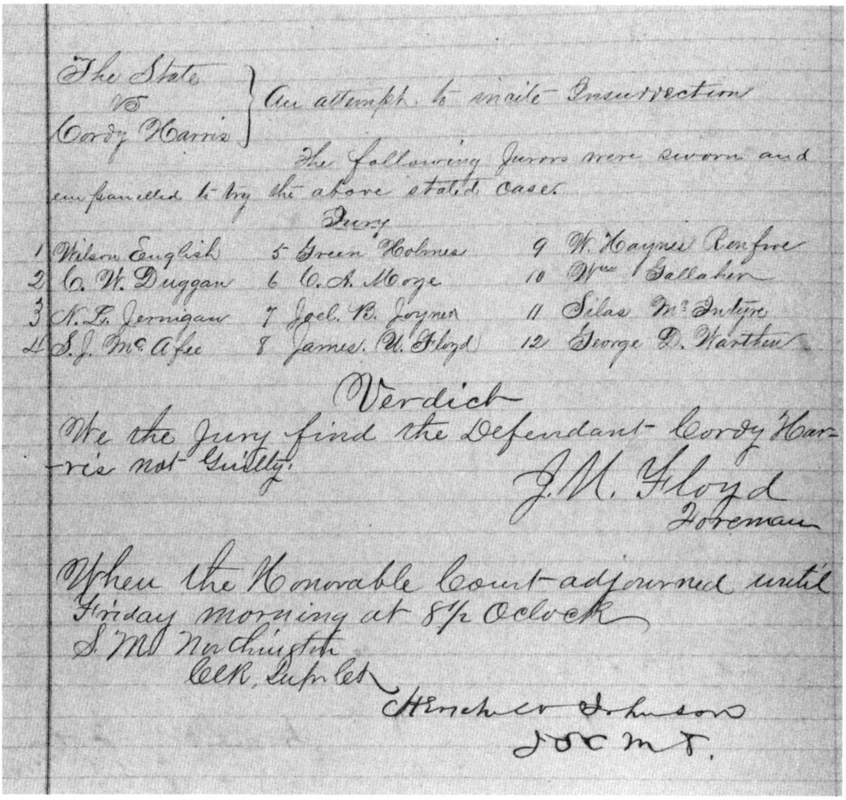

The State
vs
Cordy Harris } An attempt to incite Insurrection

The following Jurors were sworn and empanelled to try the above stated case.

Jury

1 Wilson English 5 Green Holmes 9 W. Haynes Renfroe
2 C. W. Duggan 6 C. A. Moye 10 Wm Gallaher
3 N. L. Jernigan 7 Joel B. Joyner 11 Silas Mc Intyre
4 S. J. Mc Afee 8 James M. Floyd 12 George D. Warthen

Verdict

We the Jury find the Defendant Cordy Harris not Guilty.

J. M. Floyd
Foreman

When the Honorable Court adjourned until Friday morning at 8½ Oclock

S. M. Worthington
Clk. Sup. Ct.

Herschel Johnson
JSC MJ.

Twelve jurors, all prominent white men, found Cordy Harris, a freed slave and Union League member, not guilty of "an attempt to incite insurrection."

Author's Collection

PART IV

THE LOST CAUSE YEARS 1865–1939

OVERVIEW

THE LOST CAUSE YEARS 1865–1939

The summer of 1865 found the South defeated, having paid the price of secession with the lives of a generation of young men and much of the accumulated wealth of its inhabitants. Across the greater expanse of the Confederacy, "[Northern] forces destroyed two-thirds of the assessed value of Southern wealth, two-fifths of the South's livestock, and one-quarter of her white men between ages twenty and forty. More than half the farm machinery was ruined, and the damage to railroads and industries was incalculable..., eloquent testimony to the tragic irony of the South's counterrevolution of 1861 to preserve its way of life."[63] In Georgia, Sherman's 60,000 troops carved a 300-mile-long swath of desolation between Atlanta and Savannah, living off the land while destroying homes, livestock, industries, rail lines, and other means of production in a deliberate scorched-earth campaign designed to demoralize the population and stifle all attempts at resistance. Broken but not bowed, the memories and bitterness were to become an integral part of the Southern ethos in the years to follow.

During the decades that followed the end of the Civil War, both the North and the South memorialized the conflict though the written word, veterans' organizations, remembrance days, and monuments, each side extolling the valor of its troops, the brilliance of its leaders, and the justice of its cause. In the North, a prominent example was the Grand Army of the Republic (GAR), organized in 1866 as a fraternal order open to veterans of federal forces. At its peak in 1890, it boasted nearly half a million members, serving as an advocate for veterans' rights.

In the South, similar organizations were slower to emerge, retarded, perhaps, by the devastation of the war and the presence of federal troops until 1877. Established first as local groups, these coalesced into regional

---

[63] James M. McPherson, *Ordeal by Fire: The Civil War and Reconstruction* (New York: Alfred M. Knopf, 1982): 476.

organizations, including the United Confederate Veterans (UCV), founded in 1889, and the Sons of Confederate Veterans (SCV), founded in 1896. Many of the Southern monuments erected to honor those who served in the Civil War were sponsored and promoted not by the veterans, but by their wives and female descendants through the United Daughters of the Confederacy (UDC), founded in 1894.[64] Both the SCV and UDC remain active today as benevolent organizations devoted to preserving the memory of those who served on the side of the South, and to worthy causes, including education. The SCV's stated goals include "ensuring that a *true* history of the 1861–1865 period is preserved." The objectives of the UDC include the goal "to collect and preserve the material for a *truthful* history of the War Between the States." (Emphasis in both cases is the author's.)

The question arises, if what we term "history" represents a compilation of facts, why is it necessary to be certain a "true" version exists? If semantics are to be believed, "facts" represent the truth but "history" is often mutable, presenting its own interpretation of events past. Such is the case in what has become known as the "Myth of the Lost Cause."[65] In the years that followed the Civil War, military and civilian notables alike wrote extensively on the conflict, their works taking the form of memoirs, biographies, commentary, and historical papers. The term "Lost Cause" is traditionally attributed to an 1866 book by Edward A. Pollard, *The Lost Cause: A New Southern History of the War of the Confederates*.[66] Described by its author as "drawn from official sources, and approved by the most distinguished Confederate leaders," it was a virulently pro-Southern, anti-Northern account justifying the right of secession, while defending slavery and the Southern Cause in general. The Southern Historical Society, founded in the late 1860s, promoted the cause of the Confederacy through its journal, the *Southern Historical Society Papers*, published between 1876 and 1959. *The Confederate Veteran* magazine, originally the official organ of the United Confederate Veterans, did likewise during its publication between 1893 and 1932. At times ignoring facts, at times selectively choosing them, and at times engaging in wishful thinking,

[64] The GAR was disbanded in 1956. The UCV continued to meet until 1950.

[65] The word "myth" is used in this context to mean a traditional tale or history, in part or whole based on facts, and which may or may not be true in whole or in part.

[66] Long out of copyright, *The Lost Cause* is available from several online sources in its original format.

these and multiple other publications developed a new, "Southern" account of the conflict of 1861 to 1865. No longer should the term "Civil War" be used. It was "The War Between the States," implying a battle of equally legitimate powers.

Beginning with fervor in the latter quarter of the nineteenth century and continuing on for the next fifty-plus years, a consistent narrative formed and became the accepted truth in the realm of the former Confederacy. Briefly put, despite Yankee attempts to spread contrary untruths, the War Between the States was fought over states' rights, not the issue of slavery. The South had every right to secede, and it was the North's failure to acknowledge this fact that led to the conflict. The Southern economic system (including the institution of slavery) and the Southern way of life were superior to that of the North. With regard to slavery, it was—all considered—benevolent and just. Both the civilian and military leaders of the Confederacy were wise, skilled, and brave. The women of the South, in particular, worked selflessly despite trying hardship in support of the Cause. It was only the overwhelming economic strength and available manpower of the North that allowed the war to end as it did. The wanton destruction of men like Sherman and the arduous years of Reconstruction were designed to punish the South for attempting to exert their lawful constitutional rights.

This accepted narrative insinuated itself into almost every facet of Southern (and, to a degree, national) life. Confederate Memorial Day became an official holiday in the states of former Confederacy. Hundreds of monuments commemorating the valor of the Southern soldier were erected throughout the states of the former Confederacy. The UDC sponsored contests and granted scholarships based on essay contests devoted to Southern history. The 1915 silent film *The Birth of a Nation* became the first blockbuster, holding all-time attendance and profitability records until displaced by a second movie incorporating the themes of the Lost Cause, *Gone with the Wind*.

Across the South, state school systems set up textbook committees to be certain that impressionable young minds were presented with the proper historical perspective. A 1942 state-issued school textbook, *The Story of Georgia*, is rife with elements of the Lost Cause narrative. The pre-Civil War years were described as "The Golden Age." Plantation owners were said to be "kind men" who took on great obligations in caring for their slaves' welfare. With regard to the slaves, the following quote is telling: "Negro problems, as we know them today, simply did not exist. The Negro had his job to do and his place to fill. The slave owner had his place, too, and his responsibility to the Negro. Although no one would recommend going back to slavery, it is true that the race problems became serious only after the slaves were freed." The Ku Klux Klan of the Reconstruction era is praised: "In its early days...the Klan performed a great service for independence and the right of the state to govern itself. Some of our best citizens were then members." By way of visual impact, five photos from *Gone with the Wind* were used as illustrations, including one of seemingly content slaves and another of "the memorable party scene" displaying "the grandeur that many Georgians knew during the Golden Ages before the War Between the States."

In this section, I have included three articles on subjects directly related to "the Lost Cause." The first, "Gutzon Borglum and the Lost Stone Mountain Confederate Memorial," is the account of what was destined to be America's largest and greatest monument to the Confederacy, a massive carving on the sheer north face of Georgia's Stone Mountain. The three figures depicted on the monument as it exists today are the slightest suggestion of the original plans that included columns of troops and some 700 to 1,000 individuals carved in granite. The second, "The Drum Returns Home," is the story of the Civil War battle drum of Thomas H. Sparks, a young drummer from Washington County, Georgia, and its return to its current resting place. This tale is illustrative of the reverence which many Southerners still have toward relics of the conflict. The third piece is an essay titled "The Lost Cause on the Silver Screen." It briefly examines two of America's most successful and best-known movies and is meant to be both informative and thought-provoking.

Sources and Resources

For those interested in reading about the Lost Cause in general, the following works are recommended:

Foster, Gaines M. *Ghosts of the Confederacy.* New York: Oxford University Press, 1987. An excellent and broad overview of the Lost Cause movment, including its roots and many manifestations.

McPherson, James M. *Ordeal by Fire: The Civil War and Reconstruction.* New York: Alfred M. Knopf, 1982.

The Myth of the Lost Cause and Civil War History. Edited by Gary W. Gallagher and Alan T. Nolan. Bloomington: Indiana University Press, 2000. A collection of essays on the Lost Cause and its influence on the history of the Civil War.

Wilson, Charles R. *Baptized in Blood: The Religion of the Lost Cause 1865–1920.* Athens: University of Georgia Press, 2009. A classical work on how the Lost Cause took on the aspects of a grass-roots religion in the late nineteeth and early twentieth century South.

For a stunning example of Lost Cause ideology, *The Gray Book* provides interesting reading. Published in pamphlet form in 1920 by the Sons of Confederate Veterans, it represents an aggressive attempt to adjust history's narrative. It can be obtained in digital form at little or no charge from several Internet sources, including the Internet Archive (www.archive.org/details/graybook00sons).

CHAPTER 9

GUTZON BORGLUM AND THE LOST STONE MOUNTAIN CONFEDERATE MEMORIAL

The story of Gutzon Borglum and the Stone Mountain Confederate Memorial is one of the more curious and complex sagas that are woven into the history of the South. It involves the nation's most famous sculptor, an eighty-five-year-old Confederate widow, the United Daughters of the Confederacy, the United States Mint, and the Ku Klux Klan, to name a few of the characters. It could be argued that were it not for egos, money troubles, and an internal dispute among the ruling hierarchy of the Klan, South Dakota's Mount Rushmore monument would not have been built. And if events had worked out after things in Atlanta fell apart, it is possible that the majestic carving that was once intended for Georgia's Stone Mountain would have ended up on North Carolina's Chimney Rock.

The year was 1915. The carving was to be "a memorial to a movement," in the words of its designer, Gutzon Borglum, "the biggest sculptural undertaking in the history of the world." Moreover, what better place to display it than the sheer cliff of the huge granite monolith known as Stone Mountain, located among the farms and fields of rural Dekalb County some fifteen miles northeast of the city of Atlanta. Borglum was enthusiastic. He had been commissioned to build a monument for the ages. "Stone Mountain," he said, "in its colossal proportion, makes the Pyramids small and insignificant by comparison. They are built of cut stone and long since have fallen into decay. The large figures of Egypt are little more than symbols, and awaken little interest in modern man beyond the splendid intention and mystery they suggest regarding the civilization and culture of their day. However, had the Egyptians possessed Stone Mountain there can be little doubt they would have shaped it into one of the first wonders of the world."

Half a century had passed since the end of the Civil War. In the North, tributes to those who had served were observed during memorial days and by the erection and dedication of innumerable local monuments. The famed sculptor Augustus Saint-Gaudens had received a number of commissions for works honoring Northern military figures. During the same era in the South, the accounts and history of the conflict had been spun into the legends of Lost Cause. With the memories kept alive by groups such as the Sons of Confederate Veterans (SCV), the United Daughters of the Confederacy (UDC), and others, hundreds of monuments to the valor of the soldiers of the South were erected in towns and cities from Virginia to Texas. The South's Cause had been just, its leaders wise, its soldiers heroic, and defeat had come only because of the North's overwhelming superiority in men and matériel. The majesty of Stone Mountain would make it a perfect place to erect a monument to "the South of '64." Composed of solid granite and rising more than 800 feet above the surrounding countryside, the great rock's sheer north face would provide the ideal palette for a sculptor of Borglum's acclaim.

The idea of a monument to the Confederacy at Stone Mountain is generally credited to Atlanta attorney William H. Terrell,[67] who made the suggestion in a 1914 newspaper article. It was Helen Plane, however, a Confederate widow active in the Daughters of the Confederacy, who helped bring the dream to fruition. Born on a plantation in Tuscaloosa, Alabama, in 1829, she married William F. Plane, a physician, in 1854. Their marriage was short lived; Dr. Plane enlisted as a captain in the Confederate army only to be killed at the Battle of Antietam[68] in 1862. Still in her early thirties, Plane devoted the rest of her life to the promotion of the memory of her late husband and others who had served on the side of the South in the conflict. She helped found the Atlanta chapter of the Daughters of the Confederacy and served in numerous offices in the local and national organization. Remaining quite active in spite of her age, Plane embraced the idea of building the ultimate Confederate monument at Stone Mountain, touring widely to promote the idea among other chapters of the UDC. Based on Plane's enthusiasm, the concept of such a memorial was heartily endorsed, and the

[67] Terrell served as Klonsel (General Counsel) to the Knights of the Ku Klux Klan, Inc., between 1916 and 1920 before breaking with the group in a dispute over legal fees.

[68] In the South, the Battle of Antietam was generally referred to as the Battle of Sharpsburg.

search for a sculptor with the skill to undertake the work began in earnest in early 1915.

Among the first to come to mind was John Gutzon de la Mothe Borglum, at the time considered by many to be America's foremost sculptor. Borglum was born near Bear Lake, Utah, in 1867. His father, a Danish Mormon convert, had immigrated to the United States in 1864, at once avoiding conscription into the Danish army while planning to join the growing Mormon colony near Salt Lake City. Gutzon was the son of the elder Borglum's second wife. His early years were spent in the Midwest before moving to Los Angeles, California, with his family at age seventeen. Gutzon received only a basic education, but he was highly intelligent, driven, and a quick learner. In contrast to his father, who had forsaken the frontier life to become a homeopathic physician, Gutzon chose to become an artist.

Borglum's biographers describe him as "charismatic, charming and intense." He was also outspoken, opinionated, and easily willing to defy the social and cultural standards of the day. By age twenty, he was receiving recognition in Los Angeles for his paintings. During the latter part of the nineteenth century he spent a number of years in England and France, achieving success there while influenced by the then-fashionable *beaux-arts* movement. By the turn of the century, Borglum was a rising star in the American art world. Having for the most part given up painting to concentrate on sculpture, he won an increasingly prestigious series of commissions for public art. In 1906, his flowing depiction of *The Mares of Diomedes* was acquired by the Metropolitan Museum of Art in New York. Two years later, his statue of Union general Philip Sheridan leading his troops into battle was unveiled in Washington, DC. In 1911, his lifelike *Seated Lincoln* in Newark, New Jersey, drew national praise. Thus, in 1915, it was only fitting that Helen Plane would contact Borglum in hopes that he might create an appropriate memorial to the memory of the Confederacy.

The challenge of creating a monument on a mountain immediately appealed to Borglum. He readily agreed to consider the project, journeying to Atlanta in the August heat of late summer 1915. Mrs. Plane and a delegation of UDC dignitaries were waiting as the famed sculptor arrived by train at Atlanta's Terminal Station. She greeted him warmly but did not shake his hand. He was from the North. Several years later she would confess, "Mr. Borglum, did you notice the first time that I met you I did not shake hands with you?"

"Yes, I did notice it," Borglum replied.

"I could not help thinking," Plane went on to say, "that it might be you that shot my husband."

This exchange, reported by the *New York Times*, took place in 1924 at the dedication of the first portion of the carving to be completed. Helen Plane was ninety-four years old at the time. Even though Borglum was born after the end of the Civil War, Plane's initial hesitation reflected an attitude of the era held by many older Southerners toward "Yankees."

Borglum was taken by limousine to Stone Mountain, where he would stay for three days as a guest at the home of Samuel Venable. Venable's family had owned Stone Mountain for years, extensively quarrying granite from the more gently sloping areas. He had agreed to deed the monolith's sheer north face to a group established by the UDC for the purpose of building a Confederate monument. Notably, Venable was soon to become a founding member of the revived Ku Klux Klan, taking part in a ceremony that would occur a few months later on the windswept summit of the mountain.

Borglum spent three days considering Stone Mountain. Devoting close attention to the slope of the scarp, the position of the sun and the area available for carving, he roughed out in his mind a plan for a work of massive scale, the largest carving ever attempted by man. Plane, speaking on behalf of the memorial committee, had envisioned the monument taking the form of a seventy-foot high bust of Robert E. Lee sculpted in bas-relief on the mountainside. Borglum's direct response was indicative of his personality, dismissively saying such a tiny work "would look like a postage stamp on a barn door." He returned to his home in Connecticut to consider a plan.

In early October 1915, Borglum sent an initial report back to Mrs. Plane and the UDC committee. The monument was to be nothing short of massive. Borglum estimated that there were approximately 75 acres of mountainside available for carving. He proposed "to construct, as we can, the great characters of those days and to carve them in high and full relief in action mounted and on foot, moving across the face of the granite mountain in the arrangement of two wings of an army, following the mountain contour, moving naturally across its face to the east." In all, there would be between 700 and 1,000 individual figures. At the head of the columns would be the leaders of the Confederacy and its military: Davis, Lee, Jackson, Stuart, Johnson, and others. Each state of the former Confederacy would have its own leaders portrayed; the exact choice of individuals would be left to the states. The carving, given its scale and grandeur, would be visible from many miles away. Borglum estimated that when completed, the monument would be up to a hundred feet in height and 2,000 feet in overall length. And there was to be more. At the base of the mountain, directly below the central portion of the carving, Borglum proposed to sculpt in place a "huge colonnade" of thirteen columns, one for each state of the Confederacy. The columns would serve as the front of a massive memorial hall, some sixty feet deep and forty feet high, dedicated to the Daughters of the Confederacy.

It was a colossal project indeed. Borglum projected that it would be accomplished in three phases. The first, taking three years, would be the images of the Confederate leaders, the central portion and focal point of the carving. The next two phases would require an additional decade or more, meaning the time for the completion of the entire project would likely stretch into the 1930s. Borglum anticipated a cost in the range of $2,000,000.[69]

Throughout the nation, in both North and South, the Stone Mountain memorial received endorsements and positive reviews. The horrors of the Civil War were now a fading memory. The wounds had healed. This was not to be a monument to a rebellion; it was to be a remembrance of the valor, dedication, and heroism of the men and women of the South. It was now the twentieth century. Once again, the states of the former Confederacy had resumed their rightful place in America's stream of history. It was only right that the nation's citizens should remember and learn from events of the past.

On May 20, 1916, the headlines of a front-page article in the *Atlanta Constitution* read, "Thousands Present at the Dedication of Gray Memorial. Men Who Followed Lee and Jackson Side by Side With Followers of Grant and Sherman Bare Heads at Impressive Services Conducted at Stone Mountain." With the band playing "Dixie," a huge Confederate battle flag hung over the mountain's sheer side and "a battery of motion picture men with cameras set to record for all the world the living image of the momentous event, the ceremonies began." The address was given by Emory Speer, at the time both a federal judge and dean of the Mercer University School of Law.

[69] It should be appreciated that the national per capita income in the United States in 1915 was $358 per year. Since Georgia's economy was agriculturally based at the time, this figure probably overstates the state's average.

In flowery language invoking the heroes of conflicts long past, Speer declared the monument "will perpetuate to millions yet unborn the heroism, the fortitude, the glory of the men who wore the gray." With that, the deed to the mountainside was formally presented to the Stone Mountain Confederate Monumental Association (SMCMA), the legal entity established by the UDC to hold title to the site of the carving. Next, the cornerstone was dedicated with full Masonic rites and its contents sealed with a silver trowel designed by Borglum. The trowel was given to Borglum who, in turn, presented it to Helen Plane. The construction of what was to be the greatest sculpture in the history of man was officially underway.

The difficulties faced by Borglum were more technical than artistic. The design, the making of models, and the carving of stone were skills that he had long since mastered. Logistics were the issue: how could one safely sculpt a sheer rock wall hundreds of feet high? The issue had become evident at the dedication ceremony. The simple act of suspending the Confederate flag on the rocky face required anchors and cables, as well as men willing to brave the heights to affix them. A workman on the speaker's platform volunteered to help. His name was Jesse Tucker, and he would become Borglum's supervisor, friend, and self-taught technical advisor for years beyond the Stone Mountain project. Borglum was much in demand, and he never planned for the Confederate memorial to be his only project. He was usually working on multiple commissions at any given time. Furthermore, most of the routine tasks of removing stone and roughing out the figures would be done by trained workmen, referring to working models and supervised by men like Jesse Tucker.

The next months were spent establishing platforms from which to work, surveying the mountain, and laying out the plans for the initial carving. A huge hoist had been installed on top of the mountain, and another was on order. By early 1917, Borglum had finished the plaster casts of the central group. A sketch of the proposed final work by Borglum reproduced in the *Atlanta Constitution* depicted a long line of Confederate cavalry and artillery emerging over the mountain's western edge. It was led by a group of eleven horsemen, representing the heroes of the lost struggle. The actual carving was to begin shortly.

It was not to be. The United States declared war on the German Empire on April 6, 1917, marking America's entry into World War I. On April 24th the Stone Mountain Confederate Monumental Association voted to "temporarily" abandon the project "to await the return of peace before attempting the further prosecution of this great work." It was a decision born of necessity. The wartime demands of men, money, and matériel made continued work impossible. Jesse Tucker, like many others, joined the military and saw service in Europe. It would be more than six years before the first chisel pierced the stone.

During the hiatus, Borglum devoted his time to support of the war effort. He was a national figure and politically active, friends with Theodore Roosevelt, and well known to then-President Woodrow Wilson. Under authorization of the president, Borglum personally investigated fraud and corruption in America's nascent aircraft industry, uncovering losses of hundreds of millions of dollars. Borgland, his expansive estate at Stamford, Connecticut, became a training camp for eastern European troops eager to enter the war against Germany.

Such diversions, totally unrelated to his career as an artist and sculptor, were typical of Borglum. He was a man who wanted the best for his country yet saw much that distressed him. World War I was relatively brief, ending only nineteen months after America's entry into the conflict. The years that followed were a time of rapid change. The economic upheaval caused by the war, the massive influx of returning troops, many of whom lacked employment, the growing influence of the socialist labor movement, and the lurking menace of Bolshevism must have all represented what Borglum saw as a threat to the American way of life. Action was needed, and he was a man of action. It was likely for this reason that Borglum joined the Ku Klux Klan, rising rapidly to become a member of the Kloncilium, the Klan's ruling body.

The first group calling itself the Ku Klux Klan was one of many resistance organizations formed in the South during the turbulent years immediately after the Civil War. The name was generally applied to most such groups, brought to the public eye by congressional hearings held in 1871. Both as a result of vigorous federal prosecution and changing times, the various "klans" died out by the early to mid-1870s. Over the ensuing decades, the Lost Cause movement turned what was certainly a terrorist organization into heroes of Southern resistance in the years after the Civil War. Inspired in part by the 1915 movie, *The Birth of a Nation*, William J. Simmons, an Atlanta fraternal organizer, founded a "beneficial, fraternal order" named "The Knights of the Ku Klux Klan, Inc." It was to be like hundreds of others of the day, similar to the Elks, the Moose, the Masons, or the Knights of Pythias, to name a few. So dramatic was the influence of the movie, that in December 1915 shortly after its debut in Atlanta, Helen Plane contacted Borglum to suggest adding a group of uniformed Klansmen to the proposed carving. At the time, Borglum knew little of the Klan but agreed to include an altar to them in his plans for the memorial.

There was, however, a somewhat tangential connection between the newly formed fraternal order that adopted the name of the Ku Klux Klan and Stone Mountain. Samuel Venable, the man whose family owned the mountain and Borglum's frequent host during his sojourns in Georgia, was one of the founding members of the new Klan. The hooded order was inaugurated by a ceremony on top of Stone Mountain on Thanksgiving night, November 1915. In many ways, the mountain became an alternative symbol for the group.[70] It was apparently Venable's influence that led Borglum to join the Klan.

During its early years, Klan members included many prominent, presumably well-meaning men attracted to its stated philosophy of One Hundred Percent Americanism. Allegedly, the order stood for Protestant Christian values, white supremacy, and the rule of law. It was anti-immigrant, supported Prohibition, and publically funded education and opposed socialists, Bolsheviks, and the labor movement in general. Its call to action carried wide appeal to men of power and influence. In the early 1920s, for example, both the mayor of Atlanta and the governor of Georgia were Klansmen, as were a number of members of the Stone Mountain Confederate Monumental Association.

Jesse Tucker returned to Stone Mountain in the summer of 1919 after being mustered out of the army. The platforms and rigging had suffered from neglect after more than two years and needed repair before carving could start. There were other problems as well. The UDC, despite its enthusiastic backing of the project, was unable or unwilling to provide the financial support needed. In early 1920, Helen Plane, now in her nineties, re-

---

[70] A postcard from the early 1920s in the author's collection shows a group of mounted Klansmen with flaming crosses in the foreground and Stone Mountain in the background. The caption notes that the Klan was "organized" there in 1915. Later, the image of Stone Mountain became the symbol of the Klan's venture into insurance, the Empire Life Mutual Insurance Company.

signed from the association. Nathan Bedford Forrest, grandson of the famed Confederate general and prominent member of the Atlanta Klan, was appointed. The idea of soliciting support from the Ku Klux Klan was considered. Edward Y. Clarke, a former professional fundraiser and now head recruiter for the Klan, was contacted. Even in its early years, the Klan was controversial, so Clarke agreed to solicit funds through his former business, the Southern Publicity Association, "a purely cosmetic solution that deceived no one." As such, the project became associated with the Klan, and Clarke's assistance became all the more toxic when it was later revealed that he was taking a 25 percent commission from the donations received.

Borglum, who was working on other projects, did not return to the Stone Mountain until the summer of 1921. The basic design was done, but he faced the problem of laying out the huge scale of the carving on the mountainside. With figures whose height was measured in dozens of feet, and scenes whose breadth measured in hundreds, it was impossible for anyone working closely on the rock face to have a sense of perspective. In seeking a solution, Borglum "employed two of America's most famous engineers and paid them a handsome fee." The first termed the project an "impossible madness" and advised that it be abandoned. The second suggested building a mechanism that "would cost exactly the contract price of the entire sculpture." Borglum set out to solve the problem on his own.

Borglum's initial idea was so unique as to warrant a two-page illustrated article in *Popular Science* magazine. The plan was to photograph the sculptor's models then use the cover of darkness to project the image on the side of the mountain in segments measuring 110 feet high by 220 feet wide. With the image thus displayed, workers would be lowered down the side with barrels of silver nitrate to be poured on the area of the projected image in order to "sensitize" the granite surface. After several hours of exposure, barrels of developer would be poured over the area to "set" the image, followed by barrels of water to remove any residual chemicals. With the photograph of that portion of the carving now "printed" on the sheer face, workers could be lowered down to chisel away the rock. By the time the story appeared in the June 1923 issue of the magazine, this highly innovative idea had been discarded for more practical ones.

First, Borglum tried drawing the outline of the head of General Lee directly on the mountain while suspended from an apparatus similar to a bosun's chair.[71] It rapidly became evident that this would not work. The scale was simply too large. Still considering the idea of a projector, Borglum reasoned that he could shine photographic images on the side of the mountain from a thousand or more feet away and have someone trace the outlines of the figures in white paint. With this done, the stone removal and finish work could proceed. Consulting with those in the industry, he was told "the feat was impossible." Images could not be projected beyond 250 to 270 feet, given the technology of the day, and, furthermore, the heat generated by the arc-type lamps used in motion-picture projectors would melt both the slides and lenses.

Undeterred, Borglum began experimenting with a projector at his estate in Connecticut. After months of work and a great deal of trial and error, he was able to project what appeared to be a sharp image on a snowy hillside some 1,500 feet away. Elated with his success, Borglum had a half-ton custom-made projector installed on a concrete base a quarter mile from the site of the carving. But this solution had problems as well. Of greatest importance was the fact that even at that distance, the photographic image of the sculptor's model was distorted when projected upward toward the mountain's face. To solve this problem, Borglum photographed the models from an angle, producing a distorted image that would appear correctly when projected upward at an angle toward the scarp. And if this issue were not enough, the two-and-a-half-inch photographic slide covered a square 200 feet on each side when projected over the great distance. With that degree of enlargement, even the smallest detail became an indistinct blur on the granite face. To correct this, Borglum traced the outlines of the figures directly on the slides using an extremely fine crow-quill pen. The modification worked perfectly. Within two hours two men suspended from the work platform had outlined the heads of Lee and Jackson on the granite. The projected images were so vivid that a contemporary news item described them as resembling a finished carving illuminated with a searchlight.

Borglum's time was by no means devoted solely to Stone Mountain. In addition to other artistic commissions, he was deeply involved in his work

[71] A bosun's chair (also known as a boatswain's chair) is simply a piece of plank, canvas, or leather seat with a rope on either side attached to a single rope above. Generally, it might be described as similar to a child's swing suspended from one rope rather than two.

with the Ku Klux Klan. That was soon to become a problem. In the fall of 1921, the *New York World* ran a series of articles exposing the Klan as a corrupt and at times violent organization. This was followed shortly thereafter by a congressional hearing during which the Klan's purpose and actions were defended by Imperial Wizard Simmons. Almost overnight, the Klan became a national issue. There were many who condemned it, yet there were many who believed that its purpose was to strengthen America and the American way of life. Borglum was clearly in the latter group.

In November 1922, the Klan held an Imperial Klonvocation in Atlanta to celebrate the seventh anniversary of its founding. Behind the scenes, there was concern that William Simmons's leadership was lacking. By way of a deft parliamentary maneuver, Simmons was deposed as Imperial Wizard by his elevation to the powerless office of Emperor of the Invisible Empire. Hiram W. Evans, a former Dallas dentist, took Simmons's place as Wizard. Evans hoped to stem the violence associated with the Klan and at the same time mold it into a national political organization. At first, the transition of leadership seemed to go smoothly. Initially supportive of the new regime, Borglum's political clout in the Republican Party allowed him to arrange a meeting with President Warren Harding. In December 1922, he accompanied Imperial Wizard Evans to the White House "to inform the President of the secret order's purposes."

The tranquility within the Klan leadership was not to last. Belatedly realizing that he had been stripped of power, William Simmons began a concerted effort to wrest back control of the organization from Evans. During much of 1923 the Klan's internecine power struggle figured prominently in national headlines. Borglum, Sam Venable, and Nathan B. Forrest threw their backing behind Simmons. In late May, Borglum's leadership position in the Klan was publically revealed when he was named as a defendant in a lawsuit brought by dissident Klansmen. His public response was one of denial: "I am not a member of the Kloncilium as charged, and I am not a knight of the Ku Klux Klan." Few believed him. Although only indirectly related to the Stone Mountain Confederate memorial, this political squabble within the Klan would have bearing on events to come.

While Borglum had been trying to figure out how to project the image of the proposed carving on the mountain, changes were underway in the Monumental Association. Despite wide support for the project, money remained tight. In March 1923, Hollins N. Randolph[72] was elected president. Randolph was a prominent lawyer and businessman and, like Borglum, Venable, and others, active in Ku Klux Klan affairs but a supporter of the new leadership of Imperial Wizard Evans. Hoping to run the association in a more professional manner, Randolph opened an office in a prestigious downtown Atlanta building and hired a full-time business manager. Edward Y. Clarke was fired as a fundraiser, to be replaced by a "salaried fundraising organization under the direct control of the executive committee" of the Stone Mountain Confederate Monumental Association (SMCMA). The changes brought some success in terms of increased donations over the ensuing months, but at the cost of vastly increased overhead expenses. Adequate funding for the actual work of carving remained an issue.

On June 18, 1923, in an "impressive ceremony," the first chisel blow was delivered to the mountain. A "great cavalcade" of automobiles carrying Virginia governor E. Lee Trinkle, lame-duck Georgia governor Thomas W. Hardwick, and other distinguished officials wended its way from downtown Atlanta to the top of Stone Mountain. The party descended the long set of steps to the work platform where, on the signal of SMCMA President Randolph, Borglum chiseled the first small hole. Afterwards, the group reassembled at the base of the mountain for a barbecue and a series of speeches paying tribute to the Confederacy and the Southern way of life. Nearly eight years after Borglum first viewed the mountain, the carving had begun.

The work progressed slowly over the following months. By September, the project had become a tourist magnet, visited by more than 30,000 people a month, a number greater than contemporary figures for George Washington's Mount Vernon home. The Monumental Association announced that it was working diligently to get a paved road to the base of the mountain. Despite sometimes-harsh weather conditions on the exposed granite face, Borglum pushed his crew to complete the head of Robert E. Lee in time to unveil it on the hundredth anniversary of the general's birthday, January 19, 1924. During the last six weeks before the deadline, the men worked in three shifts around the clock.

---

[72] Hollins N. Randolph (1872–1938). Randolph was the great-, great-grandson of Thomas Jefferson and was said to count among his ancestors the Indian princess Pocahontas.

Despite a light drizzle that slickened the crowded dirt roads leading to the mountain, an estimated 5,000 people were present for the unveiling. The review stand, set up across a gorge half a mile away from the mountain, was crowded with dignitaries from across the South. Helen Plane, now frail at age ninety-four, was carried onto the stage by Borglum. With a wave of a small Confederate flag, she signaled for a huge American banner draped over the carving to be drawn back. The sculpted head of General Lee appeared, "startlingly white against the dark gray surface of the imposing slope.... A deep and pregnant silence fell over the throng; a ripple of applause started on the fringe of the crowd and burst into a roar of tribute to the creation and of sentiment for its meaning." A celebratory banquet given at the Piedmont Driving Club that night, attended by five Southern governors, three ex-governors, and a host of other regional and national dignitaries, heaped praise on the memory of General Lee, the Southern Cause, and Gutzon Borglum, the sculptor. When called upon to speak, Borglum seemed overwhelmed, responding,

> But the head of Lee is on Stone Mountain! And if a tidal wave should sweep over this fair land of ours and cover it all, tearing away the last vestige our commercial, all-too-commercial, existence, and if in time the tide should break and roll away—the head of Lee would remain on Stone Mountain for all time, immutable and imperishable. The head of Lee is on Stone Mountain!

Little did he realize how ironic his words of exultation would become.

Rhetoric aside, it was funding that was necessary to complete the monument, and that remained the major obstacle. The World War I era marked the greatest single period of inflation in American history. The value of the dollar had been halved between 1915 and 1920. The original cost estimate of $2,000,000 for the completion of the memorial was now in the range of $4,000,000 or more. On top of this, the dramatic fall in cotton prices in 1920 and 1921 had severely impacted the South's agriculture-based economy. In January 1924, the new leadership of the SMCMA announced a "Children's Founders Roll" open to children "of Confederate descent" and less than sixteen years of age. In exchange for a one-dollar contribution, those eligible would have their names inscribed in "a great book of record" and receive a medal designed by Borglum. Hollins Randolph confidently pronounced, "We believe that the Children's Founders Roll is going to sweep the South."

Meanwhile, in mid-1923 the idea of a memorial half-dollar issued by the federal government to help raise funds was suggested. Credit for the idea is given to Harry Stillwell Edwards,[73] a regionally well-known author and journalist. Based on the efforts of Edwards, Borglum, and others, bills to produce a Stone Mountain memorial coin were introduced into the United States Senate in December 1923 and in the House a few weeks later. After some modification, the bill was passed and signed into law by President Calvin Coolidge in March 1924. The final act specified that in addition to recognizing the monument to the soldiers of the South, the coin should also commemorate President Warren G. Harding, who had died suddenly while in office in July 1923, and "in whose administration the work was begun." The income from coin sales would certainly solve most of the association's fiscal problems. The plan was to produce 5,000,000 half-dollars, to be sold by banks for one dollar each. Half of the proceeds would return to the Treasury while the other half—a potential $2,500,000—would go to fund the memorial.

The annual meeting and election of officers of the SMCMA was held in April 1924. Under Randolph's leadership as president, the organizational bureaucracy had grown, but the power still lay with the UDC, heavily represented on the executive committee. Randolph was easily reelected. One of his first acts was to consolidate power by restructuring the executive committee. For the most part, UDC members were replaced by "Randolph's cronies." Now in full control, he reorganized the management of the SMCMA to give himself "almost absolute control of the organization."

As work continued on the mountain, Borglum was given the task of designing the commemorative half-dollar. The design of the Children's Founders Roll medal had been relatively simple; it was a small version of the central grouping of the carving, displaying Lee, Jackson, and Davis mounted

[73] Harry Stillwell Edwards (1855–1938). Born in Macon, Georgia, Edwards was a graduate of Mercer University School of Law. He is perhaps best known for his book *Eneas Africanus* (1919, with multiple later editions). Loosely drawing its name from *The Aeneid*, Virgil's epic Latin poem about the wanderings of Aeneas after the fall of Troy, Edwards's tale focuses on the wanderings of a loyal freed slave in search of his former master in the days following the Civil War. It reiterates the "happy slave" myth that had become part of the Lost Cause movement.

on horseback. The requirements of the United States Mint were far more stringent, and both the front and back of the proposed coin needed to be laid out. In all, Borglum crafted a total of nine bas-relief models before the Department of the Treasury would give its final approval. Just as that hurdle was passed, however, the Teapot Dome affair and other scandals that had plagued the Harding administration came to light. The commission that approved the half-dollar design instructed Borglum to remove the words honoring Harding. The Mint, however, refused to produce the modified coins in light of the fact that Congress had mandated that Harding be honored. The impasse was solved when President Coolidge approved the change. The first coins were minted in January 1925.

While Borglum was distracted with the coin design during much of 1924, work continued at the mountain under the supervision of Jesse Tucker. A fissure in the stone discovered at what was to be site of Stonewall Jackson's head became the source of an unexpected delay. In the background, a storm was brewing between Borglum and the Monumental Association under Randolph's leadership. The SMCMA seemed to have ample funding for office workers while arguing with Borglum over payment for the actual carving work.

And there were other matters of lesser importance. Borglum and Randolph, two strong personalities, stood on opposite sides of issues involving both national politics and internal quarrels amongst leaders of the Ku Klux Klan. In September, Borglum accepted an invitation to visit South Dakota to discuss the possibility of a new national monument to be built in the Black Hills. This angered the members of the association, who blamed the slow progress on Borglum's lack of attention. Amid the issues of money, politics, and personalities, the working relationship between Borglum and Randolph deteriorated as the year progressed.

While behind the scenes the memorial project may have been in turmoil, the public face was quite different. On December 27, 1924, Hollins Randolph declared, "Results accomplished during 1924 were so large that they insure the complete success of the Stone Mountain Confederate Memorial." Gutzon Borglum would be finishing the figures of Jefferson Davis, Robert E. Lee, and Stonewall Jackson in time for another unveiling on June 3rd, Davis's birthday, he said. Meanwhile, Borglum's drilling crew would be roughing out the figures of the other four Confederate generals in the central group. Randolph confidently predicted that the upcoming sale of Stone

Mountain memorial half-dollars would generate sufficient income to completely fund the entire project, including the proposed Memorial Hall.

Exuberant press releases forgotten, the conflict between Borglum and the Monumental Association exploded into public view on February 21, 1925. Borglum contacted the Associated Press and issued a scathing statement declaring the association "has shrunk into a local habitation with no funds and scarcely a name." The leadership, he declared, was without "any fast or firm plans" for completing the project. Hollins Randolph, speaking for the association, responded by viciously attacking Borglum, stating "he had been a thorn in the side of the memorial chiefs for many months past, that he had created heavy liabilities and accomplished little actual work, and that he had proven generally unsatisfactory and incompetent." The conflict raged in the national press over the next few days. The *New York Times* and other papers openly speculated that the Ku Klux Klan might be behind the rift but were assured by an unnamed Georgia congressman that this was not the case.

To deal with the worsening crisis, on February 25th, Hollins Randolph called an emergency meeting of the SMCMA's executive committee, pushing through a resolution to cancel the sculptor's contract while accusing him of "inordinate demands for money..., offensive egotism and...delusions of grandeur." The association agreed to seek an injunction barring Borglum from his studio and worksite. Borglum was working at the mountain when he was notified by telephone of the committee's action. After a moment of hesitation, he ordered that the models and casts that he had prepared for the project be destroyed.

The front-page headline in the *Atlanta Constitution* the following day read, "Borglum and Tucker Are Sought on Warrants Following Destruction of Memorial Models." On discovering that the models had been smashed, the Monumental Association swore out arrest warrants against Borglum and Tucker. This was a turn that Borglum apparently did not anticipate. The word that he was being sought by the authorities reached him by way of Jesse Tucker, who burst in with the news as Borglum was speaking to a meeting of the Atlanta Chapter of the UDC. Hustling his boss out the door, they barely missed the arrival of a sheriff's deputy dispatched to arrest them. Within hours, Borglum and Tucker had crossed the North Carolina state line, temporarily safe from arrest.

The issue of Borglum versus the Stone Mountain Confederate Monumental Association raged for weeks in both public and private venues. Sam Venable and the Daughters of the Confederacy supported Borglum. The Atlanta City Council and the Atlanta Rotary Club condemned him. The Monumental Association brought suit seeking monetary damages. Many were not sure whether issues related to the Ku Klux Klan were part of the underlying cause, but all parties consistently denied this. When it was discovered that Borglum was in North Carolina, he was arrested and then immediately released on his own recognizance, based on a writ of *habeas corpus*. He departed shortly thereafter for New York. A survey of Borglum's acquaintances by the *New York Times* revealed most supported him. The one exception was a sculptor named Augustus Lukeman, a former Virginian now living in Manhattan.

Within a few days, tempers had cooled. Georgia governor Clifford Walker suggested that efforts to extradite Borglum back to Georgia be dropped. There were suggestions that the parties compromise, allowing the sculptor to resume his work. In response, Hollins Randolph was intransigent, stating "he was personally opposed to the plan and that he did not see how success was possible under Borglum's direction." On March 9th, less than two weeks after being fired by the Stone Mountain Confederate Monumental Association, Borglum announced that he had accepted a contract to carve figures of Presidents Washington and Lincoln on a mountain in the Black Hills of South Dakota. Jesse Tucker was soon dispatched to begin the preliminary surveys while Borglum worked on other projects. Although unnamed at the time, this project would later be known as the Mount Rushmore National Memorial.

Based in part on Borglum's assertions of possible financial mismanagement, Sam Venable and the Daughters of the Confederacy demanded an audit of the SMCMA's books. Having announced that the association was in good shape, Hollins Randolph had no choice but to comply. Following an examination of the group's finances by the independent accounting firm of Peat Marwick Mitchell & Company, Randolph announced the books "were in perfect order," but refused to make the results of the audit public.

On April 17, 1925, the executive committee of the Monumental Association announced that a new sculptor had been chosen to complete carving. His name was Augustus Lukeman. Under Lukeman's contract, he would be paid to create a new design and to supervise the carving work, which would be done by skilled workmen. Lukeman's concept was far more modest than Borglum's original. The initial carving, figures of Lee, Jackson, and Davis, was to be placed on the mountainside just below Borglum's head of Lee. Even though the transition to a new sculptor had taken less than two months, it would be nearly two years before actual work on the carving restarted. During this time protracted efforts to have Borglum reassume the project were unsuccessful. A week after the announcement that Lukeman had been chosen as the new sculptor, Mrs. Helen Plane died in a private sanitarium in Atlanta. She was ninety-five.

In July 1925, the *New York Times* announced that Borglum was planning to transfer his original plans for the Stone Mountain Confederate Monument to Chimney Rock, in the western North Carolina mountains. Borglum was "full of enthusiasm" about the site, stating "this granite face is more suitable to the proposed memorial than Stone Mountain because it is broken here and there by natural curves and lines by which much carving would be saved." Despite local and state support, the project never seemed to proceed beyond the discussion stage.

With a new sculptor chosen and the prospect of ample income from the sale of the commemorative half-dollars, Hollins Randolph and the Monumental Association had great hopes for the future. An aggressive sales campaign was planned, but high overhead costs consumed much of the funds received. When work on the carving did finally resume in early 1927, it progressed slowly. Plans were laid for a public unveiling of Lukeman's work in early April 1928. By then Lukeman had completed only the head and upper body of his version of the general. On the stone face, just above the Lukeman carving, Borglum's head of Lee, now abandoned, stared ahead to the east. It was an embarrassing juxtaposition. In March 1928, after expenses totaling more than a million dollars, and nearly thirteen years after Borglum took on the project, the famed sculptor's head of General Lee was unceremoniously blasted off the side of Stone Mountain in preparation for the upcoming ceremony.

The April 9th unveiling went well, with large crowds in attendance. Three days later, Hollins Randolph announced that he would not seek reelection as the association's president, citing other business concerns.

In mid-May, G. F. Willis, an Atlanta "capitalist" and real estate developer was named to succeed Randolph as president of the SMCMA. Soon thereafter, work at the mountain ground to a permanent halt for lack of funds. An audit of the finances of the Monumental Association made public some time later confirmed Borglum's suspicion that under the leadership of Hollins Randolph significantly more funds were expended on administrative costs than were devoted to the completion of the carving. For the nine-year period beginning April 1916, 57 percent of total expenditures were devoted directly to carving. Of the amount spent on "Overhead," the line item "Salaries" consumed the largest single amount, averaging approximately $5,500 per year. During the next three years, when the organization received nearly $700,000 from sales of the memorial half-dollar, only 20 percent of funds were spent carving, with 27 percent devoted to "Salaries," averaging nearly $75,000 per year. Borglum had been correct.

In the years and decades that followed, sporadic efforts were made to revive work on the monument. None produced any practical progress. In 1958, the state of Georgia acquired Stone Mountain and the surrounding land for the purpose of opening a public park. With state sponsorship, work on the carving was resumed in 1964, with final completion in 1972. It remains today a mere wisp of Gutzon Borglum's original plan. As for Borglum, he devoted the remainder of his life to the completion of the Mount Rushmore memorial, with the work continued by his son, Lincoln Borglum, after the sculptor's death in 1941.

Sources and Resources

Gutzon Borglum was a true national figure, a prominent newsmaker of the day, and the frequent subject of articles and news items in both the daily press and popular magazines. Likewise, the proposed Stone Mountain memorial and the eventual brouhaha that brought its demise were covered widely. Most of the details of the events that transpired can be reconstructed by a careful reading of contemporary newspapers and popular literature. The Emory University Manuscript and Rare Book Library in Atlanta holds in its collection a number of documents relating to Borglum, Helen Plane, and Stone Mountain. In addition to these sources, the following list of works served as resources for this chapter. Many of the details regarding the Stone Mountain Confederate Monumental Association were gleaned from Freeman's excellent work.

Borglum, Gutzon. "Engineering Problems to Be Met in Mountain Sculpture." *The Black Hills Engineer* (November 1930): 306–34. This issue of this quarterly publication of the South Dakota State School of Mines was devoted to the carvings on Mount Rushmore, then firmly underway by Borglum. Although the article is nominally about the Mount Rushmore work, Borglum has much to say about the technical difficulties he encountered in Georgia. He stated, "I am using some of my experiences on Stone Mountain, which apply equally to our work on Rushmore and reveal the difficulties inevitable in colossal design, as they will be useful to students hereafter." To illustrate some of his points, Borglum presented several drawings of technical issues at Stone Mountain that are found only in this reference.

Casey, Robert J. and Mary Borglum. *Give the Man Room.* New York: Bobbs-Merrill Company, 1952. This biography, coauthored by Borglum's second wife, presents a sanitized version of his life. The section on Stone Mountain is quite sketchy and is opened with the disclaimer: "The years have produced a variety of stories about what happened at Stone Mountain, most of them untrue, and there is little use now summing them up." Borglum's membership in the Ku Klux Klan is not mentioned. A reader of this book should be aware that he or she is being presented a selective version of the facts.

Freeman, David B. *Carved in Stone: The History of Stone Mountain.* Macon: Mercer University Press, 1997. Freeman's work is undoubtely the best single source available on the history of Stone Mountain and, in particular, the original Borglum carving. Well documented and heavily illustrated, it examines in detail not only the events of 1915 to the late 1920s, but also the subsequent completion of the current memorial carving.

Shaff, Howard and Audrey K. Shaff. *Six Wars at a Time.* Freeman, SD: Pine Hill Press, 1985. This work by the Shaffs, written in cooperation with Gutzon Borglum's daughter, Mary Ellis Borglum Vhay, is the better of two major biographies of the sculptor. The Shaffs were associated with the Center for Western Studies in Sioux Falls, South Dakota, at the time of the book's publication. While the general flow of Borglum's life is generally well-researched, there are a number of inconsistancies in the account of the Stone Mountain memorial carving. This should not deter the interested reader, but rather suggest that other parallel sources be consulted for research purposes.

Borglum, a talented sculptor with an ego to match, posed for a number of photographs during his life. Apparently somewhat sensitive about his baldness, many of them depict him wearing a hat.

Library of Congress

In this 1923 photo, Borglum surveys the as-yet-uncarved north face of Stone Mountain. The set of wooden steps leading down to a work platform can barely be seen near the top of the mountain. The first outlines of the figures to be carved have been painted on the sheer scarp below.

Emory University Rose Library Archives

Suspended on the sheer rock face in bosun's chairs, Borglum supervises while an unidentified man uses a pneumatic tool to carve the head of General Lee.

Emory University Rose Library Archives

Gutzon Borglum (right) proudly demonstrates the projector he designed to throw the image of his models on the side of Stone Mountain. The work was done at night, with men suspended from a work platform above outlining in paint the figures to be carved in the granite.

Emory University Rose Library Archives

The idea of a Confederate Memorial on Stone Mountain was originally promoted by the United Daughters of the Confederacy (UDC), with management of fund-raising and actual completion of the project later overseen by the Stone Mountain Confederate Monumental Association (SMCMA).

Emory University Rose Library Archives

Although there was no direct connection between Gutzon Borglum's proposed Confederate Memorial and the Ku Klux Klan, an association exists in the minds of many. After a hiatus of nearly half a century following the Civil War, a fraternal order calling itself the Ku Klux Klan was founded on the top of Stone Mountain in November 1915. Later, many members of the Stone Mountain Confederate Memorial Association's Board of Directors were Klansmen. In the early 1920s, Borglum himself was a member of the Klan's inner circle.

Emory University Rose Library Archives

CHAPTER 10

THE DRUM RETURNS HOME

It drummed the Boys in Gray off to war, was lost on the battlefield, and barely survived a disastrous fire. Now, more than 150 years after its creation on a plantation in rural Georgia, the drum carried by Thomas H. Sparks, Company B, 59th Georgia Regiment of the army of the Confederate States of America, has returned home.

The story of this remarkable journey begins on a plantation near the village of Warthen, Georgia, in 1861. In January of that year, Georgia became the fifth state to secede from the Union. In the months that followed, militia companies formed across the South in anticipation of the possibility of war with the North. Washington County, whose seat was Sandersville, raised several such units. In Warthen, a crossroads community in the northern part of the county, local men organized the Jackson Guards under the leadership of Capt. William Warthen, for whose family the town had been named. The company began weekly drills in May 1861, marching to the cadence of a drum crafted on a local cotton plantation.

The Guards' drum was a work of art, made completely of local materials, painted and decorated by its maker, Jasper M. Howell, who presented it to the unit. It was roughly 24.5 inches in diameter and 18.5 inches high, its heads made of fine leather and its shell and hoops of bent wood. The hoops were originally red, and the outside of the shell a shade of brown. On the front of the drum, the part that would be displayed as a drummer carried it, Howell painted a background of blue on which he painted an eagle with an American shield for its breastplate, its head surrounded by thirteen stars and its beak holding a streamer with the motto *E Pluribus Unum*. In its talons, the eagle held an olive branch on the right side and arrows on the left. The drum was designed to be carried while marching, with a rope for this purpose laced through holes in both hoops. The name "T. H. Sparks" appears on both the shell and on one head of the drum near the initials "C.S.A." Both were apparently added later during the conflict.

The Jackson Guards were mustered into the service of the Confederacy in October 1861 for a six-month rotation doing local duty within the state. J. Benton Warthen, a relative of the Guard's captain, served as the unit's drummer. In May 1862, the unit reorganized as Company B of the 59th Regiment of Georgia Infantry. George W. Sparks was elected captain and would continue to command the company until the end of the war in 1865. His brothers William, Stephen, and Thomas served together with him in the unit. Thomas, at the time eighteen years of age, took over the position of regimental drummer in July 1862. He was sent off to war wearing homespun gray, produced from the wool of sheep raised on family lands and spun and woven into cloth on plantation looms.

The Sparks brothers were members of a prominent Washington County family. Their grandfather, John Sparks, had moved to South Carolina from Virginia in the early 1770s. In the 1790s, he sold his lands there and moved to a large plantation about three miles from Warthen. Family history suggests that much of this land was granted to him for his service in the Revolutionary War. John had eleven children, including Thomas, who became a wealthy planter. Four of Thomas's sons were the Sparks boys serving together in the 59th Georgia Regiment, including his namesake, Thomas Harris Sparks, the drummer.

In May 1862, the 59th Georgia Regiment was assigned to the defense of the Macon, Georgia, area, primarily guarding Federal prisoners. In August, the unit transferred to Virginia, spending the first few months near Richmond, then reinforcing the guard at the important Confederate fort at Drewry's Bluff on the James River, a duty that lasted from December 1862 through April 1863. As the war in Virginia intensified, the unit transferred to the commands of Brig. Gen. G. T. ("Tige") Anderson and Lieutenant General John B. Hood. For the next two years, the Sparks brothers fought in some of the bloodiest battles of the war. William died of illness at Rapidan Station, Virginia, in the spring of 1863, a fate of many soldiers in the war. Stephen was killed a few weeks later at Gettysburg. George continued to serve as an officer, finally surrendering with Lee's forces at Appomattox in April 1865.

Thomas, the youngest of the brothers serving with the 59th Georgia, was to suffer a different fate. Wounded in battle, he was taken prisoner near Gettysburg on July 5, 1863, and spent the next four months in a Union military hospital. In November, he was paroled pending a prisoner exchange.

Pay records indicate he was back with his unit by February 1864, reassuming his role as regimental drummer.

Thomas Sparks's war came to a practical end at the bloody battle of Cold Harbor. Family history relates that in the heat of battle he laid down his drum, picked up a rifle, and went to the front to help defend the Confederate lines. It was there on June 1, 1864, that he was once again captured by Federal troops. He was held captive at the infamous Federal prisoner-of-war camp at Elmira, New York, where he remained until his release on July 11, 1865. Sparks was fortunate to survive. At Elmira Prison, named "Hell-mira" by its inmates, approximately a quarter of those imprisoned died of disease, malnutrition, and lack of medical care.

It was on the Cold Harbor battlefield that the drum and Thomas H. Sparks parted ways, seemingly forever. Like so many other personal objects belonging to soldiers in battle, it had been lost in the fog of war, assumed to have been destroyed. With the war over, Sparks was required to sign an oath of loyalty to the Union and given a train ticket home. In the years that followed, he married, raised a family, became a successful businessman, and served in public office as county treasurer. Little thought was given to the drum, its loss overshadowed by the memories of the horrific loss of life at Gettysburg, Cold Harbor and other battles, and the months spent in near-starvation in the Federal prisoner-of-war camp.

But such was not to be the fate of this drum. In September 1915, a news item appeared in the *Atlanta Journal* under the headline "Who Beat This War Drum of the Sixties?" It told of a letter received by Adjt. Gen. J. Van Holt Nash, head of the Georgia National Guard, in regard to a drum carried by a Southern soldier during the Civil War. A New York man, William F. Scott, was seeking "the owner of the drum, or some of the owner's relations," hoping to return it (for a nominal fee of $25). In his letter to General Nash, William Scott wrote, "The drum, which is 19 inches across the head, is in a fine state of preservation, with the exception of a bullet hole through its side which was made during the battle of Cold Harbor." The inscriptions "T. H. Sparks," "Georgia Vol.," and "C.S.A." could still be clearly seen, but the unit number was indistinct.

Thomas H. Sparks, who at the time was quite active in the United Confederate Veterans organization, immediately contacted Scott. After an exchange of correspondence to prove that Sparks was in fact the "T. H.

Sparks" whose name appeared on the drum, Scott agreed to sell it to him for $15, plus the cost of shipping.

As it turned out, the drum had in some ways saved itself. It was an object of beauty to be sure, which is perhaps why it was picked up on the battlefield by a soldier from New York. He, in turn, gave it to a soldier from New Hampshire who had in some way been kind to him. After "knocking about from owner to owner in the North," it was acquired by William F. Scott, who later set out on the quest to repatriate the relic with its original owner.

The drum arrived in Sandersville in January 1916, remarkably intact, the only change being the replacement of the rope around its top. It was originally kept in Sandersville's Masonic Temple, the only public building on the City Square to survive General Sherman's torch on his March to the Sea in the fall of 1864. It became part of an irreplaceable collection of historical memorabilia, joining relics from colonial days, the American Revolution, and the Civil War. A 1916 photo of a gathering of the county's remaining Confederate veterans taken in front of the Masonic Temple shows Thomas H. Sparks once again holding the drum he had carried during the war. For several months, newspapers carried stories of the return of the drum thought lost forever a half century earlier. Sparks died in December 1920 at the advanced age of seventy-seven, less than five years after he was reunited with his drum.

In February 1921, only two months after Sparks's death, disaster struck. A freak mid-winter lightning storm ignited a wooden building near the Masonic Temple. Despite the best efforts of the local fire brigade, the conflagration spread down the block toward the Temple. Among the crowd gathered on the square was one of Thomas Sparks's daughters. Terrified at the prospect of her father's drum being lost in the fire, she persuaded Hines Wood, a young lawyer and member of the Masonic lodge, to make an attempt to recover it. The drum was in the lodge room on the second floor of the building. Wood was a lodge member and knew its exact location. Using a ladder, he climbed into the burning structure and rescued the drum, the only one of many unique historical objects to be saved from the fire.

Over the following decades, the drum remained in the Sparks family, passed down from eldest son to eldest son, most recently to Thomas H. Sparks's great-great-grandson, Thomas W. Sparks, the last male heir in the line. With his death, his family made the decision in the spring of 2014 to return the drum to its home in Washington County, its original birth site more than a century and a half earlier. It is now in the collection of the Washington County Historical Society, on display at the Old Jail Museum and Genealogical Research Center on the Sandersville City Square, just a few dozen yards from where it was nearly destroyed in 1921.

Seventeen-year-old Thomas Sparks in his Confederate Gray uniform. In 1862 he took over the position of regimental drummer for Company B of the 59th Regiment of Georgia Infantry. He served in that role until captured by Northern troops on June 1, 1864 at the Battle of Cold Harbor.

Washington County Historical Society

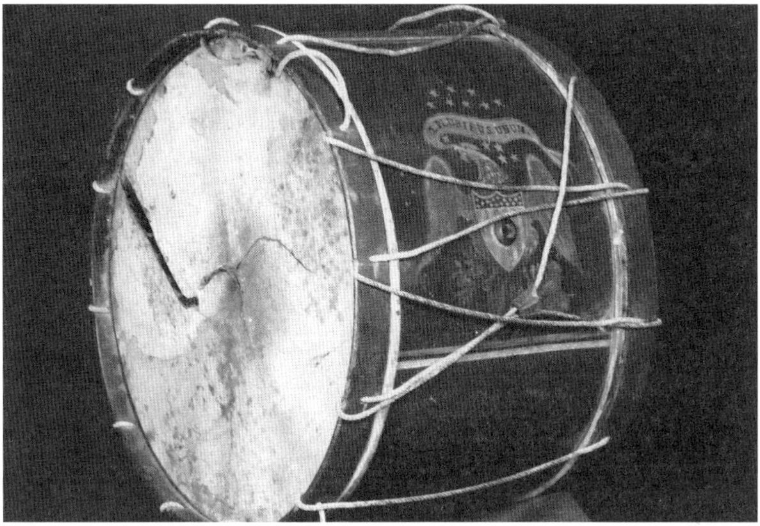

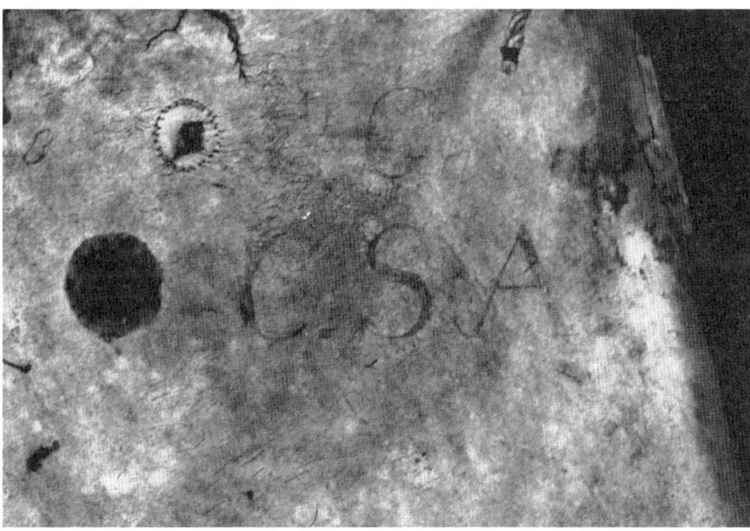

Above, the regimental drum was presumed lost forever with Thomas Sparks's capture in 1864. Somehow, it miraculously survived and ended up in the hands of a New York collector. Through a serious of fortuitous events, it was returned to Sparks in 1916. Below, the letters "CSA" can be seen on one of the drumheads, next to what is alleged to be a repaired bullet hole.

Author's Collection

In 1916, more than half a century after the end of the Civil War, the Washington County chapter of the United Confederate Veterans met for one of the last times. Thomas Sparks can be seen holding his battle drum near the left end of the front row. The building in the background, Sandersville's Masonic Temple, became the home of the drum after Sparks's death in 1920 at age 77. The following year the drum barely escaped destruction when the building burned following a lightning strike.

Washington County Historical Society

CHAPTER 11

THE LOST CAUSE ON THE SILVER SCREEN

A few years ago I found myself in Beijing on my way to visit the steppes and deserts of Mongolia. It had been a long flight from the West Coast, and I was quite exhausted. I checked into an upscale hotel in the central part of the city near Tiananmen Square, thinking that I would take a nap and try to adjust to the time change. I flopped on the bed and began surfing through the television channels, looking for something to watch as I drifted off to sleep.

As chance would have it, I had arrived in China on the same day it was announced that Beijing would be the host of the international Olympic Games several years hence. The offerings on the state-run television channels were scant, and most were in Chinese anyway, so I settled on a somewhat grainy black-and-white movie that appeared to have something to do with Greece or the Olympics—I wasn't sure, and at the moment didn't really care. I watched idly for a few minutes as half-naked athletic figures cavorted on the screen, apparently in praise of the Olympic spirit. Soon the screen was filled with the image of a huge stadium with marching athletes and cheering crowds, many of them raising their arms in the Nazi salute. I propped up and began to take notice, just as Adolph Hitler announced the opening of the 1936 Berlin Olympic Games.

I sat bolt upright. "My god!" I murmured half out loud. "They're showing Leni Riefenstahl's *Olympia*. Unbelievable."

To understand my reaction, one has to be familiar with the work of Leni Riefenstahl. She was, and is, considered one of the most talented cinematographers of all time. Born in Germany in 1902, she achieved early success as an interpretive dancer, later turning her talents to acting and appearing in several successful films. In 1932, she directed her first film, winning a silver medal at the Venice Film Festival. That same year she met Adolph Hitler, head of the National Socialist (Nazi) Party and future German chancellor. Thus began a relationship that would last until the end of World War

II. Riefenstahl became a favorite of Hitler's and of his propaganda minister, Josef Goebbels. Over the next several years she would write, produce, and direct a number of propaganda films for the Third Reich, the most famous of which was the 1935 *Triumph des Willens* ("Triumph of the Will"), documenting the 1934 Nazi Party Nuremberg rally. *Olympia*, the film I was viewing in Beijing with some degree of morbid fascination, was a celebration of Germany's new place in the world order of the day.[74] It premiered on Hitler's forty-ninth birthday in 1938.

I was initially taken aback that any civilized country would air Riefenstahl's documentaries. She was, after all, intimately associated with a regime that was—directly or indirectly—responsible for the deaths of more than 60 million people. After a moment of reflection, however, I realized that I was in China, far removed from horrors of Nazi Germany. Yes, millions of Chinese died in World War II as well, but mostly in conflict with Japan. To most in Beijing, Hitler with his concentration camps and goose-stepping minions were half a world away, a conflict of the West. Riefenstahl's association meant little here. The movie was a work of art, relatively devoid of political content.

From a cinematic standpoint, *Olympia* was a work of beauty. Its use of what were then cutting-edge techniques made it unique for the day. Riefenstahl was among the first to use extreme close-ups, tracking shots accomplished by mounting cameras on a rail or moving dolly, scenes of the reaction of the crowds juxtaposed with footage of athletic competition. The film became popular in late 1930s America for, among other things, its "heroic treatment" of Jesse Owens, the African American sprinter and four-time gold medalist in the 1936 Berlin Olympics.

Following the war, Riefenstahl was arrested and held in detention for three years before being freed without punishment for her involvement with the Third Reich. Her artistic skills remained widely acclaimed until her death at age 101 in 2003. In her obituary, the *Guardian* noted her *Triumph of the Will* was "renowned and reviled as the best propaganda film ever." A writer for the *Daily Telegraph* opined, "She was perhaps the most talented female cinema director of the 20th century; her celebration of Nazi Germany in film ensured that she was certainly the most infamous." Despite the con-

[74] *Olympia* was originally released in two parts: "Part I. Festival of Nations," "Part II. Festival of Beauty."

troversy that surrounds it, Riefenstahl's *Olympia* remains on *Time* magazine's "All-Time 100 Best Movies" listing, the only one of the group directed by a woman.

More pertinent to the theme of this essay, there are two American movies from the first half of the twentieth century that are also consistently cited for their dramatic and cinematographic excellence yet remain mired in controversy because of their themes. Both were wildly successful in their day and, despite the decades that have passed since their creation, continue to rank among what many consider the best movies ever made. *The Birth of a Nation* (1915) and *Gone with the Wind* (1939) are both listed, for example, on the "American Film Institute's 100 Greatest Movies of All Time" and on Filmsite's "100 Greatest Films." On a certain thematic level, the two have much in common. They are both "Southern" films, with the story unfolding during and after the Civil War. Much of the conflict and drama takes place in the devastated South during the Reconstruction years. Most importantly, from the standpoint of twenty-first century controversy, they embody a graphic visual representation of the themes of the Lost Cause.

In the years that followed the end of the Civil War, there were spontaneous movements in both the North and South to commemorate the valor and sacrifice of those who fought in the conflict. On the Union side, this took the form of the Grand Army of the Republic (GAR), initially organized in 1866 as a fraternal order of veterans. The GAR was instrumental in the designation of May 30 as a national Memorial Day and in the erection of hundreds of monuments commemorating those who fought in the war. Rapidly morphing into an advocacy group for veterans' rights, at its peak it boasted nearly half a million members.

In the defeated South, memories and public opinion of the war took another direction. Like their counterparts in the North, the numerous local Southern remembrance organizations coalesced into regional groups such as the United Confederate Veterans (UCV), the Sons of Confederate Veterans (SCV), and the United Daughters of the Confederacy (UDC). Collectively, many of their purposes were similar to corresponding organizations in the North, sponsoring the erection of monuments to the soldiers of the Confederacy and active in the designation of April 26 as Confederate Memorial

Day.[75] But in addition, these groups and others were in large part responsible for the not-so-subtle rewriting of history in their promotion of the so-called Lost Cause.

It is generally agreed that the name "Lost Cause" was derived from the title of an 1866 book by Virginia journalist Edward A. Pollard titled *The Lost Cause: A New Southern History of the War of the Confederates*. Virulently pro-Southern, in the book's introduction the author refers to his narrative as "a severely just account of the War on the basis of contemporary evidence," and "above political misrepresentations." The conflict, he averred, was fought over states' rights, not slavery. The Southern Cause was just, with the invading North the malefactor in the struggle. Pollard's book was followed not only by many others advocating the Southern viewpoint, but also by scholarly articles sponsored by the Southern Historical Society that embodied what would become the South's standard narrative of the history of the war, the myth of the Lost Cause.

The Lost Cause interpretation of the events of the Civil War presents a number of primary elements: First and foremost, secession was a legitimate option for the South under the Constitution. Therefore, the war was fought over states' rights, not the existence of slavery. Second, slavery as it existed in the antebellum South was a benevolent institution, beneficial to all parties, and characterized by the "faithful slave." Third, Confederate soldiers and their military leaders were heroic and beyond reproach. The defeat of the South was not due to a lack of valor or military skill, but rather the overwhelming advantage of the North in men and matériel. Topmost in the pantheon of military leaders was Robert E. Lee, the consummate Southerner and gentleman, followed by a number of others including especially Thomas J. "Stonewall" Jackson. At home, Southern women, aided by loyal servants, selflessly supported the war effort in spite of trying privations. Finally, the postwar period known as the Reconstruction era was a deliberate effort on the part of the victorious North to destroy the Southern way of life and at the same time inflict additional punishment on the South for secession and the formation of the Confederacy.

---

[75] Confederate Gen. Joseph E. Johnson surrendered to Union General William T. Sherman on April 26, 1865, marking the practical end of the war for most in the South.

By the beginning of the twentieth century, this narrative had become the accepted truth for most in the South and, indeed, for many in the North. Variations on the Lost Cause theme were often woven into popular literature, music, and stage performances. In 1914, a struggling movie producer named David Wark Griffith was contacted by Frank E. Woods, a scenario writer, with a possible idea for a feature-length movie. It was still the dark days of motion picture production. Films were silent, with the "soundtrack" supplied by a local orchestra, and the dialogue, such as it was, displayed for the audience to read as annotations to the action on the screen. Woods called Griffith's attention to a touring stage play titled *The Clansman*, thinking it might do well in a movie adaptation. The play was based on a 1905 book of the same name, written by Thomas Dixon, a former minister/lawyer/politician/lecturer turned author and playwright. In its adaption for the stage, the play had toured the country successfully for five years. *The Clansman* was part of Dixon's "Reconstruction Trilogy," books portraying a postwar South occupied by Union troops and ruled by unscrupulous carpetbaggers and scalawags. The black former slaves are portrayed negatively while the heroes of the day are the Ku Klux Klan.

Working on a shoestring budget and with unknowns for actors, Griffith managed to produce what would become the world's first blockbuster movie, an innovative adventure tale beginning just prior to the Civil War and concluding in the Reconstruction era. In those early days of the motion picture industry, movies were commonly referred to as "photoplays." Many were. With minimal adaptation, a producer would simply set up a camera in front of a stage and film the scene. Griffith was among "the first to realize that the conventions of the stage were not suitable for the screen."[76] Working closely with his cameraman, Billy Bitzer, and without the aid of artificial lighting, Griffith's innovative use of camera angles, scene transitions, and action shots made *The Birth of a Nation* a technologic marvel of the day. A retrospective review of the movie in 1937 gushed,

> Without today's artificial light and with the crudest sort of technical equipment, *The Birth of a Nation* still stands up as a great picture. The harshness of the light gives it an authenticity that all the camera work of today cannot equal. The panoramic battle scenes are tremendous;

[76] Milton Mackaye, "The Birth of a Nation," *Scribner's Magazine* 102 (1937): 42.

> they have no smell of artifice, but, instead, seem to be photographs of actual war. I have never seen a more moving or significant shot than the one utilized by Griffith to tell the story of Sherman's March to the Sea. The camera "irises in" (Griffith invented the iris by focusing the camera through a hole in a cigar box) on a starved mother with two crying children hanging to her skirts. Then the perspective enlarges; the mother and children are on a hilltop. The camera shifts and with the mother's eye we look down into a broad valley where far in the distance an army column shaped like a scythe moves along while haystacks and houses burn.[77]

Griffith also realized that the visual aspects were only part of the cinematic experience. Working with composer Joseph Carl Briel, *The Birth of a Nation* was among the first silent films to have a synchronized musical score designed for an orchestra to perform as the film rolled. Drawing from a wide musical palette, the works were chosen for their emotional impact: there are adaptations of black folk music, Sherman attacks Atlanta to the strains of Grieg's "In the Hall of the Mountain King," and the Ku Klux Klan gallops in to save the day accompanied by Wagner's "Ride of the Valkyries."[78]

For all of its technical beauty, *The Birth of a Nation* displayed an ugly side in its portrayal of African Americans. To quote the same reviewer who gave the film such high praise, "One cannot escape the fact that the emotions aroused by the dramatic incidents give the audience a definite feeling of Negro depravity and white virtue." Simply put, the depictions of persons of color were patently racist. This fact was not missed by the public of the day. The National Association for the Advancement of Colored People (NAACP), then less than a decade old, vigorously opposed the movie's release. In its early days, showings were accompanied by protest demonstrations outside of some theaters. Despite all, the consensus of most seemed to hold that the movie was the finest ever made.

As a measure of its success, *The Birth of a Nation* drew sell-out crowds with ticket prices of one to two dollars in the days when normal admission prices were ten to fifteen cents. It toured continuously for years, not only in

---

[77] Mackaye, *Birth of a Nation*, 69.

[78] "The Ride of the Valkyries" was used by director Francis Ford Coppola as a leitmotif for the (in)famous helicopter attack scene in the 1979 film, *Apocalypse Now*, itself an adaptation of Joseph Conrad's 1899 novella, *Heart of Darkness*.

the United States, but also in Europe, Australia, and South Africa. Those who had invested in its production became wealthy. The film held all-time attendance and profitability records until edged out by America's second great blockbuster movie, the 1939 epic *Gone with the Wind*, also based on the themes of the Lost Cause.

Like *The Birth of a Nation*, *Gone with the Wind* was based on a book, in this case Margaret Mitchell's thousand-page opus of the same name. Both movies focus on war and its aftermath, but the former is a tale of action and conflict while the latter focuses on love, loss, hope, and redemption. In the twenty-four years that elapsed between their creations, there had been dramatic strides in the technical aspects of movie production. The somewhat wooden and exaggerated acting of the silent screen had morphed into a more natural style. The actors were now stars, in this case Vivien Leigh, Clark Gable, Olivia de Havilland, and Leslie Howard. Jerky black and white silent images had been replaced by full Technicolor, with a coordinated soundtrack, custom-composed musical themes, and what had become known as "special effects," all designed to enhance the reality of the movie experience. The musical score, composed of ninety-nine separate compositions in all, drew heavily on both classical Southern tunes as well as music contemporary to the era of the story. The keynote piece, "Tara's Theme," remains a classic decades after its composition. *Gone with the Wind* was designed to be a movie for the ages. It was.

There is no doubt that the movie's producer, David O. Selznick, was aware of the controversy generated by *The Birth of a Nation*'s negative portrayal of blacks. Early in the film's production stage, Selznick, himself a member of the Jewish faith, was contacted by prominent members of the Jewish community and urged to avoid arousing "anti-Negro antipathy." Acknowledging the persecution that Jews were then suffering in Nazi Germany, Selznick replied that he was "most sensitive to the feelings of minority people," promising to avoid controversy in this regard.[79] Two African Americans played prominent roles in *Gone with the Wind*'s screen narrative, Hattie McDaniel as Mammy and Butterfly McQueen as Prissy, both house servants. While their roles were generally positive ones, other blacks were depicted in a less flattering light, at times buffoonish and at times menacing.

[79] See Wilson's *The Making of Gone with the Wind* for a more complete account of this issue.

The use of disparaging racial epithets was avoided, but the slaves seem generally content with their lot in life. The freedmen are seen as shiftless and easily manipulated by corrupt Yankee carpetbaggers. The presence of the Ku Klux Klan with its anti-black bias is implied, but never mentioned directly.

Gone with the Wind was a stupendous success. Its premiere in Atlanta on December 15, 1939, was perhaps the largest public event hosted by the city up until that time. Georgia governor E. D. Rivers declared the day a state holiday. An estimated 300,000 lined the parade route as the stars arrived in town for the gala at Lowe's Grand Theater on the corner of Peachtree and Forsyth streets. Clark Gable and Vivien Leigh were the center of attraction, but Hattie McDaniel, who would later win an Oscar as Best Supporting Actress for her role as Mammy, did not attend. Given the state's segregation laws of the day, she would have been required to sit in the "colored" section.

Selznick's magnificent production of Mitchell's book went on to win a then-record eight Oscars at the 12th Academy Awards Ceremony held in February 1940 in Los Angeles, including Best Picture. Despite its length of nearly four hours, the movie would tour continuously for years, remaining among the all-time favorite of American motion pictures, often based on surveys of viewers who had not been born when it was filmed. Adjusting for inflation, it remains at or among the top money-making movies of all time more than three-quarters of a century after its release.

With that said, as I write this essay in early 2016, it is quite a simple matter to find calls in the current media for suppression of the showing of *Gone with the Wind*, accusing it of being an anachronistic paean to a shameful period in American history. Opinions of this movie are often regional. Whether its visual motifs are true to history or exaggerated, Southerners are known to defend it as a tribute to an idyllic past. In sharp contrast, others see it as romanticizing slavery and racism.

How should one approach movies such as *The Birth of a Nation* or *Gone with the Wind*? Were they originally produced to disparage persons of color or to glorify the long-discredited institution of slavery? Does their undisputed technical wizardry and artistic beauty offset their often not-so-subtle racism? Should they be viewed in the context in which they were made, in an earlier era when the world was different and social justice less of a personal and national priority?

There is no simple answer to these and similar questions. Many of our reactions are intimately related to events long past: the North-South schism that manifest itself as the American Civil War of the 1860s; the institution of slavery, allowed under the Constitution yet condemned by those who authored it; the ingrained human trait to consider others different from ourselves as somehow lesser beings. In my way of thinking, we should celebrate both films for what is positive about them, recognizing at the same time that they are of an earlier time when life was guided by a different ethos.

The films of Leni Riefenstahl have been condemned not so much for their content, but rather for the association of their creator with the Nazi regime of 1930s Germany. As my experience in Beijing revealed, absent the cultural context, her cinematic work could be and often is considered a thing of beauty. Most Americans have no desire to forget our past or ignore our shared cultural history, warts and all. At the dawn of the Germany's Third Reich in 1933, there was a campaign for the suppression of works considered subversive or "un-German." Josef Goebbels himself called for an end to "decadence and moral corruption." The result was the May 1933 public burning in cities across Germany of thousands of books deemed antithetical to the new German order. The call for the suppression of *The Birth of Nation, Gone with the Wind,* and other symbols of the day that some find incongruent with constantly changing cultural norms seems to me to be history's effort to repeat itself. We are what we are. We cannot change the past by pretending it never existed. We can only hope to make the future better.

Sources and Resources

One cannot properly appreciate a movie by reading about it. I would suggest that anyone wanting to review *The Birth of a Nation* or *Gone with the Wind* obtain a copy and view it for themselves. Both movies are readily available from multiple sources in various formats and at a reasonable price. *The Birth of a Nation* can be viewed online without cost, but in many versions the quality of the images is often poor and the soundtrack is not Griffith's original. There are seemingly innumerable books on *Gone with the Wind*, reflecting the movie's lasting popularity. To supplement the actual viewing of the movie, I would suggest two:

Howard, Sidney. *GWTW—The Screenplay*. Edited by Richard Harwell. New York: Collier Books, 1980. With a long and informative introduction, and illustrated by a number of contemporary photos taken at the time of filming, this book provides the complete script for the movie, together with stage directions and notes. It serves as a useful adjunct when viewing the film.

Wilson, Steve. *The Making of Gone with the Wind*. Austin: University of Texas Press, 2014. Released to coincide with the seventy-fifth anniversary of the movie, this well-researched book focuses on many behind-the-scenes aspects of *Gone with the Wind*'s creation and directly addresses the concerns of racial animus.

There is relatively little recently written about *The Birth of a Nation*. Newspapers of the day were full of reviews of the movie, mostly positive, with the occasional negative comment or letter to the editor regarding its depiction of blacks. Perhaps the best (and most widely quoted) single reference is Milton Mackaye's 1937 retrospective review in *Scribner's Magazine*:

Mackaye, Milton, "The Birth of a Nation." *Scribner's Magazine* 102 (1937): 40–46, 69.

For further reading on the Lost Cause, please see the introductory overview for this section.

Based on the book, *The Clansman*, by Thomas Dixon, D. W. Griffith's 1915 *The Birth of a Nation* became the world's first block-buster movie, holding all-time attendance and income records until dethroned by *Gone with the Wind* in 1939. Patently racist even by then-current standards, it extolled the role of the Reconstruction Era Ku Klux Klan in "saving" the South from Federal occupation.

Public Domain

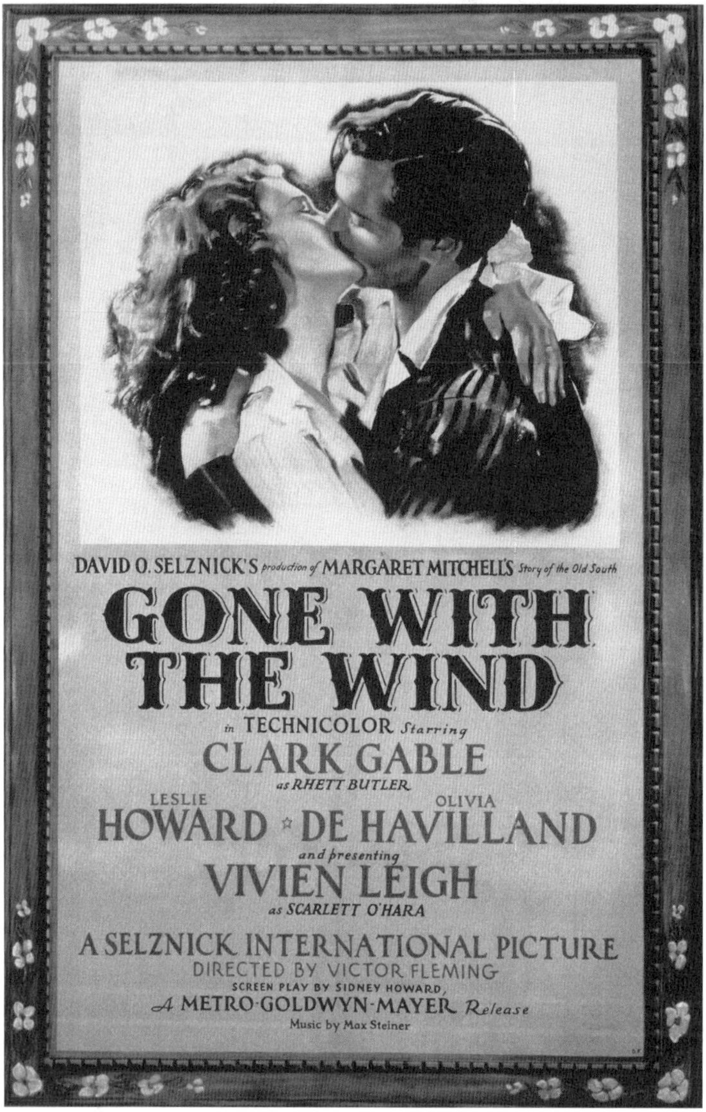

Gone with the Wind, based on the book by Margaret Mitchell, featured themes based on the Myths of the Lost Cause, glorifying the Southern way of life in the years that preceded the Civil War. Popular but at times controversial, it still holds attendance and income records three-quarters of a century after its release.

Public Domain

Leni Riefenstahl (center in this photograph) was a pioneer in the techniques of modern cinematography, and is often cited as among of the greatest directors of the first century of movie-making. In this photo she directs filming of the 1936 Berlin Olympics.

Public Domain

Riefenstahl's skill and fame as a cinematographer have often been overshadowed by her association with Germany's Nazi hierarchy in the 1930s. Here she meets with Reich Chancellor Adolph Hitler in 1933.

Public Domain

PART V

THE GOLDEN AGE OF COTTON AND ITS AFTERMATH 1915–1925

OVERVIEW

THE GOLDEN AGE OF COTTON AND ITS AFTERMATH 1915–1925

For those curious few who choose to venture off Georgia's expressways when traveling about the state, it is often difficult to not view the rural countryside and its myriad of small towns with a bit of wonder. Driving slowly down the tree-lined Main Streets or situated on a country highway miles from the nearest village, one often encounters huge old homes, their wide, welcoming front porches or columned entrances now sagging with age and sadly in need of a coat of fresh paint. Shaded by hundred-year-old oaks or surrounded by ornate Victorian cast-iron fences, they beg the question, "Why would *anyone* build such a mansion here, in the middle of *nowhere*?"

Today, Georgia, like many Southern states, is dominated by her urban centers. Depending on how one defines urban versus rural, roughly six out of every seven Georgians live in a city or its suburbs. These are the hubs of wealth, commerce, education, and sophistication, or so the story goes. Yet the evidence seems to point to a long-gone era of glory days enjoyed by now-rural areas of the state. What was different in the past? Why did things change? Overall, the answer is quite complex, but it can be summed up in a single word: cotton.

At one time, a century or so ago, a traveler venturing down Georgia's rutted dirt roads between Atlanta and Savannah in late summer or early autumn would pass mile after mile after mile of white fields of cotton, their fuzzy bolls being hand-harvested by a drove of workers dragging long sacks bulging with the fruits of their labor. And for several months of the year, the Cotton Avenues of the small towns one passed through would be jammed from dawn to dusk with mule-drawn wagons filled to the brim with cotton waiting to being ginned. It was this one crop that made many Georgians wealthy, and the dependence on this one crop that, for the most part, presaged the end of the economic heyday of the state's small towns.

Historians of the South often refer to two "Golden Ages of Cotton." The first, from about 1850 until the start of the Civil War, was fueled by the plantation system at its apex: vast fields, labor furnished by slaves, a system of commerce and distribution that held potentially rich rewards for those at each level in the chain, and a steady and growing demand for the white fiber, especially by the textile mills of Great Britain. Georgia in 1860 held the distinction of being the wealthiest state in the Union, an honor made dubious by the fact that half of the state's wealth was accounted for by the value of human capital; that is, by slaves. The war brought an end to slavery and with it the plantation system. Although there were ups and downs, for the next half century the state weathered what one agricultural historian termed "The Long Depression."[80]

Georgia's second Golden Age of Cotton began in the second decade of the twentieth century and came to a crashing halt in the first years of the next. Fueled initially by the demand for cotton generated by World War I, and spurred on by economic policies undertaken by agencies of the federal government, cotton prices soared, rising as much as six- to ten-fold over the few years between 1914 and 1920. Farmers prospered, allowing merchants to prosper, which in turn allowed banks to prosper. Cotton, a commodity, was effectively monetized; bales of cotton in the warehouse became equivalent to cash in the bank.[81] Folks had money to spend—or invest, as the case might be. As cotton appeared to be the way to riches, many bought more cotton land, often on credit secured by cotton. And then it all came to an end.

Much of the run-up in the price of cotton during the World War I era and the years that followed was due to inflation. The price of cotton went up but the cost of everything that one could buy with its proceeds went up as

---

[80] See Willard Range, *A Century of Georgia Agriculture 1850–1950*, Athens: University of Georgia Press, 1954.

[81] The term "to monetize" means "to convert into, or make equal to, money." Gold ingots, for example, are an example of a commodity that has a generally accepted but variable value quoted in dollars (or other currencies). The problem here is that the price of commodities can change rapidly over very short periods of time based on supply and demand. If, for example, a discovery were made that allowed nuclear energy to be produced safely and very inexpensively, the price of coal, oil, and natural gas might plummet as demand dropped and their cost of production remained the same.

well. Meanwhile the boll weevil was advancing steadily eastward, arriving in Georgia in 1915. The same financial largess displayed by the Federal Reserve and central monetary policy during the war years soon turned in another direction. There were calls to "restore the true value of dollar." The policies that had tolerated inflation turned to deliberate deflationary tactics. America plunged into the Great Recession of 1920 to 1921. Cotton prices tumbled, falling to levels below those of 1914 (when corrected for inflation). Farmers were unable to pay their bills, merchants declared bankruptcy, and nearly half of Georgia's banks failed or otherwise went out of business. Which brings us back to the large homes often seen along the major thoroughfares of the state's small towns. The vast majority of them were built prior to the early 1920s. Beyond that date, they became unaffordable for most. The bubble had burst.

The three chapters in this section recount events of this Second Golden Age of Cotton. The first, "A Vast Pool of Oil," details the "discovery" of an alleged massive deposit of oil in Washington County, Georgia, a most convenient way for those with a little (or a lot) of excess cash to invest their funds. It did not end well.

The second chapter, titled "A Killing on Ring Jaw Bluff," is the saga of Charles Graves Rawlings.[82] In 1920 he was one of Georgia's wealthier men; by 1925 he was serving a life sentence for the conspiracy-murder of his first cousin, Gus Tarbutton. This crime (or accidental death, as the case may be) led to one of the state's most publicized criminal trials of the 1920s. This chapter originally appeared as a magazine article in *Georgia Backroads*. I was attracted to the story in some small way as the protagonist was a relative, but more so because I initially saw this as a tale of a very wealthy man who suffered a precipitous fall based on his own greed. As I delved further into my research, however, I realized that the tale of Charlie Rawlings was, in reality, that of the small-town businessman who lost everything in the Great Recession. The theme was indeed one of morality, but it was also one of economics. This article later was incorporated into a book by the same name, but with added subtitle, *The Great Recession and the Death of Small Town Georgia*, published by Mercer University Press in 2013.

The final chapter, "The Myth of the Boll Weevil," makes the case that—in spite of popular opinion—it was not the boll weevil that caused the

[82] The author's great-uncle.

crash of the cotton economy in Georgia. Instead, it was a combination of both unique and then-new external economic factors, including the globalization of America's economy, the system of agriculture that developed in the post-Civil War South, and well-meaning, but in practice toxic, economic decisions on the part of the federal government.

Sources and Resources

Two older references provide an interesting view of Southern agricultural and economic history. Economics is at its best a fuzzy science, characterized by constantly changing truths lucidly explained by the theory *du jour*. As such, it is often illuminating to read facts and opinions that predate the current day.

Hawk, Emory Q. *Economic History of the South*. New York: Prentice-Hall, 1934. A fascinating and very much dated view of "Southern" economics from the perspective of the post-boll weevil years of the Great Depression. The discussion of "Present Economic Problems of the South" (chapter XVII) bears witness to the dramatic and fundamental changes that have taken place since this book was written.

Range, Willard. *A Century of Georgia Agriculture 1850–1950*. Athens: University of Georgia Press, 1954. An excellent summary of the state's agricultural economy from the beginning of the first Golden Age of Cotton through the World War II period. Beginning in the 1950s and beyond, the state's rural-to-urban migration intensified. In many ways, this book is among the best in its review of Georgia's pre-modern agricultural eras.

CHAPTER 12

A VAST POOL OF OIL

On Wednesday, April 23, 1919, the *Sandersville Progress*, a local weekly published in the east-central Georgia town of the same name, announced that oil and gas had been discovered in Washington County. It was a startling revelation, and one that promised to bestow fortunes on the people of the already prosperous local community.

The facts of the discovery were quite simple and appeared to be well documented. Some three months earlier a convict chain gang digging a new roadbed through the farm of W. R. Beach had encountered what appeared to be oil seeping from the earth, accompanied by "a very strong odor of petroleum." Realizing the potential significance of the find, Beach quietly began an investigation, submitting samples from the site to "two of the most prominent chemists in the state." Both "declare[d] emphatically that an analysis disclose[d] the existence of oil and gas in the samples," concluding "that it is hardly possible for it to be from any source but a pool of oil."[83]

With confirmation of the existence of oil beneath his plantation, Beach recruited five prominent local citizens to join him in exploiting the find. They were among "the most substantial and conservative business men in the county," including the wealthy banker Lake B. Holt, attorney Willis Evans, as well as the owner of the local Coca-Cola Bottling Company and two other large landowners. By mid-April they had formed the Middle Georgia Oil & Gas Company. Evans spoke for the group in declaring, "We would be unpatriotic and derelict in our duty as good citizens in not developing it." The paper hinted that there might be future opportunities for other local investors.

---

[83] Quotes in this initial section are drawn from contemporary issues of the *Sandersville Progress* and advertisements of the Middle Georgia Oil & Gas Company.

Within weeks, the Middle Georgia Oil & Gas Company had established an office on the fifth floor of the prestigious Flatiron Building on Peachtree Street in Atlanta. Having purchased 500 acres of the Beach farm, lots would be available for sale to the public for $35 each, payable either in cash or in monthly minimum installments of $10. Each lot, measuring 25 by 25 feet, was said to be of sufficient size for the purchaser to drill his or her own oil well, if so desired. A third of the proceeds from lot sales was to be set aside as an exploration fund, with drilling to begin as soon as an appropriate sum had been raised.

By early May 1919, the sales blitz had begun. Huge ads in the *Progress* featured sworn affidavits from the warden and chain-gang guard who were present at the discovery of the oil seepage earlier in the year. Letters from the two chemists offered "conclusive proof" of oil, while reminding potential investors that "a few dollars now may mean a return of a thousand fold in the near future." As additional reinforcement of the significance of the discovery, a parade of "oil men" from Texas and Oklahoma began to arrive like the Magi of old, each expressing his confidence in riches to come. J. C. Nix from Beaumont, Texas, averred that he expected "to see this section among the greatest oil producers in America." D. B. Duskin of Oklahoma City "stated he had never seen a more favorable indication of securing oil in abundant quantity." All agreed that "Washington County will soon be the oil center of the southeast."

Sales of lots soared. Within the first three weeks more than 600 lots had been sold to purchasers within the county alone, not to mention other sales across the state. The list of local investors spanned the social and economic spectrum, ranging from plumbers and mechanics to physicians and attorneys. Prominent among them was the editor of the *Sandersville Progress*, whose confidence (and investment) assured frequent front-page news articles extolling the looming probability of hitherto unimagined prosperity.

Whether or not the promised pool of oil existed would have to wait on the drilling of the first well, but the mere possibility of its presence was enough to warrant enthusiasm. Commercial quantities of oil were first discovered in the United States near Titusville, Pennsylvania, in 1859. While widely used in commercial and industrial operations, it was in the second decade of the twentieth century that America's dependence on oil began to raise the specter of eventual shortages. Fueled by the widespread use of the internal combustion engine and the industrialization that accompanied

World War I, demand for petroleum products increased by 75 percent between 1913 and 1921. The United States was the world's leader in petroleum production, but by the early 1920s many geologists felt that production had reached its peak. A 1923 report by the Geologic Survey of Georgia noted that "the world's supply of crude petroleum is perhaps most generally placed as being sufficient to last sixteen to eighteen years." With depletion of the world's oil just over the horizon, a new discovery in Georgia could change the course of history.

The possibility of liquid black gold hidden beneath Georgia's red clay was not a new dream. Among the acts of the first post-Civil War Georgia General Assembly in 1865 to 1866 was the incorporation of several businesses whose charters included the specific purpose of searching for petroleum. The Trenton and Lookout Mountain Mining, Manufacturing and Petroleum Company, for example, was organized to explore for "iron, petroleum, coal, lead [and] other valuable minerals" in Dade County. The Madison Petroleum Company's stated purpose was to extract "oil and other fluids" by boring. The North Georgia Petroleum and Mining Company sought not only oil, but also copper, iron, gold, silver, lead, coal, and anything else of value that might lie beneath the earth's surface.

Northwest Georgia was the site of the first serious attempt to find petroleum in the state. The topography and geology of the area somewhat resembled that of the oil fields in Pennsylvania, making it ripe for exploration. In 1902, the Rome Petroleum and Iron Company drilled two wells to depths of 1,200 and 1,850 feet, respectively. Both were abandoned without signs of oil or gas. In 1905, Capt. A. F. Lucas, the famed discoverer of the Spindletop oil field near Beaumont, Texas, drilled a test well to a depth of 500 feet in southern Jefferson County, Georgia, some twenty-five miles to the east of the Middle Georgia Oil & Gas Company's discovery. Nothing was found. Two years later, another company extended the well to a depth of 1,143 feet before encountering bedrock. The first two decades of the new century saw a number of exploratory wells bored, almost all of them in the south of the state below the geologic Fall Line. Hints and suggestions of oil and gas were found, but there was nothing to indicate commercially significant quantities.

If the year 1919 seemed a propitious time to explore for oil from a national standpoint, it was even more of an ideal time in Georgia. Since the turn of the century, rural areas of the state had become relatively wealthy based on a slow but steady rise in cotton prices. With the onset of war in Europe and changes in national fiscal policy that effectively monetized cotton, the white fiber's value began a meteoric upward trend. By mid-1919, cotton that had sold for seven to eight cents a pound some four years earlier was now fetching more than thirty cents a pound, and over the coming year would continue to increase to nearly forty cents. Farmers of all stripes, from sharecroppers to plantation owners, seemed financially secure. The boom in the agricultural economy in turn produced a boom in the sale of consumer goods, enriching merchants and bankers. Those who were directly involved in cotton production had money to spare. Those who were not sought other investment opportunities that might yield such handsome returns. The offering of the Middle Georgia Oil & Gas Company could not have come at a better time.

The one dark cloud in the otherwise sunny outlook was the boll weevil. First appearing in south Georgia in 1915, the pest had spread rapidly throughout the state. The devastation that the weevil had wrought in Texas, Louisiana, Mississippi, and Alabama was well recognized, but somehow Georgia's overall cotton crop had been only slightly reduced by 1919, perhaps lulling some into the false assumption that the state would be spared. Capitalizing on the threat of the weevil, ads promoted the sure-fire investment in oil as a reasonable hedge against disaster, not to mention a sound way to sock away one's hard-earned profits. Thus, as the spring of 1919 melted into summer, sales of lots in the oil field continued at a frantic pace. Based on a well-organized regional sales campaign that extended even into South Carolina, the number of investors rose from hundreds to thousands, all confident of obscene profits from an oil well that had yet to be bored.

As the man on whose land the oil had been discovered, W. R. Beach emerged as the president and chief spokesman for the Middle Georgia Oil & Gas Company. "Roger" to his friends, he was already a well-known man about town. A native of Washington County, he spent his early years farming before moving to town to open a furniture store, helping "newly weds and old folks, too, enjoy the comforts of a well-furnished home, while making convenient payments." He later opened the Beach Garage ("with modern equipment and skilled mechanics in attendance") and acquired the local Buick dealership. Coupled with his furniture store was an undertaking business featuring "a full stock of caskets, coffins and burial robes" and offering service from the first automobile hearse in the county—a Buick, of course.

Meanwhile, he maintained his farm in the country, raising purebred hogs and offering milling services to the public.

Beach's leadership of a fledgling oil company would seem to be another worthy feat for an already accomplished businessman. And as a man of commerce, he had fared well initially, as did the company. Local property records reveal that the 500 acres he sold to the company for $60 per acre had for the most part been acquired some fifteen or so years earlier for a price of less than $5 per acre. With each acre now divided into approximately seventy lots for resale, the per-acre value rose to $2,450. Deducting the one-third set aside for the drilling fund, the company's gross profit margin was nearly $1,600 per acre, an astounding sum in an era when a small farmer's cash income might be only a few hundred dollars a year.

Such profits were sure to attract attention, if not envy. In mid-June, the Middle Georgia Oil & Gas Company's ad in the *Progress* ran under a bold headline reading, "Swindlers Are Running Riot Throughout the Nation Today." It reprinted the entire text of a current article from the *Atlanta Georgian* warning the public about "oil stock swindlers," while urging local, state and federal authorities to investigate all such enterprises. The writer opined, "An ordinary band of card sharks, openly playing their game in every city, would do less harm and steal infinitely less money than is stolen by these promoters of fake oil schemes." Not ones to let any publicity—good or bad—go to waste, the company's ad stated: "To the above we heartily say AMEN. The moral is, deal with your own people and help in the development of your own state." Reassurance was given that the company's directors "are men whose integrity is undoubted, who have been successful in business, [and] whose patriotism and loyalty are unquestioned."

While assurances might have calmed local investors, they did not deter the scrutiny of the state authorities. While the company's ads touted the positive reports of the two "prominent chemists" to whom Beach had submitted soil samples, they failed to mention a third report from Dr. Edgar Everhart, chemist for the Georgia Geologic Survey. In a February 1919 letter to Beach, he stated, "I have been unable to extract anything from the dirt you sent in.... The odor of gasoline or kerosene is strong, but no oily mass could be recognized by sight." Thinking the matter had been put to rest, little more was heard of it on the state level for some months. In late May, Dr. H. W. McCallie, the state geologist, received word that a company named the Middle Georgia Oil & Gas Company was "selling stock at Savannah and other points" and had been "advertising in a moving picture show in Atlanta." To his dismay, he discovered that the shares being sold were from the Beach property that had earlier been given a negative report by Dr. Everhart. He immediately set out to investigate the situation. After careful assessment of the evidence, McCallie issued a report to the state geological board "finding no evidence to support the belief" that oil would be found in commercial quantities in Washington County.

The news was prominently reported in the *Atlanta Constitution.* The *Sandersville Progress* ignored it, instead choosing to focus on the new discovery that a rod pushed down two or three feet at the site of the oil seepages (several more had been discovered by this time) would release a gas that would burn with "a blue flash flame from six to twelve inches high." "The boll weevil would be forgotten," the editor speculated. "Millions of dollars changing hands. Sandersville a town of 50,000 people and everybody happy." Sales of lots continued at a vigorous pace.

If common sense and a negative report from the state geologist could not slow the sales of shares, it was possible that state regulators might. In late August 1919, Secretary of State Guyton McLendon announced that he would be holding public hearings on the sale of oil well stock in the state. The matter had been brought to his attention by a local banker from Sandersville who questioned the appropriateness of lots being sold by the Middle Georgia Oil & Gas Company as collateral for loans. Interest in the enterprise seemed to have reached such a peak that investors were borrowing to purchase shares. Having examined the deed and an oil drilling agreement issued by the company to investors, McLendon pronounced them "carelessly prepared" and in direct conflict with each other. The investor was indeed given a title to the property, but it was anticipated that the company would retain physical possession of the land. The company, he concluded, was "boring with two augers. With one auger it would be boring into the pockets of...lot holders for profit to its own stockholders, which would be assured and would be very large.... With the other auger it would be boring into the ground for the benefit of...lot owners, if by chance, any oil should be discovered."

McLendon concluded that the company was, in fact, not selling lots or stock, but instead "certificates of participation," which were subject to regulation under state law. The company quickly agreed to comply with the state's requirements. The *Progress* presented the agreement in a positive light, hiding the story on an inside page, while the company's ads touted that the enterprise had passed the secretary of state's "rigid inspection." Now blessed by the government with an aura of legitimacy, additional salesmen were hired as purchases of the newly renamed "certificates" continued with renewed energy into the fall of 1919. Ads reminded potential investors of others who had become rich from oil investments: The two girls—mere library clerks in Texas—who had pooled their holdings of $100 and received back $1,200 each in a few months; a man named Rowe in "Homer," Louisiana, who a year earlier had been a driller but had taken in $7 million since May 1 of the year. In fact, the ads said, "Every dollar you invest in oil generally [means returns of] a hundred to one."

By mid-fall, the drilling rig had been ordered, a 110-foot-high derrick capable of drilling to a depth of 4,000 feet. It arrived in mid-January as the fever pitch of excitement increased. The company sponsored sales events with motivational speakers such as Frank Cragie of Atlanta, whose oratory mimicked that of an old-fashioned tent revival, questioning how anyone could be so stupid as to not invest in the as-yet-unproven oil well. How could one go wrong? "If you lose, you haven't lost a bit more than if you bought a hog that died." But, "You may hit it rich, and to hit it rich in the oil game means—RICH!" Sales of certificates reached a record thousand units a week.

In early March 1920 the drilling finally got under way, with the well christened the "Lillian B. No. 1" in honor of the wife of one of the company's directors. The rig—according to newspaper reports—was capable of drilling some 40 to 50 feet a day through the hardest rock. Under normal circumstances it was estimated that the well would progress at about 400 feet a week, with a depth of "several thousand feet" in a matter of weeks. A celebratory barbecue (and sales event) was held at the local resort of Brooks Springs, attracting "great crowds of prominent visitors from various sections of the state."

Problems with the well began almost immediately. Within a matter of weeks, drilling stopped due to a shortage of well casing that had to be ordered from Texas and Louisiana. A surprise discovery was the existence of extensive beds of white clay, first identified as Fuller's earth but later recognized as kaolin. It was speculated that the clay might sell for as much as twelve dollars a ton and have uses in crockery and paper manufacturing, as well as providing body for axle grease. The true significance of this finding would come later, for the moment overshadowed by oil fever.

By mid-May, the casing had arrived. The well had reached a depth of 200 feet. It was now estimated that drilling would proceed at a rate of a hundred feet a day. The oil pool was predicted to lie at a depth between 1,500 and 2,000 feet. Some three months later the well had reached a depth of only 400 feet. The company made various excuses about encountering quicksand and the necessity of reinforcing the derrick because of the heavy casing.

While the company's salesmen continued to sell interests in the Washington County lots, a quiet search for other sites had been underway. In May 1920, Roger Beach signed an agreement to acquire the right to drill on 5,000 acres of oil leases in Jeff Davis County, near Hazlehurst in south Georgia. The company was banking on completing a failed oil exploration project that had sunk a well some 900 feet in 1908. The original well had supposedly shown positive signs of oil before the project was scuttled due to an alleged disagreement among the owners. The main evidence for oil's presence was the memory of one of the drillers, John A. Chromartie. While Mr. Chromartie was quite specific in his memory of the details of the well, all the data, including the well log and analysis of specimens, had been destroyed in a fire some years earlier.

Once again, the pattern repeated itself. In June 1920, the *Hazlehurst News* reported that a group of prominent businessmen would be drilling for oil in the local area. The proposed site had been inspected by "several experienced oil men," who pronounced the area "truly and really the best prospect for finding oil that Georgia has yet offered." The company was said to be "backed by a million dollars." A limited number of shares would be made available for purchase. Company ads proudly displayed affidavits of acknowledgement—if not support—from a "Geologist of National Reputation" (who just happened to be one of the men from whom the leases were obtained) as well as the state geologist and the secretary of state. This well was to be christened "The Lillian B. No. 2."

On September 16, 1920, drilling began under the direction of the same man who had been in charge of the Washington County well. In a cleverly worded press release carried as news in the *Macon Telegraph* the next day, Middle Georgia Oil & Gas Company president W. R. Beach announced that "oil has been struck in Georgia." It was unclear if he was referring to the alleged findings of the 1908 well or the results of a few hours drilling of the Lillian B. No. 2.

While the drilling crews at the two wells bored into the earth and the company's salesmen continued to offer opportunities for savvy investors to "get in on the ground floor," other forces were at work. The prolonged period of prosperity that had accompanied the World War I era was grinding to an abrupt halt and was to be followed by a relatively brief but severe recession. Inflation, which had reached record levels in the 1916 to 1920 era, rapidly turned to deflation. The agricultural sector of the American economy was most severely affected, ushering in years of falling commodity prices and farm foreclosures. Cotton prices, which had stayed above thirty cents a pound since mid-1919, reached a peak of nearly thirty-eight cents a pound during the summer of 1920. But, as the so-called Great Recession took hold, the price of cotton plummeted, closing the year at less than twelve cents a pound and reaching a low point of less than ten cents by mid-1921. When the corrosive effect of inflation was factored in, the true worth of cotton was less than six cents a pound[84], a level not seen in decades.

Farmers who had taken on debt to expand their cotton operations were suddenly unable to meet their financial obligations. Banks and merchants who had extended credit faced failure. The boll weevil now struck with full force, drastically reducing the state's cotton crop in 1921 and the years that followed. An investment in an unproven oil venture, which might have at one time seemed an affordable bit of speculation, now was seen as the risky investment that it was and always had been.

Despite whatever financial plight the people of the state might have been facing—or perhaps because of it—sales of the company's certificates continued. An October 1920 ad boasted of continued sales of a thousand lots a week, while warning that the opportunity could be closed any day. The ad speculated that each $35 investment could net an annual $730 return to investors, provided, of course, the wells struck oil.

By December, the company admitted the Lillian B. No.1—now referred to fondly as "The Old Mother"—has "had her troubles." Drilling had stopped at 426 feet, approximately where it had been in September. This was attributed to quicksand, a broken cable, and "white lightning." But the problem had now been solved. A double crew had been assigned and "white

[84] In 1916 dollars.

lightning is barred from the camp." Meanwhile the Lillian B. No. 2 was said to be making "good progress." In what should have been a sign of things to come, the sales manager announced that he had moved back to Sandersville, ostensibly to be closer to the well. The Atlanta office had been closed.

In January 1921, a news item noted an oil strike was expected in "a matter of days." In February, it could be "almost any day." The Lillian B. No. 1 was said to be at 492 feet. One of the chemists who had endorsed the well initially now found "a small quantity of Petroleum oil" in a test sample. Meanwhile, in Jeff Davis County, the Lillian B. No. 2 was at 1,150 feet depth. Even at this late date, the ads explained, it was still possible to get in "on the ground floor." The editor of the *Sandersville Progress*, ever hopeful, speculated, "When the drill reaches the expected gusher there will be a stampede of people from everywhere to this point and there will be such a development in business that no one can predict how many millionaires will be created by the dormant wealth of Washington County which has been hidden under the ground all of these years." His words would prove prophetic, but in ways he could not have anticipated.

In February 1921, the company's ads abruptly stopped as the local economy began to feel the full brunt of the recession. An occasional news item was still seen, but the mood was far more subdued. In a front-page letter to the *Progress* published in late March, Roger Beach continued to express optimism about the Jeff Davis County well, now at 1,400 feet, reaching 1,735 feet by mid-July. No mention was made of Washington County's Lillian B. No. 1.

On September 7, 1921, the *Progress* published without comment a "self-explanatory" letter from W. R. Beach to the patrons of the Middle Georgia Oil & Gas Company. "We very much regret to inform you...," the letter began, going on to say that drilling operations had been suspended at both well sites citing the "financial depression" as well as "a malaria epidemic among our drilling crew." According to records filed with the state, the Washington County well had reached a depth of 605 feet before striking bedrock. The Jeff Davis County well achieved a depth of 1,975 feet. Neither found any significant evidence of oil or gas.

As the year 1921 came to a close, much of the nation was emerging from the severe effects of the recession, soon to enter a phase of national prosperity fondly remembered as the Roaring Twenties. In rural Georgia and in much of the agricultural South, however, the Great Recession of

1920 to 1921 merged almost seamlessly into what would later be known as the Great Depression of the 1930s. Washington County, for example, a prosperous agricultural community in 1920, would see nine of its eleven banks fail by the end of the decade that followed. Businesses failed, fortunes were lost. With the end of the Middle Georgia Oil & Gas Company's operations, W. R. Beach moved to Florida, his name and accomplishments in Washington County seemingly forgotten with time. Others suffered a more public exit. Lake B. Holt, the banker, was at the center of a spectacular series of bank failures in the late 1920s, eventually being convicted on multiple charges of fraud, conspiracy, and embezzlement and sentenced to federal prison.

The search for oil and gas in Georgia continued sporadically over the following decades. From 1902 through the mid-1980s somewhat fewer than 200 exploratory wells were drilled, none of them finding significant quantities of petroleum or natural gas. The last burst of exploration took place in the 1980s. Five additional oil wells were drilled in Washington County, one of them reaching a depth of nearly 10,000 feet. A well drilled by Chevron in Jeff Davis County plunged 11,470 feet, the deepest ever drilled in the state. As predicted by State Geologist McCallie in 1919, there was no oil. There never had been.

In an ironic twist of events, the presence of the vast beds of kaolin clay revealed by the Lillian B. No. 1 led to Washington County emerging as the geographic center of a multi-billion-dollar mining industry in the mid- to late years of the twentieth century. The "dormant wealth of Washington County which has been hidden under the ground all of these years" did indeed produce many millionaires, not from the black gold of oil, but from the white gold of the nation's largest and purest beds of kaolin clays. By the 1980s, the area had become the world's leading producer of kaolin, accounting for two-thirds of the total value of Georgia's mineral production and 90 percent of the nation's kaolin exports.

Today, the site of the Middle Georgia Oil & Gas Company's Washington County well has disappeared, the landscape having been totally reshaped by extensive strip mining of kaolin. Along the sides of the unpaved country road where hordes of investors once flocked to see the Lillian B. No. 1 are lakes and rolling pine-covered hills, the remains of reclaimed mining pits. Few if any remember the failed dream of hidden riches nearly a century earlier.

SOURCES AND RESOURCES

The story of the Middle Georgia Oil & Gas Company was carried in contemporary newspapers of the day, especially the *Sandersville* (Georgia) *Progress*. For those interested in further reading on the subject, a number of publications of the Georgia Geologic Survey provide data on the search for petroleum in the state over the years. There has never been confirmed evidence of economically significant oil deposits within the land area of Georgia.

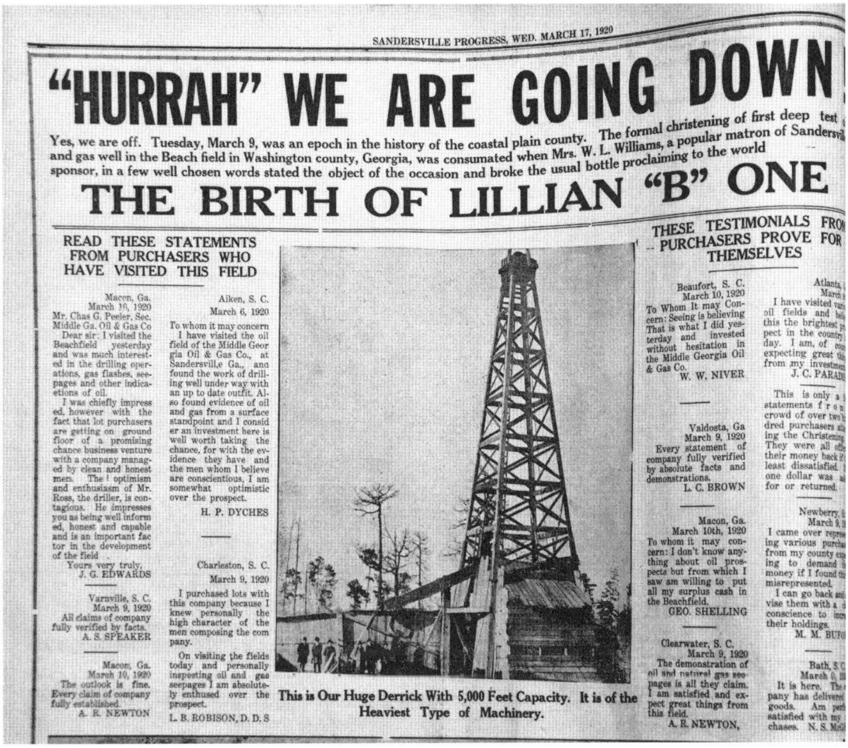

SANDERSVILLE PROGRESS, WED. MARCH 17, 1920

"HURRAH" WE ARE GOING DOWN

Yes, we are off. Tuesday, March 9, was an epoch in the history of the coastal plain county. The formal christening of first deep test and gas well in the Beach field in Washington county, Georgia, was consumated when Mrs. W. L. Williams, a popular matron of Sandersvi sponsor, in a few well chosen words stated the object of the occasion and broke the usual bottle proclaiming to the world

THE BIRTH OF LILLIAN "B" ONE

READ THESE STATEMENTS FROM PURCHASERS WHO HAVE VISITED THIS FIELD

Macon, Ga.
March 10, 1920
Mr. Chas G. Peeler, Sec.
Middle Ga. Oil & Gas Co

Dear sir: I visited the Beachfield yesterday and was much interested in the drilling operations, gas flashes, seepages and other indicaetions of oil.

I was chiefly impressed, however with the fact that lot purchasers are getting on ground floor of a promising chance business venture with a company managed by clean and honest men. The ! optimism and enthusiasm of Mr. Ross, the driller, is contagious. He impresses you as being well informed, honest and capable and is an important factor in the development of the field .

Yours very truly,
J. G. EDWARDS

Varnville, S. C.
March 9, 1920
All claims of company fully verified by facts.
A. S. SPEAKER

Macon, Ga.
March 10, 1920
The outlook is fine. Every claim of company fully established.
A. R. NEWTON

Aiken, S. C.
March 6, 1920

To whom it may concern

I have visited the oil field of the Middle Georgia Oil & Gas Co., at Sandersvill,e Ga., ana found the work of drilling well under way with an up to date outfit. Also found evidence of oil and gas from a surface standpoint and I consider an investment here is well worth taking the chance, for with the evidence they have and the men whom I believe are conscientious, I am somewhat optimistic over the prospect.

H. P. DYCHES

Charleston, S. C.
March 9, 1920

I purchased lots with this company because I knew personally the high character of the men composing the company.

On visiting the fields today and personally inspecting oil and gas seepages I am absolutely enthused over the prospect.

L. B. ROBISON, D. D. S

This is Our Huge Derrick With 5,000 Feet Capacity. It is of the Heaviest Type of Machinery.

THESE TESTIMONIALS FRO PURCHASERS PROVE FOR THEMSELVES

Beaufort, S. C.
March 10, 1920
To Whom It may Concern: Seeing is believing That is what I did yesterday and invested without hesitation in the Middle Georgia Oil & Gas Co.
W. W. NIVER

Valdosta, Ga
March 9, 1920
Every statement of company fully verified by absolute facts and demonstrations.
L. C. BROWN

Macon, Ga.
March 10th, 1920
To whom it may concern: I don't know anything about oil prospects but from which I saw am willing to put all my surplus cash in the Beachfield.
GEO. SHELLING

Clearwater, S. C.
March 9, 1920
The demonstration of oil and natural gas seepages is all they claim. I am satisfied and expect great things from this field.
A. R. NEWTON,

Atlanta,
March
I have visited va oil fields and bel this the brightest p pect in the country day. I am, of co expecting great th from my investme
J. C. PARAD

This is only a statements from crowd of over two dred purchasers at ing the Christening They were all off their money back if least dissatisfied. one dollar was a for or returned.

Newberry,
March 9,
I came over repre ing various purcha from my county ex ing to demand money if I found th misrepresented.
I can go back an vise them with a conscience to incr their holdings.
M. M. BUF

Bath, S. C
March
It is here. The pany has delivere goods. Am per satisfied with my chases. N. S. Mc

The latter part of the second decade of the twentieth century was a time new wealth for many Georgians, especially those profiting from the boom in cotton prices. The Middle Georgia Oil and Gas Company saw a way to relieve many gullible investors of their money. The first well was begun in 1920 based on dubious evidence of a vast underground pool of oil.

Sandersville Progress, 1920

Based on the success of investors attracted to its first well in Washington County, the Middle Georgia Oil and Gas Company started a second well in Jeff Davis County, Georgia. Neither well ever produced any objective evidence of oil.

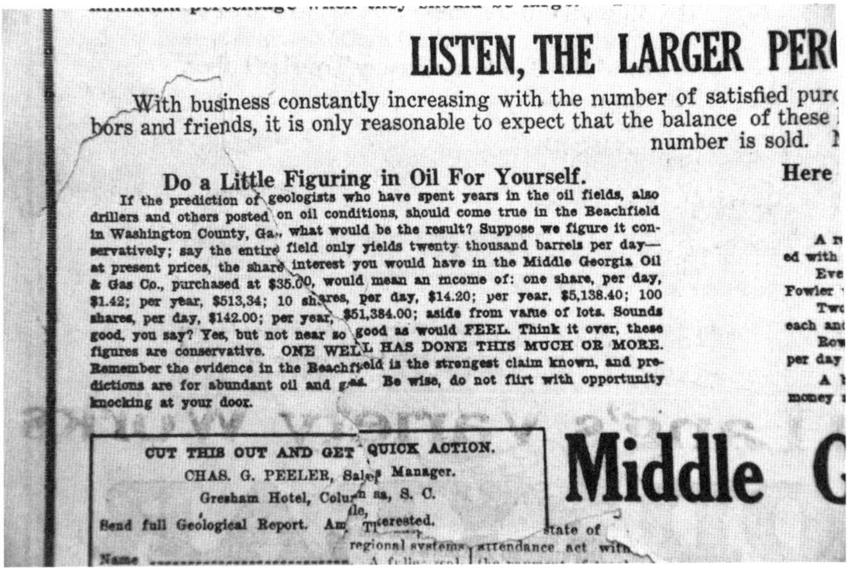

LISTEN, THE LARGER PER

With business constantly increasing with the number of satisfied pur
bors and friends, it is only reasonable to expect that the balance of these
number is sold.

Do a Little Figuring in Oil For Yourself.

If the prediction of geologists who have spent years in the oil fields, also drillers and others posted on oil conditions, should come true in the Beachfield in Washington County, Ga., what would be the result? Suppose we figure it conservatively; say the entire field only yields twenty thousand barrels per day—at present prices, the share interest you would have in the Middle Georgia Oil & Gas Co., purchased at $35.00, would mean an income of: one share, per day, $1.42; per year, $513,34; 10 shares, per day, $14.20; per year, $5,138.40; 100 shares, per day, $142.00; per year, $51,384.00; aside from value of lots. Sounds good, you say? Yes, but not near so good as would FEEL. Think it over, these figures are conservative. ONE WELL HAS DONE THIS MUCH OR MORE. Remember the evidence in the Beachfield is the strongest claim known, and predictions are for abundant oil and gas. Be wise, do not flirt with opportunity knocking at your door.

CUT THIS OUT AND GET QUICK ACTION.
CHAS. G. PEELER, Sales Manager.
Gresham Hotel, Columbia, S. C.
Send full Geological Report. Am Interested.
Name

Here

Middle

In an era when the national per capita income was less than $700 per year, ads like this from the Middle Georgia Oil and Gas company suggested that an investment of a mere $35 could yield as much as $51,384 annually. Those behind the scheme are estimated to have made millions through slick promotion.

Sandersville Progress, 1920

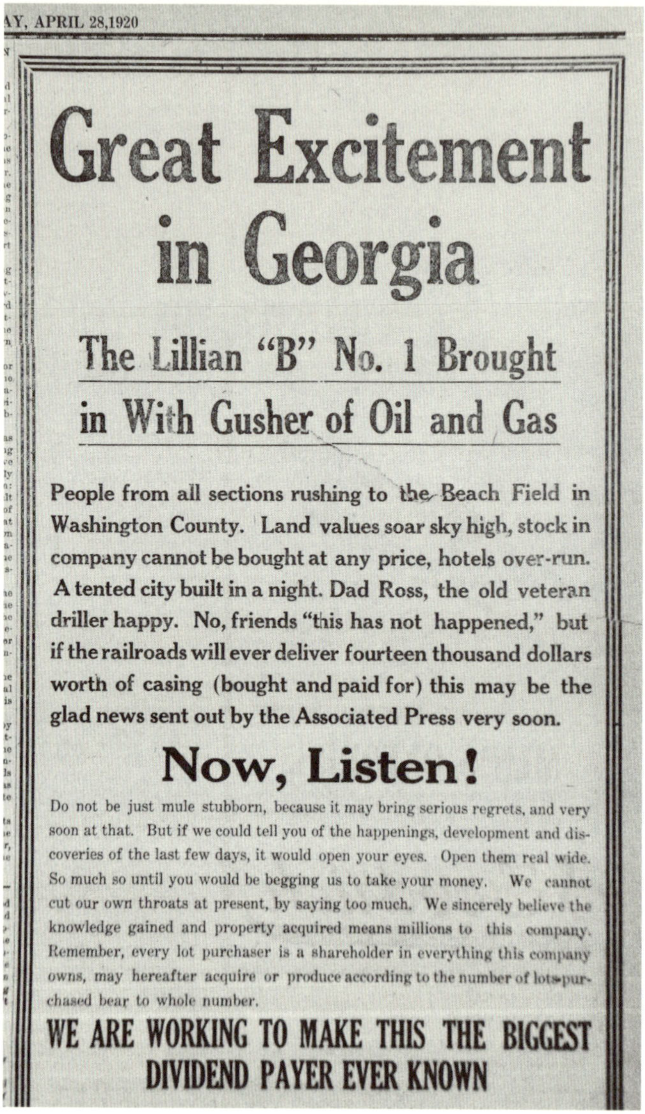

AY, APRIL 28,1920

Great Excitement in Georgia

The Lillian "B" No. 1 Brought in With Gusher of Oil and Gas

People from all sections rushing to the Beach Field in Washington County. Land values soar sky high, stock in company cannot be bought at any price, hotels over-run. A tented city built in a night. Dad Ross, the old veteran driller happy. No, friends "this has not happened," but if the railroads will ever deliver fourteen thousand dollars worth of casing (bought and paid for) this may be the glad news sent out by the Associated Press very soon.

Now, Listen!

Do not be just mule stubborn, because it may bring serious regrets, and very soon at that. But if we could tell you of the happenings, development and discoveries of the last few days, it would open your eyes. Open them real wide. So much so until you would be begging us to take your money. We cannot cut our own throats at present, by saying too much. We sincerely believe the knowledge gained and property acquired means millions to this company. Remember, every lot purchaser is a shareholder in everything this company owns, may hereafter acquire or produce according to the number of lots purchased bear to whole number.

WE ARE WORKING TO MAKE THIS THE BIGGEST DIVIDEND PAYER EVER KNOWN

The Middle Georgia Oil and Gas Company's ads, which appeared in newspapers across the South, fueled interest and sales by speculation as to what *might* happen, and how disappointed folks would be if they failed to invest. In the end, the only ones who profited were those who created and promoted the scam.

Sandersville Progress, 1920

CHAPTER 13

A KILLING ON RING JAW BLUFF

A visitor standing on the front lawn of the Methodist Church in the east-central Georgia town of Sandersville in late February 1925 might have thought this a prosperous community, one with both a distinguished history and a bright future. The church, crafted of red brick with white marble accents and a suitable number of stained-glass windows, faced the main east-west highway, appropriately named Church Street, but as yet unpaved. Directly across the street stood a simple white frame house on whose porch the body of a dead Confederate cavalryman had lain, killed in a skirmish during Sherman's March to the Sea in November 1864.

A few hundred feet to the west of the church, a small forest of white marble monuments sprouted from the Old City Cemetery, their sheer quantity and ornateness confirming the fact that Sandersville had produced a significant number of citizens who felt their wealth should be on display long after having shed their mortal coils. Just inside the cemetery entrance that faced the church, two family plots lay on either side of the wagon path. To the left, Rawlings. To the right, Tarbutton. A freshly covered grave in the Tarbutton plot awaited its permanent tombstone.

A block to the east, the spire of the First Baptist Church loomed over the intersection of Church and Harris streets, the latter being the local name for the main north-south highway through the town. On the opposite side of the intersection, a large white Victorian house dominated the crossroads, its location and size a testament to the wealth of its owner. A broad covered porch lined with turned balusters was shaded from the harsh afternoon sun by two huge magnolia trees. The ornate door opened into a wide hall lined with raised-panel walnut, its glass window etched with the initials "CGR" for Charles Graves Rawlings, the home's owner. It was in this home that on the night of February 18, 1925, Rawlings was arrested for the murder of his first cousin, George Augustus Tarbutton.

By any measure, Charles Rawlings was a wealthy man. Known as "C. G." to his business associates and "Charlie" to his friends and family, he was nearly seven years old when Sandersville felt the scorched-earth wrath of Sherman's army, the punishment being worse because of casualties suffered while securing the town. He was the youngest of seven children born to Fredrick Cullen Rawlings and Susan Malone Tarbutton. The forebears of each family had moved to Washington County around the first decade of the nineteenth century, settling near the crossroads town that had grown up around Saunders's Store, later known (and misspelled) as Sandersville.

The Rawlings were an accomplished and successful family. Charlie's oldest brother, William, graduated with highest honors from Emory College before studying medicine in Europe and achieving national fame as a surgeon. Another brother, "B. T." (for Benjamin Tarbutton), was a prominent attorney, judge, and legislator.[85] And with time, Charlie followed in their footsteps. A 1912 book containing the biographies of "eminent men" refers to him as "one of the most prominent and successful businessmen" in his part of the state.

The years following the Civil War were ones of opportunity for a man willing to work hard and take risks. Perhaps overshadowed by the achievements of his older brothers in medicine and law, Charlie poured his efforts into business. He was successful far beyond the dreams of most men. The 1870s and the decades that followed were ones of dramatic growth in what are today rural areas of Georgia. Rawlings began, modestly enough, in the livery business, stabling the horses and mules that provided transportation and power for agriculture. He imported mules and soon branched into the lucrative business of supplying farmers with their fertilizer and other agricultural needs.

Washington County, of which Sandersville is the county seat, sits astride the geologic Fall Line. In the northern part of the county, the land is gently rolling. The red clay hills topped by poor sandy soil are ideal for timber production. To the south, on the northern edge of the Coastal Plain, the topography is more suited to agriculture, with vast flat fields separated by meandering streams and wide river swamps. In the late nineteenth century, the main Central of Georgia rail line between Atlanta and Savannah split the county, and other short-line railroads connecting to points north and

[85] The author's grandfather.

south converged on the railroad town of Tennille, three miles south of Sandersville. Cheap labor, good transportation, a long growing season, and abundant natural resources of land, timber, and water led to fortunes made in agriculture and manufacturing and the support services they required.

Rawlings's businesses thrived. A November 1899 issue of the Sandersville *Progress* noted he was selling 1,500 to 2,000 mules per year, or thirty to forty per week. By the first decades of the new century, Rawlings reputedly owned up to 40,000 acres of land plus livery stables and farm supply stores, a bank, a hotel, and a substantial interest in the Sandersville Railroad, a short-line, wide-gauge track that leased its rolling stock from the Central of Georgia but boasted of owning one locomotive and one passenger car. In 1888, he married Tallulah Perkins, the eighteen-year-old daughter of a well-respected lumberman. Over the next eighteen years she provided him with four children.

Because the primary source of his wealth was agriculture, the majority of Rawlings's land holdings were to the south of Sandersville in Johnson County. Besides being in the agricultural supply business, his personal farm operations took on a huge scale. A 1917 *Progress* article noted that his farms had produced more than 3,000 bales of cotton that year.[86] While quite profitable in good times, his direct involvement in such large-scale farming and lack of greater investment diversification would later pose a threat to his economic survival.

George Augustus Tarbutton, "Gus" to his friends and family, was Charlie Rawlings's first cousin, born in 1875, the third child and second son of Susan Tarbutton Rawlings's brother. Gus's father died when he was five, followed by his mother two years later. At age fourteen, he came to live with his Aunt Soonie and Uncle Fred, Charlie's parents. His cousin Charlie, newly married and rising in the world of business, was appointed his legal guardian, later assuming the role of mentor and surrogate older brother. As court proceedings would later reveal, Charlie managed Gus's small inher-

---

[86] Assuming a yield of a half bale per acre, this would suggest that he had at least 6,000 acres in cotton alone. In those days, one plowman and a mule could cultivate 30 acres. This would imply that he may have had as many as 200 plowmen. Again, assuming one overseer per ten plowmen, he might have employed as many as 20 overseers.

itance, tried to keep him out of trouble, and helped him get started in farming once he'd reached manhood.

Despite the differences in their ages, both men's lives took strangely parallel courses. Both lost brothers to violence in which they played a role. On July 15, 1893, Charlie's brother Fred died in a shootout on Sandersville's City Square, but not before killing his opponent, the brother of his sister's husband. The root cause of the fight seemed to be a minor land dispute between Charlie and his brother-in-law, then mayor of the city. The resulting lawsuit had managed to find its way to the Georgia Supreme Court and in late 1892 had been decided in favor of the mayor. Marital ties notwithstanding, the case had created bad blood between the two families. Fred was overheard to say disparaging remarks about the mayor and was confronted by the mayor's brother. They exchanged blows, then gunfire, each dying within minutes of being shot.

The exact details of the shootings were never clearly established, but Charlie and two other Rawlings cousins were observed on the scene "with weapons in their hands" immediately after the shooting. They were arrested, but in deference to his prominence in the community, Charlie was allowed to remain at his home under guard. A coroner's jury soon found that "Charles G. Rawlings only acted as a peacemaker." He was never formally charged with any crime.

The events that led to the death of Gus Tarbutton's older brother, Herschel, were also related to a land dispute. A man named Young had sold a 600-acre tract of land to J. Letcher Tyre, a "prominent Laurens County lumberman," with payments to be made in installments. According to Young, Tyre failed to make payments in a timely manner and was thus in default. Young then sold the land to Herschel Tarbutton of Sandersville. Tyre, meanwhile, maintained he had a superior claim to the land and began logging operations. Gus Tarbutton, apparently acting on behalf of his brother, had Tyre's men arrested. The matter was pending in court in the fall of 1906 when word reached the Tarbutton brothers that Tyre was preparing to resume cutting on the land. Accompanied by Gus's brother-in-law, Joe Fluker, they rode on horseback to the property to confront Tyre and his men.

Tyre had been squirrel hunting and was carrying a shotgun. He exchanged words with Herschel, who shot him in the abdomen with a .44 caliber pistol. Tyre fired back, striking Tarbutton in the right eye. According to a newspaper report, Gus and Joe Fluker also fired their pistols, but it was the shots exchanged between Herschel and Tyre that proved fatal. Tyre died within a matter of hours, but not before implicating the Tarbuttons and Fluker to witnesses in a dying declaration. Herschel died the next day at the Rawlings Sanitarium in Sandersville, declaring he had been the first to be shot.

Gus Tarbutton and Joe Fluker were arrested in Sandersville on a charge of murder and taken to Dublin to stand trial in Laurens County. They were granted bail and the trial scheduled for February 1907. Charlie Rawlings, stepping in to assist his cousin, helped assemble "perhaps the greatest league of defense attorneys ever to appear in a Laurens County courtroom." The star among them was the popular young Thomas W. Hardwick, congressman from Georgia's 10th District and future governor and United States senator. The irony of this choice would become evident later.

The trial began with much legal wrangling. A request from the defense for a continuance was granted on multiple grounds, including a question of exactly where the homicide had occurred. Tarbutton and Fluker were under indictment in Laurens County, but the exact line demarking the boundary with Johnson County had never been clearly established.

Governor J. M. Terrell appointed an Atlanta civil engineer to mark the county line based on the original legislative act of 1857. In doing so, it was discovered that Tyre was in fact killed in Johnson County, effectively nullifying the Laurens County indictment. The venue was thus moved to what could only be considered a friendlier political environment, and the case was never brought to trial.

In spite of various bumps in the economic road, the half century marked by the end of the First World War was generally one of growth and prosperity in Georgia. This era came to a sudden and crashing halt with the economic recession of 1920 to 1921. Perhaps little remembered because of the lengthier Great Depression that began less than a decade later, it delivered a body blow to the agrarian economy of the South. The most striking event was deflation, evidenced by a 37 percent drop in wholesale prices over the course of a year, the sharpest decline since the American Revolution nearly a century and a half earlier. The proximate causes were economic changes brought on by the end of the Great War, but the local result was a dramatic decline in prices paid for agricultural commodities and a near collapse of the farm economy.

As if the deflationary recession were not enough, the boll weevil first appeared in south Georgia in 1915, spreading rapidly through cotton-producing areas of the state. From a high 2.8 million bales produced in Georgia the year before, the yield fell rapidly to a low of only 600,000 bales in 1923. By January 1925, the Sandersville *Progress* noted things had scarcely improved "as farming has become too risky [since] the boll weevil appeared to eat up all the profits of the cotton crop." They opined hopefully that the arrival of a new shipment of mules signaled an upturn in the farm outlook.

While neither of these events could have been reliably predicted, both must have had devastating effects on the fortunes of Charlie Rawlings. In addition, there were other events whose very nature must also have affected him deeply. Two of his three daughters had married and moved away. His mother, Susan, who was living in his home after the death of his father, died at the age of 91 in 1919. His brother B. T. died of cancer in November 1921, followed two weeks later by the unexpected death of Charlie's fifty-one-year-old wife. The details of her apparent sudden fatal illness are unclear. Rather than listing a cause of death, the certificate—signed by a physician who was in practice with Charlie's brother—states, "Was called Dec. 10, 7:30 PM. Found her dying. She expired in a few minutes."

The friends, enemies, and contemporaries of Charlie Rawlings are no longer here to give the interested reader their opinion of him as a man, but there were persistent rumors of marital infidelity and tales of suspicious fires that destroyed well-insured properties. None of these can be confirmed with accuracy. As of February 1925, Rawlings had been a highly successful businessman with a career of nearly a half century behind him. The events that followed may have been driven by desperation, but may also have reflected Rawlings's underlying character. The act that subsequently thrust his name onto the front pages of newspapers statewide so altered perceptions of him that statements about his character and personality are often tinged with prejudice.

For a more objective viewpoint, a reader might consider a Georgia Supreme Court decision issued more than a decade earlier. In 1908, Rawlings was approached by a family of three siblings who owed him, and others, debts they were unable to pay. They owned two tracts of property worth several thousand dollars and asked him to loan them money to pay their obligations, using the land as collateral. According to the court, they were "unlearned in legal matters" and looked to Rawlings for help with their situation. "He professed great friendship for [them] on account of his friendship for their father, and said that he would treat them fairly and properly in the matter." He did, however, insist on an absolute deed to the property, which he prepared and they signed.

Two years later, the three discovered that Rawlings claimed to be the owner of their land. They realized they had been tricked into signing a deed confirming the fact, giving him full title to the property for a mere fraction of its true value. The siblings offered to pay him back, but Rawlings refused, stating he was now the rightful owner. They sued and eventually the case was appealed to the Supreme Court, who ruled against Rawlings on procedural issues. Charlie Rawlings may have grown wealthy through his business dealings, but he was clearly willing to ignore ethical considerations if the outcome was to his benefit.

The year 1924 ended with a bleak outlook. The economic engines that had provided steady growth over the prior decades had weakened, and future prospects were uncertain at best. Local newspapers speculated that a proposed road project might bring travelers and new commerce. One bright spot reported by the *Progress* in late December was the optioning by a New York corporation of 2,000 acres in Wilkinson County for the mining of "bauxite" to be used in the production of crockery. As an entrepreneur, as well as one of the largest landowners in several counties, Charlie Rawlings no doubt sensed a possible solution to his current financial situation. He had test pits dug on several of his farms, focusing on those in Johnson County adjacent to the Oconee River.

February 17, 1925, was warm for the season, with temperatures rising to the mid-60s despite overcast skies and intermittent rain. The events of nearly two decades earlier now forgotten, Gus Tarbutton had risen to prominence as a wealthy farmer closely associated in his business dealings with his older cousin, Charlie. So it came as a shock when word reached town near dusk that day that Gus had been killed in a horrific accident at Ring Jaw Bluff on the Oconee River. The initial accounts reported that toward the latter part of the afternoon, Charlie and his driver, accompanied by Rawlings's overseer, J. J. Tanner, picked up Tarbutton and drove to the Page Place, a large tract on the river nominally owned by the firm of Tarbutton & Rawlings. Test pits had been dug looking for bauxite, and Charlie and Gus wanted to see what they had found.

They were not alone in the woods. A man named Alexander who was looking at some timber met them and exchanged a few words with the three men before heading back to his vehicle. A few moments later, he heard a shotgun blast, but thought little of it as it was hunting season. The story emerged that the three men had just arrived at the Bluff and were going down a slight incline toward the river. As was his custom when walking in the woods, Tanner carried a double-barreled hammerless shotgun to shoot snakes or other varmints. Apparently tripping on the steep bank, he pitched forward and the gun discharged, striking Tarbutton squarely in the back of his head, killing him instantly. Helped by Rawlings's chauffeur, who was waiting with the car, the men loaded the body in the back of Rawlings's vehicle and drove to Tarbutton's house to report the tragedy.

Widowed for more than a year, Gus Tarbutton shared a home with his only surviving offspring, his twenty-three-year-old son, Fluker. As friends began to gather, Fluker expressed belief that the so-called accident had been staged and, in fact, his father had been killed in cold blood. He sought out the sheriff and demanded an inquiry.

The following morning, the county coroner assembled a jury and convened an inquest. Sworn statements were heard, with members of the jury traveling to Ring Jaw Bluff, where measurements were made in an attempt to corroborate the story given by Tanner and Rawlings. The news of the death of a wealthy farmer while in the company of an even wealthier banker made front-page headlines across the state. The *Atlanta Constitution* reported, "Rawlings told an impressive and plausible story at the inquest," not failing to mention he was a "member of one of the most prominent families...in middle Georgia," in case any readers might have doubts about the significance of the story.

While Gus Tarbutton's death might have on the surface appeared to be accidental, the jury also heard testimony that Rawlings was in a financial bind and stood to benefit from several large insurance policies taken out on his cousin. Furthermore, Rawlings testified Tarbutton, "considered one of the wealthiest landowners in the county, did not own an acre of property when he died, and in fact, never had. He (Rawlings) owned it all."

The jury reached the conclusion that Gus Tarbutton's death was the result of willful homicide and gave the recommendation that Rawlings and Tanner be taken into custody on a charge of murder. On the night of February 18th, Rawlings was arrested at his home in Sandersville. J. J. Tanner and two blacks, the latter charged as material witnesses, were arrested in Wrightsville. As befitting his status, Rawlings was held under guard in a hotel while the other three were locked up in the Johnson County jail.

The populace and local press rapidly took sides. The *Wrightsville Headlight*, clearly supporting the murder-conspiracy theory against a local citizen, wondered, "Was Gus Tarbutton killed in cold blood by accident, or was it a case of wanton murder?" The *Sandersville Progress*, meanwhile, was supportive of Rawlings, declaring with a headline that "Rawlings Wants Early Hearing—'I Am Innocent' He Tells Reporters." The article further asserted, "[He] is expected to be exonerated on any connection with the horrible crime which is charged against him."

Not missing an opportunity to defend the honor of a wealthy local citizen, the *Progress* reported that Rawlings "stated that his heart was crushed because he was charged with planning the death of a man who had almost been a son to him." Referring to the Tyre murder years earlier, he continued, "Why, I raised the boy. I started him off in life. I loved him as my own child and I have stood by him in fair weather and foul. I spent thousands of dollars on him when he was on trial for murder. Tarbutton knew that in my heart I never had anything but the highest and best feeling for him."

A commitment hearing was scheduled for February 27th. With local sentiment in Wrightsville running strongly against Rawlings, he was moved from the comfort of a local hotel to the county jail in Swainsboro, some twenty-six miles distant. Unaccompanied by guards, the local sheriff drove him there in his personal vehicle, where he was kept under loose guard pending the hearing.

As the day for the hearing approached, rumors of a secret witness to the crime began to circulate in Wrightsville. "A thousand people" were expected to attend. The site of the killing became a popular tourist spot. The *Headlight* reported that "Great streams of the populace from five counties...pushed their way to the banks of the Oconee [creating] a beaten path and open route to this dismal, secluded spot that marked the fate of Johnson's beloved citizen." There were rumors of lynch mobs, which required the sheriff to post extra guards at the jail. Despite all this, the *Headlight* assured readers, "No color is attempted or desired in this story, one way or the other, and our people are and have been cool and level-headed all the while regardless of the wild reports to the contrary since the tragic death of Mr. Tarbutton."

The Johnson County solicitor, Fred Kea, decided to hold separate commitment hearings, Rawlings first, then Tanner. Rawlings's defense team was composed of seven of the best lawyers money could buy, led by Georgia's venerable ex-senator and ex-governor Thomas W. Hardwick, the same man who two decades earlier had defended Tarbutton against his own charge of murder. Three local justices of the peace presided over the spectacle, attended by "hundreds" of curious townsfolk. Hal Hooks, Rawlings's chauffeur, was the first witness, recounting how he heard the shot, then rushed to the scene to find his employer "crying and wringing his hands" over Tarbutton's body. The *Sandersville Progress*, ever supportive, reported "During Hooks's testimony Mr. Rawlings openly wept in court and seemed deeply affected by Hooks's recital of the scenes leading up to the killing of his first cousin."

The state's goal was to provide enough evidence of a crime to warrant holding Rawlings in custody. Witnesses cast doubt on the origin of the bauxite samples Rawlings said had come from Ring Jaw Bluff. Evidence was presented that the War Finance Corporation was suing both Rawlings and his bank for unpaid debts. Insurance agents testified Tarbutton's life was insured for more than $200,000, part of it payable to Rawlings and part to his bank. Two physicians who had examined the body and viewed the death scene opined Tarbutton's wounds suggested he was shot directly from behind, rather than from a lower angle as would be expected if the gun had gone off as Tanner fell.

The most damning testimony came from Noah Covington, the state's surprise witness. He said on the day of the killing he had been nearby on the river's edge, drinking from a spring. Unseen by Tanner and Rawlings, he observed the shooting first-hand. The three men were walking single file, Tarbutton in front, with Tanner and Rawlings close behind. Covington stated he saw Tanner look back at Rawlings, then raise the gun to his shoulder and fire, hitting Tarbutton squarely in the back of his head. Fearing for his life, Covington said he fled through the swamp, then waited several days before contacting the sheriff with his tale of deliberate murder. Despite the defense's efforts to discredit him, Covington stuck to his story.

Rawlings spoke in his own defense, basically repeating his version of the now-familiar events of the accident, explaining the insurance was "taken out to help my credit and to help Mr. Tarbutton's credit." Again, he wept on the stand.

Both sides made lengthy closing arguments. The *Headlight*, clearly believing a murder had been committed, reported solicitor Kea's "appeal to the three justices was one of the best speeches ever delivered in this courthouse here in the trial of any case, many said. He drew down from the house an applause seldom heard." The *Progress*, on the other hand, stated simply Kea made "a very strong plea for the state," while ex-governor Hardwick "made a brilliant plea for his client." The latter was apparently enough to sway the justices; Rawlings was ordered released pending further action by a grand jury. Solicitor Kea seemed shocked and "stammered" when asked to read the verdict to the court.

Now free, Charlie Rawlings headed to Sandersville, where "quite a number of his friends gathered at his home to congratulate him." He then disappeared from public view.

Back in Johnson County, the commitment hearing for J. J. Tanner began on Wednesday, March 4th, after some delay in finding three new justices to hear the case. The original three from the Rawlings hearing had refused to render judgment a second time. With the exception of ex-governor Hardwick, who took on the role of observer, Tanner's attorneys were the same as those hired to defend Rawlings. The same evidence was presented once again, with Covington as the star witness. The defense presented new evidence that the shooting could have occurred as the accused testified. The justices took "only fifteen minutes" to determine that Tanner should be held in jail pending indictment and trial.

For more than two weeks, Charlie Rawlings's whereabouts were unknown. Rumors and speculation swirled back and forth. A reporter for the *Atlanta Constitution* contacted his daughter in Monroe, North Carolina, looking for him. She said she hadn't been in contact with her father. An insurance investigator was in town looking into the policies that were involved with Tarbutton's death. It was reported he was worth more than $270,000 dead, including at least one double-indemnity policy which increased the value if his death was "accidental." Of these funds, "a very small amount" was payable to the estate of Gus Tarbutton, with the remainder going to the Citizens Bank of Sandersville and "the surviving partner of the firm of Rawlings & Tarbutton, *viz.*, Mr. C. G. Rawlings." Rawlings's creditors began to file liens on the future proceeds of the policies, if and when they were paid. The *Progress*, now seeing the handwriting on the wall, reported, "It is freely predicted here that both Tanner and Rawlings will be indicted by the Grand Jury."

On March 17th, arrest warrants were issued for J. J. Tanner and C. G. Rawlings on a joint indictment for murder. Judge Earl Camp, who would be presiding over the trial, was praised by the *Wrightsville Headlight* for his charge to the grand jury stating, "He is starting off well." The trial date was set for Monday, March 23rd. Tanner remained in jail. Rawlings remained in hiding.

The trial of the *State vs. C. G. Rawlings and J. J. Tanner* began as scheduled on Monday morning, six days after the indictments were issued. Rawlings appeared on time in the company of his lawyers and was promptly arrested. As both had been jointly indicted, Rawlings's attorneys moved for severance, which was granted. A motion for bail was denied. The state declared its intention to try Tanner first, a logical choice as he was the accused triggerman. The facts in evidence would be the same for either case, but a conviction for Tanner would pave the way for the conviction of the alleged mastermind, Charlie Rawlings. Ex-governor Hardwick withdrew once more to resume his role of observer of the Tanner proceedings, with A. W. Evans of Sandersville taking over as Tanner's lead counsel. Rawlings was taken to the county jail to await his fate as the legal circus began in the Johnson County courthouse's second-floor courtroom.

It was clear from the outset that while J. J. Tanner, the illiterate overseer dressed in his Sunday best, was on trial for his life, the state's real goal was the conviction of C. G. Rawlings. Since Tanner had pulled the trigger, it would take proof of a conspiracy to get a jury to convict Rawlings of murder, as Rawlings was the only one who stood to gain directly from Gus Tarbutton's death. The legal maneuvering of the state and Tanner's high-priced attorneys were to be a dry run for the real battle to come later in Rawlings's trial.

The state opened with a series of witnesses who testified as to the sequence of events surrounding Gus Tarbutton's death. Even though he was not on trial, much of the questioning focused on the actions and demeanor of C. G. Rawlings, frequently punctuated by the objections from A. W. Evans, Tanner's attorney. Judge Camp rarely agreed with the defense's concerns, stating it was up to the jury to sort out what facts or lines of questioning were appropriate. Two physicians who had examined the body and participated in the coroner's inquest testified the gunshot wound to Tarbutton's head seemed to have struck from directly behind him, but neither saw evidence of powder burns. In contrast, the undertaker who embalmed the body insisted that he found "powder burns" on the dead man's neck.

A friend of Tanner's testified Rawlings wanted Tanner to do something—the implication being that it was criminal—that would mean "big money for Rawlings." Despite the fact that this "something" seemed to refer to a disputed case of fire insurance pending in South Carolina, Judge Camp allowed the testimony, stating the jury should "give it just such weight and credit as they think it is entitled to receive."

Next to testify was Noah Covington, the man who said he'd witnessed the shooting at Ring Jaw Bluff. His account was simple and direct. He'd spent the entire day along the river, looking for a place to fish. He was getting a drink of water from a small spring at the base of the bluff when Tarbutton, Tanner, and Rawlings came into view. Referring to Tanner, he stated, "He looked around that way toward Rawlings, which was behind him, and then throwed the gun up and shot Tarbutton right in the back of the head." Fearing for his life, Covington said he ran downriver until he came to a road then walked all night to reach home, some twenty miles away.

Noah Covington was an interesting character. In the cross-examination that followed, and based on the testimony of subsequent witnesses, his cut-and-dried story of deliberate murder took on a new light. He was seventy years old at the time, an itinerant farm hand by trade, and in poor health for the three years prior to the trial. He readily admitted to a history of doing time on the chain gang for bootlegging and a conviction for "cheating and swindling" (although he pointed out he'd been acquitted of "hog stealing"). A month earlier, witnesses had seen him on the platform of the train station in Bartow, not far from Wrightsville, dressed in a convict's striped uniform, preaching on how he'd spent seven years in a Mississippi prison on a charge of murder, but had since found the Lord. Under cross-examination he admitted the prison story was not true, but he made a few dollars by passing the hat after his sermon. He had a history of morphine addiction, describing himself as a "dope fiend" until the Harrison Narcotic Act thwarted his ability to buy the drug.

Toward the end of the week after witnessing the killing, Covington wrote an anonymous letter to the sheriff of Johnson County saying there had been a witness to Tarbutton's killing. The next week he presented himself to the sheriff, admitting he was that person, but initially denying writing the letter.

Cross-examination established that Tarbutton's death took place between 5:00 and 5:30 in the afternoon. There was intermittent rain, and it would have been dark by 6:00 or shortly thereafter. Covington said he'd fled "four or five miles down the river swamp" but managed to do so before night fell. To accomplish such a feat in broad daylight would have been difficult; to do so at twilight, nearly impossible. In a final blow to his credibility, it was established that at the time of the trial, Covington was living with and being supported by the family of Gus Tarbutton.

Insurance agents once again testified on the policies taken out on Gus Tarbutton's life, but cross-examination confirmed that Tarbutton was aware of them and had signed the policy applications. None were payable to C. G. Rawlings directly, rather to the Citizens Bank, of which Rawlings was the majority shareholder, or the partnership of Tarbutton & Rawlings, which carried substantial debt in both men's names.

Fluker Tarbutton, Gus's son, testified for the state. He had instigated the investigation into his father's death, and, according to newspaper accounts, often sat at the prosecution's table during the trial. Fluker stated that as his father's only offspring and sole heir, he was entitled to the proceeds of any insurance policies on his father's life. Reacting hostilely to cross-examination by Tanner's attorney, he denied there had ever been a Tarbutton & Rawlings partnership and implied that since the crash of the farm economy in 1921, Rawlings had taken advantage of his father. The name of Jim Tanner, the poor farm overseer who was on trial for his life, was rarely mentioned.

Before resting its case, the state called a series of witnesses to confirm that the exact details of the shooting could not have occurred as Tanner and Rawlings had previously alleged. Battered by intense cross-examination, the testimony soon turned into a litany of uncertain facts, conflicting theories, and speculative opinions. The only persons in court who claimed to know the truth were J. J. Tanner and Noah Covington. One of them was a liar.

The defense had no exculpatory evidence to present, so its case consisted chiefly of casting doubt on the character and veracity of the state's witnesses against Tanner (and Rawlings). Witness after witness swore that those who'd testified for the state were of poor character and couldn't be believed under oath, each citing nothing more in support of this than his opinion.

In dealing with Covington, however, the witnesses were more specific. Elisha Coleman, who had been jailed in Soperton on a charge of murder, swore that Covington had approached him and offered to "swear him out" of jail for a price. He testified that Covington told him "he didn't know anything, but if I would pay him he would know something." Another witness testified he'd spoken to Covington the day following the Tarbutton killing and that was the first time Covington had heard of it. Most tellingly, four seemingly credible witnesses placed Covington more than twenty miles away on the day Tarbutton was killed.

Given the calumny that was being heaped on the head of their star witness, the state took an equally aggressive stance. One defense witness who had worked with Covington said he could not be believed under any circumstances. In response, he was asked if he agreed that "if a man is black today as far as sin is concerned, and tomorrow is made as white as snow, or do you deny the Divinity of Christ?" Forced to confirm his Christian beliefs, the witness was then asked if he thought Noah Covington had been forgiven. He replied, "No, sir. If he has, it's been lately."

Hoping to undo the damage done to their witness, the state managed to produce two new witnesses, one of whom was Covington's son, to support their side of the story. Covington's daughter, with whom he allegedly had spent the night after the incident, had been subpoenaed but disappeared and could not be found.

The defendant, J. J. Tanner, made a brief unsworn statement to the court, again stating the killing was an accident and proclaiming his innocence. Given the confusing nature of the forensic evidence about how the accident might have happened, the defense requested that the jury be allowed to visit Ring Jaw Bluff themselves. Judge Camp dismissed the motion "on the ground of the inconvenience, expenses, and the fact that there is evidence in the record thoroughly describing the scene of the homicide." He had heard enough, even if the defense thought the jury hadn't.

After closing arguments the case was given to the jury at 6:00 P.M. on Thursday, the 27th, after less than three day's testimony. The twelve men deliberated for four hours undecided and met again the next morning to deliberate another six. "There was a death-like silence as the foreman read the verdict" of guilty with a recommendation of mercy. The judge immediately sentenced Tanner to life in prison. Charlie Rawlings's case was scheduled to begin the following Monday, March 30th.

Tanner's conviction dimmed whatever chances Rawlings might have had for acquittal, especially in Johnson County. When his case was called on the 30th, ex-governor Hardwick filed a motion asking bail for his client and a change of venue for the trial. Both were denied at a hearing in early April, and the slow process of appeals began. His trial was rescheduled for the June session of court.

While Charlie Rawlings sat in the Johnson County jail, his business empire was unraveling. A week after denial of his bail, his creditors filed a petition in Washington County Superior Court to appoint a receiver for his assets. The court picked Lake B. Holt, a prominent businessman and banker from Sandersville. He reported that Rawlings's debts totaled about $200,000 to two banks and "a number of other creditors" while his assets were estimated "to be from $700,000 to $1,000,000, consisting chiefly of farm property in Washington and Johnson counties." The *Progress* noted with some awe that "the petition which was filed aggregates in dollars and cents the largest sum that has ever been filed in the courts of this county."

For Rawlings, the bad news kept coming. On April 21st, the Georgia Court of Appeals rejected his demand for a change of venue. The matter was appealed to the state supreme court. On April 23rd, it was announced that the Citizens Bank of Sandersville was being placed in the hands of the state banking department and would be liquidated. On April 28th, Prudential Insurance filed a claim in federal court in Augusta asking that the policies on Gus Tarbutton's life be declared void on the basis of fraud and conspiracy.

In late May, Judge Camp heard an appeal for a new trial for J. J. Tanner. The defense filed a total of twenty-five motions, the principal one supported by affidavits from three of Noah Covington's children that he "swore falsely" at Tanner's trial. The son, who earlier had testified in support of his father, now averred he had been recovering from an illness and his earlier testimony was in error. Two other children, including the missing daughter who had been subpoenaed for the trial, gave sworn statements that their father was lying and that he could not have been at Ring Jaw Bluff on the day of the killing. They described him as "a dope fiend." Nevertheless, Camp denied the various defense motions.

By the first of June, the trial and its aftermath were becoming old news. On June 10th, Fluker Tarbutton filed suit against Tanner and Rawlings for

$250,000. The *Headlight* advised that it was uncertain that Rawlings's trial would get underway as scheduled on June 22nd, but that "the safest thing to do if an interested party or witness is to be in the city Monday morning."

By late June the summer doldrums had set in. Rawlings's appeal was still pending and the trial was once more deferred to August. Despite two gory sawmill accidents, the *Sandersville Progress* complained that there was "nothing much of general interest" happening and asked readers to submit news that is "out of the ordinary." (They were rewarded some weeks later with a report of a mother of thirteen who was gored to death by a cow.) Meanwhile, in Wrightsville, the sheriff reported that Rawlings was "whiling away his time in jail and has for his only companionship his Bible and J. J. Tanner, his former farm overseer who constantly aids and consoles him."

In mid-July, the Supreme Court of Georgia denied the appeal for a change of venue. The *Headlight*, apparently hoping to revive interest in the case, noted in a mid-August headline that "Rawlings Likely to Face Jury Monday: Aged Banker and Wealthy Farmer Will Appear in Court on High Charge of Murder." Despite the fact that the state had promised "new and startling evidence against Charles G. Rawlings," the *Progress* reported that "farmers are busy and interest in the case is waning."

The trial began on Monday morning, August 17th, exactly six months after Tarbutton's killing. Jury selection was not completed until the following day. When asked for his plea, Rawlings replied, "I'm not guilty, of course." The crowds were smaller this time, owing in part to the farming season and in part to the hundred-degree heat which blanketed the state. As with Tanner's trial, this one was also closely watched by reporters for the state's daily and weekly papers.

The trial basically followed the same course as that of J. J. Tanner. The state's "new and startling evidence" was testimony from Ray Hewitt, another inmate in the Johnson County jail. Hewitt testified "he heard Tanner upbraid Rawlings for 'not doing what he promised to do,' and the reply from Rawlings that 'he would fulfill his promise when he got the insurance money all straight.'"

Other than Charlie Rawlings, who testified on his own behalf, the defense offered no witnesses. The *Headlight*, still convinced of his guilt, reported "Rawlings sat on a chair just in front of the jury and told his version of it all, at one time breaking down and weeping. His story was about the same, only longer and covered more than the former statement at the commitment." The jury deliberated five and one-half hours before finding him guilty, with a recommendation of mercy. Judge Camp immediately sentenced him to life in prison.

With both Rawlings and Tanner convicted, the cases were soon forgotten except by the attorneys and those who had a financial interest in one or another of the various aspects of the matter. The lawsuits multiplied. Two days after Rawlings's conviction, Lake Holt filed suit demanding $143,750 in payments for legal fees and his work as court-appointed receiver. This and various other cases were settled in November 1925 with the awarding of $17,000 in insurance proceeds to Fluker Tarbutton as the executor of his father's estate. With a touch of coincidental irony, the same day that the Supreme Court of Georgia denied Rawlings's request for a new trial it granted Tanner one on grounds that the *Headlight* referred to as "strictly technical." In December, several of the insurance companies and those suing Rawlings and his receiver reached an out-of-court settlement for an undisclosed amount.

J. J. Tanner's retrial began on March 25, 1926. Judge Earl Camp once again presided. The trial, by newspaper reports a reprise of his earlier one, ended three days later when he was found guilty "soon after deliberation began." The attorneys immediately filed another motion for a new trial.

In December 1926, the *Atlanta Constitution* reported that a federal judge in Atlanta ruled that Gus Tarbutton "did not come to his death by accident," thus thwarting Lake Holt's attempt to collect on the double-indemnity life insurance policy.

With their appeals exhausted, Rawlings and Tanner were transferred to the state prison in Milledgeville to begin serving their life sentences on February 17, 1927, two years to the day after the incident on Ring Jaw Bluff. In small notices in 1928 and 1929, the *Constitution* reported the State Prison Commission's rejections of Charlie Rawlings's pleas for clemency. The last lawsuit involving Rawlings's estate was settled by the United States Fifth District Federal Court in New Orleans in June 1935. The "bauxite" deposits that drew the three men to Ring Jaw Bluff were, in fact, kaolin. In the decades that followed, its mining and processing became a multi-billion dollar industry, creating fortunes for many large landowners.

Every family has its secrets, those embarrassing incidents and shady relations consigned to the dustbins of history and best left unmentioned in polite company. For my father and grandfather's generation, it was the killing that took place on Ring Jaw Bluff on that overcast day in the winter of 1925. Charlie Rawlings was my great-uncle, my grandfather's brother. He died long before I was born, and all I knew of him as a small boy were the tales told by men of his generation overheard in the barbershop and cafes of the small town where I grew up and still live. Little else was left. His once-stately home had become a faded, down-at-the-heels boarding house named the Magnolia Inn, his hotel pulled down to make way for a filling station and grocery store.

I assumed what my grandmother told me was true: Charlie Rawlings was an evil man, so motivated by material greed that he committed the ultimate crime, the murder of a close relative. Now I am not so sure. The question remains, was Gus Tarbutton's death an accident or a murder? The juries saw the matter one way, and that has become history's record. But to me it became clear that Noah Covington, the state's star witness, was lying. He repeated in unsophisticated detail the publicly known facts of the killing, turning it from an accident to murder and thus confirming what everyone believed to be true: Charlie Rawlings was not a good man. Wealth had corrupted him. If he didn't stage the accident on Ring Jaw Bluff, it was something he *might* have done, and for that he deserved punishment.[87]

Charlie Rawlings was eventually released from prison in the mid-1930s, having served the minimum seven years to make him eligible for parole. He spent the last few years of his life living on his niece's comfortable plantation to the north of town and was occasionally seen hanging out on the benches of the city square with other old men whose productive lives were behind them. In those days, many smoked Bull Durham tobacco, rolling their own cigarettes from a drawstring pouch sealed with a folding metal clip about the size of a dime. The streets were littered with these discarded clips, appearing to the casual observer as lost coins in the gutter. One man, a relative of both families, sadly recalls Charlie as a bent old man with a cane poking at the discarded clips in hopes of finding a bit of change. Charlie Rawlings died at age eighty in November 1938. He is buried in an unmarked grave in Sandersville's city cemetery.

[87] See chapter notes for additional comments on Charlie Rawlings's trial and conviction.

Sources and Resources

The sources on which this story is based include interviews with family members and others who had known the characters, contemporary newspaper articles, and an existing copy of the transcript of Charlie Rawlings's trial. During the writing process, it became evident that while the tale of Gus Tarbutton's death was a fascinating one, the bigger story was the era in which it occurred, the early 1920s during the time of the boll weevil, the crash of the cotton-based economy, and the rise of the Ku Klux Klan. As a result, the account of the Rawlings-Tarbutton murder case became one of the central themes in a nonfiction history book bearing the same name, *A Killing on Ring Jaw Bluff*, published by Mercer University Press in 2013. The book goes into far more detail regarding the alleged crime, but more importantly, addresses the critical economic issues of World War I and the early 1920s. On a practical basis, the Great Depression of the 1930s began in Georgia a decade earlier. In the expanded book version, the tale of Charlie Rawlings serves as an example of the fate of the small-town businessman of the day, a fall from heady wealth to abject bankruptcy.

Charles Graves Rawlings, known to his friends as "Charlie," was among, if not *the*, wealthiest man in Washington County in 1920. His financial empire included as much as 40,000 acres of land, a railroad, a bank, a hotel and other businesses. In this undated photo, probably taken in the middle of the second decade of the twentieth century, many of Sandersville's prominent citizens sit in front of the local cotton exchange. Although undocumented, it is believed that Charlie Rawlings is the man in the overcoat seen sitting on the cotton bale just over the left shoulder of the man seated on the curb.

Washington County Historical Society

The Citizens Bank of Sandersville was among Charlie Rawlings's many businesses. It was located downstairs from the Rawlings Sanitarium, his brother's hospital. The bank is on the left, and the Post Office on the right. The store in the middle is the W. R. Beach Furniture Company. Beach was behind the oil well scam of 1919. (See Chapter 12, "A Vast Pool of Oil")

Author's Collection

The Hotel Santon, located at the junction of the main north-south and east-west roads in Sandersville, was owned by Charlie Rawlings.

Author's Collection

The trials of J. J. Tanner and C. G. Rawlings took place in the Johnson County Courthouse in Wrightsville, Georgia. The building, and courtroom in particular, has changed little since the 1925 trials.

Author's Collection

ille Headlight

and Georgia Press Association

N COUNTY, GEORGIA AUGUST 20 1925 $1 50 TH YEAR

TOBACCO MEN ARE HIGHLY RECOMMENDED

TOBACCO EXPERTS HAVE HIGH ENDORSEMENTS FROM HOME PEOPLE. MUCH INTEREST IN COUNTY IN PRODUCTION.

Johnson county is still talking tobacco and what it means to the farming people. A great influx of ready cash into all south Georgia counties has served as a large incentive to investigations into the growth, marketing and sale of tobacco in this county and it looks now as if there will be a large

RAWLINGS FACES TWELVE MEN'S VERDICT ON TRIAL NOW IN PROGRESS AT COURTHOUSE

A DOZEN FARMERS OF COUUTY COMPOSE JURY TRYING FAMOUS MURDER CASE. JURY SELECTION CONCLUDED TUESDAY A. M. GOV HARDWICK CONDUCTING DEFENSE QUESTIONING. JUDGE KENT QUESTIONS FOR STATE.

Judge R. Earl Camp opened Johnson Superior court here at 10:45 Monday morning, a delay occuring when Ex-Governor Thomas W. Hardwick, was late in showing up owing to car trouble enroute here from Dublin. A hundred men as jurors were called. More than a fourth of them went off for cause, sickness and age being an excuse. Three doctors had patients and couldn't serve. A total of 31 were excused, 4 were out of the county, 1 sick and 5 absent, leaving 59.

After a series of delays and failed appeals, the murder trial of C. G. Rawlings began on Monday morning, August 17, 1925. By the end of the week he had been found guilty and sentenced to life in prison.

Wrightsville Headlight, 20 August 1925

Despite his one-time wealth and social prominence, Charlie Rawlings is buried in an unmarked grave near his father, F. C. Rawlings, in one of the family plots in Sandersville's Old Cemetery.

Photo by Author

CHAPTER 14

THE MYTH OF THE BOLL WEEVIL

Among those of us who trace our Georgia roots back more than a century, an oft-heard tale goes something like this: "Back years ago, my great-granddaddy was a big cotton farmer in a little town down in south Georgia. Owned thousands of acres of land. And then the boll weevil came along and wiped him out." Such stories, often delivered late at night and in the context of explaining why one is forced to work for a living, have a ring of truth. To the traveler on Georgia's back roads, the empiric evidence of a past economic collapse is abundant. In small towns and villages across the rural reaches of the state, one finds decaying Main Streets, abandoned rail stations, and once-grand homes gone to seed.

Indeed, the decade of the 1920s was one of wrenching economic and social change for Georgia and much of the South. In context it equals in importance other pivotal times and events in the state's history, on a par with the invention of the cotton gin, the Civil War, and the civil rights era of the 1960s. The popular myth holds that cotton production, which had so richly rewarded Georgia's agriculture-based economy for more than a century, was irreparably damaged by the arrival of the boll weevil. Farmers and businessmen alike suffered a blow from which recovery was impossible, or so the story goes. Historians and others who have studied the era point out there were other factors, including the post-World War I crash in cotton prices and the brief recession of 1920 to 1921. Still, in popular thought, the boll weevil is assigned blame.

In writing this essay, it is not my purpose to attempt to exonerate the boll weevil. It was—and in fact remains—a potentially devastating plague for cotton farmers. Rather, I would like to suggest that *in context* the boll weevil was a relatively minor factor in the 1920s agriculture-based economic collapse in Georgia. I will postulate that the state's economy would likely have collapsed anyway due to other factors. Despite the havoc the bug wreaked in

Louisiana, Mississippi, and Alabama, in Georgia the weevil became more of a *coup de grace* for an already moribund economic system.

Economics poses as a science, but as such, its discoveries are often those derived from *retrospective* observation. Even then, the lessons supposedly learned may not be of value in predicting *future* events as the myriad of factors that influence outcomes are often far removed from the outcomes themselves. In popular thought, the more simple and accessible the explanation, the more readily acceptable it seems to be, hence the assignation of blame to the boll weevil. The events of the second and third decades of the 20th century were complex, unique, and new. Accordingly, I propose that the collapse of Georgia's economy in the 1920s and the subsequent demise of the state's rural economy can primarily be ascribed to three factors:

1. The effects of what we refer to today as "globalization," the intertwined nature of the world economy.
2. The lingering aftermath of the plantation-based agricultural system and the Civil War of 1861 to 1865 that ended it.
3. Well-meaning, but in the end erroneous, monetary and tax policy on the part of the federal government, aided and abetted by lax state regulations controlling banking and finance.

An understanding of what happened requires a bit of historical perspective. In today's urbanized Internet age, we tend to forget that up until World War I and for a number of years afterwards, the United States was primarily a rural, agrarian nation. There were exceptions, of course, but it was not until 1920 that a bare majority of Americans were city dwellers. There were mines and mills and industrial development, but in terms of agricultural products and national wealth, cotton was all-important. It was profitable and the economy of the South was almost completely dependent upon it. Between the first decade of the nineteenth century and the 1930s, cotton exports alone accounted for 100 percent of the positive balance of trade of the United States. Sen. James Hammond's assertion that "Cotton is King" was true in 1858 when he said it, and still true more than half a century later.

The South following the Civil War was a defeated land. While the victorious North held the moral high ground with the abolition of slavery, the freed blacks were not welcomed there as immigrants. The geographic distribution of the African American population in 1900 was roughly the same as it had been in 1860. Slavery had been abolished, but on a practical basis the now-freed slaves were offered little hope of migratory freedom and economic advancement. With few other options available, most of them returned to farming, most commonly as laborers and later as tenant farmers. Few in that day seemed to acknowledge the obvious fact that the former slaves, disenfranchised and relegated to the class of second-class citizens, were an integral and irreplaceable part of the agricultural economy.

As the decades progressed, the system of tenant farming (also referred to as "sharecropping") became the mainstay of cotton production in much of the South. In Georgia, the average farm shrank in size from 430 acres in 1860 to a mere 82 acres by 1920, an operation of insufficient size to achieve economies of scale. A tenant held no interest in the land yet his livelihood and that of his family was almost totally dependent on the outcome of the harvest. If the crops failed, there was little to keep him from walking away. By 1920, about half of all white farmers were sharecroppers, but among blacks, the figure was closer to 90 percent.

Another feature that came to characterize the cotton culture of the South was the system of credit that financed most activities of daily life. The majority of the population was directly dependent on agriculture as a source of income, but crops were generally harvested only in one season of the year. Lien laws enacted shortly after the Civil War allowed the farmer to operate almost entirely on credit, with debts to be paid in cash following the fall harvest. It was, in fact, the chain of credit that linked banker to broker, merchant to farmer, liveryman to landowner, and so on in a network whose successful function was often dependent on a crop yet to be planted and yet to be sold at a price yet to be determined. Whatever the system's faults and weak points, it managed to persist and grow from the latter third of the nineteenth century well into the World War I era.

The post-Civil War nineteenth century was a difficult time for Georgia. Despite Henry Grady's vision of the New South, for years the vast majority of the state remained rural, mired in a lifestyle little changed from a century earlier. By 1900, however, solid progress was being made. The state's network of railroads had grown steadily, opening trade and opportunity for once-isolated communities. The spinning and weaving mills that formerly characterized New England had begun to move south, closer to their raw materials and ready sources of labor. The number of banks in the state exploded, peaking near 800 in number by the middle of the second decade of the twentieth century. Every hamlet and country crossroads seemed to have one or more banks, loosely regulated and uninsured yet integral links in the chain of agricultural credit.

It is hard to predict the exact beginning of the end of Georgia's cotton economy. Personally, I would date it to January 1914, when Henry Ford offered a minimum wage of $5 per day at a time when the average income of a tenant farmer might be a tenth this amount. Though relatively few took advantage of it at the time, the lure of regular working hours and steady paychecks was tempting to a struggling farmer in the rural South.

Another seminal event occurred in 1914 with the start of World War I. The year was shaping up to be a record one in terms of number of cotton bales produced, most grown on credit. Since cotton was a commodity, an abundant supply meant lower prices, but the advent of war in Europe added a particularly vicious twist. Cotton, which had been trading at around 12 cents a pound at the time of Archduke Ferdinand's assassination in Sarajevo in June, was to plummet to under seven cents a pound by the end of the year, the lowest figure in nearly two decades. Cotton was America's leading agricultural export and integral to her positive balance of trade. War in Europe could mean a sharp decrease in cotton exports, further increasing the already abundant supply. As much of the crop had been given as collateral for outstanding liens, farmers faced the risk of being forced to sell at rock-bottom prices to satisfy their creditors. The looming financial loss could be devastating.

The potential effect of this crisis was recognized by the US Department of Agriculture. In August 1914, an emergency meeting convened in Washington to address the situation. In attendance were the secretaries of the Treasury and Agriculture as well as the newly formed Federal Reserve Board. The net result was a decision to allow nationally chartered banks to loan money against receipts for cotton stored in certified warehouses, effectively monetizing the commodity. This credit bailout would allow farmers to hold out until prices rose, thus cutting losses and avoiding bankruptcy. The policy was later formalized in the United States Warehouse Act of 1916. Shortly thereafter, the balance sheets of many banks, both nationally and state-chartered, began to show significant line-items labeled "Advances on Cotton." As prices for the white fiber began to rise to previously unheard-of levels in the ensuing months, the nature of this collateral as a commodity—subject to sudden and unpredictable changes in value—seemed forgotten.

Whatever the horrors of the Western Front, World War I was good for the American economy. Officially a noncombatant nation until April 1917, the demand for war-related goods spurred the already burgeoning growth of the industrial North while at the same time raising demand (and prices) for Southern cotton. Meanwhile, the necessary loosening of credit to finance the rapid economic expansion brought with it the seeds of inflation. Essentially nonexistent in 1914 and 1915, inflation began with a vengeance in 1916, peaking at an annual rate that approached 20 percent in 1918. Based on the newly measured Consumer Price Index, a dollar in 1920 purchased only half of what it could have some four years earlier.

Not that any of this seemed to matter in the cotton-producing South. While inflation was gnawing away at the value of the dollar, the price of cotton zoomed more than 500 percent compared to its low point in 1914. By the summer of 1920, it was selling for near 40 cents a pound on average, far exceeding even the unprecedented rate of inflation. While there were forces to legitimately increase the price, in retrospect it was clearly an economic "bubble." Not unlike the seventeenth-century Dutch burghers' affinity for tulips, or the early twenty-first-century bankers' love of mortgage derivatives, everyone seemed to believe that it would go on forever, with cotton being the one true path to riches. So banks were willing to lend and farmers were willing to borrow, sure that the costs of their debts would be more than covered by the rich harvests ahead. Speculators and those eager to get in on the game drove up the price of land while the basic costs of crop production were driven up by inflation.

It is reasonable to postulate that many in the South did not recognize the specter of inflation and the disastrous consequences it could bring. Much of the commerce of daily life was based on credit, and often at interest rates that were quite high as the collateral against the loan was based on as-yet-to-be-harvested crops. Otherwise, many folk were in large part self-sufficient, sustained by the products of their farms and fields. While the price of consumer goods might rise, it still cost about the same to plant a home garden or allow cattle to feed in one's pasture. Above all, cotton production finally seemed outrageously profitable, and that was what mattered.

Meanwhile, the actions and inactions of both the state and federal governments helped plant the seeds of economic destruction. The Federal Farm

Loan Act of 1916 gave those in the agricultural segments of the economy access to long-term credit to enlarge and maintain their operations. Income tax rates increased to help fund the costs of the nation's entry into the war in 1917, effectively reducing the "bottom line" profit of business enterprises, including farming. Bank regulation was minimal, consisting mainly of perfunctory audits and public reporting requirements, leaving these key players in the financial system at risk of failure.

Much of cotton production was based on the labor of those who tilled the land but held no equity in it, and for these, the wartime lure of well-paying jobs in the North was tempting. Labor agents were dispatched to the South to recruit workers while Southern farmers and governments alike urged tenants and laborers not to leave, citing the importance of agricultural production to the war effort. Some left, but the massive exodus was yet to come.

With the end of the war in 1918 it was forecast that a rebuilding Europe would keep demand for cotton high. The American economy seemed to be booming as well, perhaps attributable to the loosened credit and increase in commerce that had accompanied the war. Returning veterans helped ease the labor shortage, making the year 1919 a prosperous one for the nation. The future appeared to be bright.

The astute reader will note thus far I have not mentioned the boll weevil. The pest had crossed the Rio Grande into Texas in 1892, gradually working its way eastward and destroying cotton crops along the way. It was first identified in Georgia during the summer of 1915, its potential for destruction well recognized. Yet nothing happened—or so it seemed. For more than two decades, agricultural scientists had been seeking ways to stop the weevil. By the time it arrived in Georgia, reports were widely circulating that they were on the cusp of success. Fertilizer and proper farming techniques were of help. Pesticides were soon to be available, although expensive and labor-intensive. With local exceptions, the state's total cotton production was little affected. During the years 1915 through 1920, cotton production remained in its historic range, driven by high prices and apparent apathy toward the risks of insect-borne destruction.

In 1920, things began to fall apart. The period between January of that year and August 1921 has been termed by economists as the Great Recession. It was characterized by severe deflation and falling prices, especially in the agricultural sector. As it immediately followed the most intense bout of inflation in American history, the whipsaw effect on the economy was brutal. The presidential campaign of 1920 focused in large part on the economy. Warren Harding, the winner, promised to "restore" the value of the dollar through a sharp decrease in governmental spending. The Federal Reserve obliged by increasing the discount rate[88] to a level not seen again until the Carter years of the late 1970s, effectively squeezing credit availability.

Farm commodity prices in general fell sharply. From its all-time high in mid-1920, the price of cotton dived deeply, finally scraping bottom in the spring of 1921. When corrected for inflation, cotton's true price was near five cents a pound in 1915 dollars. Suddenly, cotton became an unprofitable crop, setting off a series of events that would spell the end of a way of life that had developed and persisted in the rural South for more than a century.

Damage from the boll weevil began to severely affect Georgia's cotton production in 1921. The state had produced on average from 1.5 to 2 million bales a year between 1915 and 1920. In 1921, fewer than 800,000 bales were harvested, and by 1923, fewer than 600,000. Tenant farmers began to leave in droves, some for the North and others to mill towns that offered steady salaried employment. Blacks streamed to the cities of the North, economic and social refugees from a system that had failed them. Farms were abandoned by the thousands, as cotton producing areas suffered massive depopulation over the coming decades. Some counties lost as many as one out of three citizens in the decade of the 1920s alone. The absence of available labor caused further curtailment of farm crops. Merchants who had extended credit to farmers declared bankruptcy. Banks that had loaned to farmers and merchants failed. Between 1916 and 1925, approximately 45 percent of Georgia's banks ceased operation. In Washington County, where I live, the number of banks dropped from eleven in 1920 to two by 1929, all *before* the onset of the Great Depression of the 1930s. Railroads that had linked rural areas to the outside world ceased operation as their lifeblood of commerce declined.

---

[88] Banks often borrow money to relend it at a higher rate, with the difference in their cost and the consumer's cost representing profit. The "discount rate" is the rate at which banks borrow money from the Federal Reserve System. This number, which can be raised or lowered depending on economic conditions, serves as a benchmark for the "cost" of borrowing. If the discount rate is increased, borrowers pay more to incur debt and profits fall.

Those who stayed behind often continued to pursue the only occupation they knew—that of farming. By the latter part of the decade, it was quite possible to achieve per-acre yields of cotton that equaled or exceeded those prior to the advent of the boll weevil. Cotton prices rebounded, but when weighed against the inflation-driven cost of production and the relative unavailability of labor, planting this once-valuable crop entailed significant financial risks for meager profit potential. Over the ensuing decades, Georgia's rural populations continued to fall while that of its cities grew rapidly. By 1970, half a century after the onset of the Great Recession of 1920 to 1921, many former cotton-producing counties had lost half of their residents.

It is interesting to speculate what might have happened if the boll weevil had not appeared or if a cost-effective treatment had been found prior to its arrival in Georgia. All things considered, it is likely that things would have turned out the same. The bubble in cotton prices would have eventually ended in a crash. The heavy and necessary use of credit to finance the economic system of the day would have resulted in bankruptcy for many whose livelihoods were dependent on cotton, either directly or indirectly.

The severe monetary inflation that characterized the World War I era masked the "true" value of the inflated price of cotton. The use of a commodity as collateral effectively weakened banks and other lenders whose financial futures depended on its maintaining its inflated value. In those pre-Keynesian days, economists might have expected deflation to follow as it did, while bankers seemed to turn a blind eye. Few realized that when it came, deflation would most greatly impact the agricultural sector of the nation's economy.

Pure economics aside, the system of farm labor on which cotton production was based was one that developed not because of its benefits for all involved, but instead because it seemed at the time the best among the alternatives. If good jobs and regular wages had been available earlier in the history of the South it seems likely many would have sought them instead of struggling year-to-year as tenants. If the freed slaves had been afforded true economic and social equality after the Civil War, the system of cotton production that depended upon their labor would not have developed. When such freedom was available, many availed themselves of it, depleting agricultural labor pools in what came to be known as the Great Migration.

In Georgia, at least, the boll weevil began to do its damage after the tipping point for economic collapse had been reached. Unschooled in the corrosive effects of inflation, the wisdom of monetizing a commodity, or the inevitable failure of a labor system based on near-peonage, the average farmer or man on the street would have more easily blamed the problems on an invasive insect. The failure was of such magnitude as to permanently damage and in some cases destroy the very underpinnings of the system that had brought wealth to so many. As the rest of America sped into the glitter of the Roaring Twenties, the simple and uncomplicated story of a culture destroyed by the boll weevil took on a life of its own, an accepted but erroneous bit of historic fact, a myth that exists to this day.

SOURCES AND RESOURCES

This essay is drawn in part from the conclusions examined in greater detail in the book *A Killing on Ring Jaw Bluff—The Great Recession and the Death of Small-Town Georgia*, published by Mercer University Press in 2013.

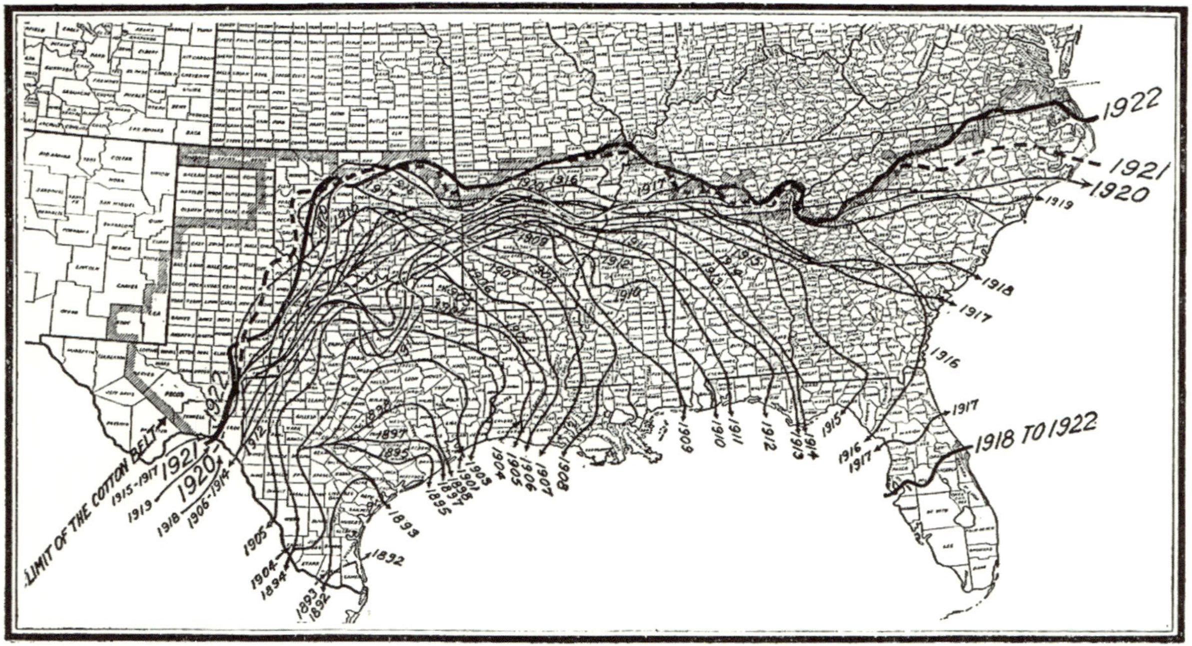

After first crossing the Rio Grande River in 1892, the boll weevil spread eastward, reaching essentially all of the cotton producing areas of the United States by 1922. While devastating to cotton production in the early years, by the end of the third decade of its spread, countermeasures had been developed to mitigate its damage. Despite this, the crash of the cotton economy in the 1920s is often primarily attributed to the dreaded weevil.

U.S. Department of Agriculture Circular 266, 1923

The famed Boll Weevil Monument was erected by the people of Enterprise, Alabama in 1919 as a tribute to the boll weevil forcing diversification of the local agriculture. However, the crash of the cotton economy that followed in the early 1920s was based not so much on the weevil, but rather on a series of national and international events that rocked the nation's fiscal structure in the early days of the Federal Reserve system.

Library of Congress

PART VI

THE KU KLUX KLAN 1915–1930

OVERVIEW

THE KU KLUX KLAN 1915–1930

History, when viewed objectively, is oftentimes ugly and disturbing. This is the case when considering the secret, hooded order of the early twentieth century known as the Ku Klux Klan. My interest in the story of the Klan of the era found its roots in the research for my first nonfiction book, *A Killing on Ring Jaw Bluff*. That work, the combined tales of a sensational murder and the crash of the cotton economy in the 1920s, was centered about the sad fate of Charlie Rawlings, a very wealthy man who was convicted of the murder of his first cousin and spent many of his latter years in prison. Uncle Charlie—he was my grandfather's brother—had an unfortunate run-in with the Klan of the day, who targeted him for punishment because of marital infidelity. I felt it necessary to include the story of the Klan in the book. In fact, it is virtually impossible to say anything about Georgia in the early 1920s without mentioning the Ku Klux Klan.

One cannot write about history without understanding it. Consequently, I spent one long vacation reading a tall stack of books on the Ku Klux Klan. Being reasonably well educated, I thought I knew most of what I needed to know about the organization. I was mistaken. The more I read, the more evident it became that I possessed very little insight into this alleged revival of the Reconstruction era secret order. I had vaguely assumed that "the Klan," or some manifestation of it, was founded in the 1860s, persisted quietly until it found new life in the 1920s, then lay dormant until it reared its ugly head in protest of the civil rights movement of the 1960s and beyond.

In truth, there have been three "Klans" that have marked their place in American history since the 1860s. The first, a series of loosely affiliated groups of the Reconstruction era, arose as regulatory and resistance cadres in response to the social and political turmoil of the day. They were, in both contemporary and modern parlance, terrorist organizations. The second manifestation, formally known as "The Knights of the Ku Klux Klan, Inc.," was a fraternal order not unlike hundreds of others of the day. It was well organized and at its peak boasted of millions of members in all of the then-forty-eight states. At its heart corrupt and at times violent, it sought political power, eventually failing for those very reasons. The third group of Klans that arose after World War II are simply white supremacist "hate groups." They attract few followers and exist courtesy of the First Amendment. At their heart, the most that the three "Klans" have in common is their name and little more.

The research that I did on the Klan for *A Killing on Ring Jaw Bluff* led me to write a magazine article on the topic, *The Second Coming of the Invisible Empire*, and that, in turn, led to a book of the same name. There have been other books written over the past few decades on the second Ku Klux Klan. In terms of historical research, the availability of online research material has opened new vistas for historians. Newspapers, magazines, and other ephemera often paint a different and more detailed portrait of events of days past. In writing a new history of the second Klan, I had access to material that enabled me to fill in a number of details missing in previous works.

The first chapter in this section is a slightly modified version of the original magazine article on William Simmons's Knights of the Ku Klux Klan. It is a broad overview of the subject, which I pursue in far greater detail in the book. The second chapter is titled "Reign of Terror: The Ku Klux Klan of the 1920s in Macon, Georgia." It also appeared originally as a magazine article and is an expanded version of an account detailed in the book. I think it is an important story for several reasons. Many are aware of the Klan's violence, but few realize how pervasive it was in the early 1920s. The details of the Klan's excesses in Macon are unusually well documented, a rarity for the day. Also, these events discount two often preconceived notions, the idea that Klan members were ignorant lower-class whites and that the hooded order's violence was primarily directed toward blacks. Several of those kidnapped were white, educated, and of high social standing, of which the same can be said about those responsible for these criminal acts.

CHAPTER 15

THE SECOND COMING OF THE INVISIBLE EMPIRE: THE KU KLUX KLAN IN THE 1920S

To the average American of the early twenty-first century, mention of the Ku Klux Klan evokes images of burning crosses and hooded men espousing a foul agenda of white supremacy, far from the mainstream of the nation's core values. Indeed, such an image would be correct. Those fringe elements that today make up the loose-knit groups that represent themselves as the Klan are nearly universally reviled, existing on the margins of society and protected in their rights of free speech under the First Amendment. But less than a century ago, the Ku Klux Klan was a major force in American life and politics, active in every state in the Union, promoting its nativist agenda of "One Hundred Percent Americanism" while democratically electing officials on all levels from local councilmen to congressmen, senators, and state governors. Though never firmly representing the consensus of American thought, the Klan represented "an authentic folk movement," in the words of one contemporary commentator. Equally importantly, its phenomenal membership growth from perhaps 2,000 members in 1920 to several million in 1925 is the story of one of the most successful marketing efforts in American history.

The organization known as the Ku Klux Klan has had three separate and distinct incarnations since its founding in the post-Civil War era. While bearing the same name, each "Klan" has been different in organization, agenda, and impact on society at large. Though each iteration is of social and historical interest, it was the second Klan of the 1920s that rose to a position of national prominence and is the subject of this review.

The original Ku Klux Klan was formed in the Reconstruction South of the 1860s. The name was derived from the Greek word *kyklos* (*κύκλος*), meaning circle, with "klan" added for alliteration. Originally organized by Confederate veterans as a resistance movement to Northern occupation and imposed Republican rule, it was but one of many similar groups that spontaneously arose across the vast expanse of the former Confederacy during the Reconstruction era. The Ku Klux Klan, like many others, rapidly became a terrorist organization whose methods included intimidation, beatings, and murder. Its targets were freedmen, carpetbaggers, and politically active Republicans, with the goal being the suppression of black voting rights and restoration of the rule of the Democrat Party. For a brief period of time between 1867 and 1869, the Ku Klux Klan had a semi-public incarnation under former Confederate Gen. Nathan Bedford Forrest, who assumed the office of Grand Wizard. Overall, however, the Klan had little formal central organization, and most local chapters operated independently. Importantly, the name of this particular secret society was rapidly adopted in the general term "Ku Klux movement," which came to include other similar organizations of the day.

By 1869, the Klan's violence and excesses had perverted its original purpose, and Forrest ordered it disbanded. Given the lack of a formal hierarchal structure, many chapters ignored the mandate. The Klan, or individuals representing themselves as members of the Klan, continued their paramilitary activities until finally suppressed by martial law, aggressive federal prosecution, and the eventual return of Democratic rule in the late 1870s. By 1880, the Klan had ceased to exist. For whatever good or evil the Klan accomplished, its legacy became enshrined and embellished in the lore of "the Lost Cause" as the South remembered the history of the Civil War in the late nineteenth and early twentieth centuries.

The Klan of the 1860s and 1870s would have been merely a footnote in history were it not for the vision of a failed Methodist minister named William Joseph Simmons. Simmons belonged to a dozen or more fraternal organizations and relished their secrecy and rituals of brotherhood. He imagined a revived Ku Klux Klan, a secret fraternal order based on his vision of authentic American values with respect for "old-time religion" and conventional moral authority. In practice, this meant aggressive disdain for Negroes, Jews, Roman Catholics, and foreigners in general, not to mention extramarital sex and infidelity, bootlegging and alcoholism, night clubs and bawdy houses, and dope. From modest beginnings in Georgia in 1915, the revived Klan's power peaked in the mid-1920s, followed by a rapid decline in membership. By the end of the decade it had, for practical purposes, ceased to wield significant influence, politically or otherwise. The second

Klan was formally disbanded in 1944 under pressure from the federal government.

The current group of white supremacist organizations that carry the name of Ku Klux Klan sprang up in the years following World War II. At present, it is estimated that there are more than forty different "Klans" in existence in the United States, with a total membership of around 5,000. There is little or no affiliation between individual groups. While adopting the regalia and iconography of the 1920s Klan, the actions and agendas of present-day Klans vary widely.

Some years later, W. J. Simmons would recall that in reviving the Klan in 1915, his purpose was "to establish a fraternal, patriotic, secret order for the purpose of memorializing the great heroes of our national history, inculcating and teaching practical fraternity among men, to teach and encourage a fervent practical patriotism toward our country, and to destroy from the hearts of men the Mason and Dixon line and build thereupon a great American solidarity and a distinctive national conscience which our country sorely stands in need of." Despite the eloquence of his high-minded statement, the truth was likely far more complicated.

Simmons, known to his friends as "Joe," was a tall, bespectacled redhead of Irish ancestry, born in north Alabama. Prior to the founding of the Klan, he had led a singularly undistinguished life, failing as a Methodist minister and subsequently drifting from one job to another without great success. By 1914 he was employed on a commission basis as a district manager for the Woodmen of the World, a fraternal organization founded in the late nineteenth century. By Simmons's account, he had dreamed for years of creating a secret society founded on the preservation of American values but had taken no action. Early in 1915, while confined to bed following an automobile accident, Simmons laid out the structure and ritual of what was to become the revived Ku Klux Klan. His timing, while fortuitous, could not have been better.

The era of World War I and the years that followed were a time of dramatic social change in America. The country was on the verge of transition from a predominantly rural, agricultural society to one dominated by its cities. The census of 1920 confirmed for the first time that the majority of Americans were city dwellers, but with the obvious implication that many would have rural roots. Fraternal organizations, though numerous in the late nineteenth century, grew dramatically in number as newly minted urbanites sought identity in the midst of strangers. The evolving technologies of the telephone and the automobile were often seen as a threat to the family unit for the freedom and mobility they offered. Women were soon to win the right to vote, usurping the dominant role of men. Later in the 1920s, the growing popularity of movies and the advent of commercial radio offered new sources of unfiltered information, while in cities the easy availability of now-illegal liquor was often construed as a further indication of a society gone astray.

One of the more significant events associated with the reemergence of the Klan was the murder of young Mary Phagan. In April 1913, the thirteen-year-old factory worker was found strangled to death in the basement of the National Pencil Company on Forsyth Street in Atlanta, where she had been employed for approximately a year. Despite conflicting evidence and testimony, the factory's manager, Leo Max Frank, was convicted of her murder and sentenced to death. The case was a highly controversial one, all the more so because Frank was Jewish and from New York. For the next two years the appeals process wended its way through the system, finally reaching the United States Supreme Court in April 1915. In a split decision, the court upheld his sentence.

His legal appeals exhausted, Frank appealed to the Georgia State Prison Commission for a commutation of his death sentence to one of life in prison. The commission, voting to deny his request, forwarded their report to Gov. John M. Slaton. The governor, after exhaustively studying the records of the proceedings, was uncertain of Frank's guilt. He commuted his sentence to life imprisonment. In a reflection of public outrage, an angry mob assembled near Slaton's home, requiring the intervention of the National Guard and local police.

The unpopular decision created a firestorm of protest in the press. Tom Watson, the populist former congressman, railed against Slaton and suggested the creation of "another Ku Klux Klan." Frank was moved to the state prison farm in Milledgeville, where it was thought he would be relatively safe. Meanwhile, in Marietta, Phagan's hometown, a group of men calling themselves "The Knights of Mary Phagan" openly discussed freeing Frank from prison in order to lynch him. And they did. On the night of August 16, 1915, the organized mob traveled to Milledgeville, handcuffed the prison warden, and departed with Frank, driving all night to arrive in Marietta early on the 17th. There, at approximately seven in the morning, they lynched the prisoner in front of a house that was once Phagan's home.

A second and perhaps more important influence on the decision to create a fraternal order named after a terrorist organization of the Reconstruction era was, surprisingly, a movie. In the years prior to America's entry into World War I, the motion picture industry was still in its infancy. Films were silent, with captions displayed on the screen and a musical soundtrack provided by the local theater, most commonly a single piano or organ player. In 1914, D. W. Griffith, a rising star in America's nascent motion picture industry, acquired the movie rights to Thomas Dixon's best-selling 1905 novel, *The Clansman*. The fictional work focused on events in the post-Civil War South of the Reconstruction era, portraying freed blacks and occupying troops as savages bent on looting, pillage, and rape. The Klan, depicted in flowing white robes and bearing flaming crosses, arrives to save the day (and the fair maiden, portrayed by Lillian Gish). The silent-film version (under the original name, *The Clansman*) opened in January 1915 in Los Angeles. It was a runaway success, with the name soon changed to *The Birth of a Nation* before a tour of theaters nationwide. The film became the first motion-picture blockbuster, garnering wide press coverage and playing to packed audiences across the country before reaching Atlanta in December of the same year.

Congressional hearings of 1871 had established beyond any doubt that the Ku Klux Klan and related resistance and regulatory groups of the 1860s fully deserved to be labeled terrorist organizations. Yet the passage of time, the Lost Cause movement, and *The Birth of a Nation* had almost completely reinvented the Klan's reputation as that of a band of patriots. Simmons realized that a new fraternal order, allegedly embodying the mystery, courage, and bravery of the now-mythical Klan of the 1860s, might have wide appeal. Gathering together nearly three dozen men, including several members of the Knights of Mary Phagan and a few who were alleged to have been members of the original Klan some four to five decades earlier, he staged a ceremony atop Stone Mountain on Thanksgiving night, November 1915. There, under a flaming cross and with the Bible open to the twelfth chapter of Romans, Simmons led the group in the oath of allegiance to his new creation. The initial charter from the state was issued December 4, 1915, with an additional charter from the Superior Court of Fulton County the following year. Within weeks, Simmons had enlisted several dozen members and set out to create what would become one of the most controversial organizations in American history.

Simmons had developed a detailed and complex set of rituals and oaths for the Klan's ceremonial use, based in some measure on the Prescript of the Klan of the 1860s.[89] Membership was limited to "native-born, Gentile, white American citizen(s)" who were willing to swear allegiance to the United States government, the Christian religion, as well as loyalty to and brotherhood with fellow Klansmen. Expanding on the "kl" alliteration of the order's name, chapters became "klaverns," recruiters "kleagles," chaplains "kludds," meetings "klonclaves," and so on in a long list. Members were given secret signs and passwords: "AYAK?" meaning "Are you a Klansman?" to which a member would reply, "AKIA," or "A Klansman I am." The secret book of Klan oaths and rituals was known as the "Kloran." While members gave a vow of secrecy as to its contents, Simmons wisely registered its copyright with the Library of Congress in January 1917, duly depositing two copies for public view.

Seizing on the popularity and imagery of the Klan as portrayed in *The Birth of a Nation*, Simmons based the regalia and iconography of his new organization directly on that seen in the film. The Klan of the 1860s had indeed worn frightening masks and other disguises, but there was no standard in either design or color. In the newly revived Klan of 1915, the white flowing robes and conical caps were nearly identical to those worn by the valiant heroes of the silver screen. The flaming cross, something invented by Dixon in his novel and never used by the 1860s Klan, was adopted as the essential symbol of its successor.

For whatever high-minded or altruistic motivations Simmons might have had, there were practical considerations in starting one's own fraternal order: There was money to be made. Each new recruit was required to deliver a nontaxable "donation"—a "klectoken" in Klan parlance—of ten dollars on being accepted as a member. And as one advanced to higher levels of membership, additional payments were necessary. The order required costumes, regalia, and jewelry, additional sources of income. One of the first things Simmons did was to contract with a local company to make robes to be sold to Klan members. There was the potential for newspapers and maga-

[89] A "prescript" is generally defined as a rule or ordinance. In this case, the term is used to describe a constitution laying out the rules of the organization.

zines—the Klan would eventually have dozens nationwide. Recalling his former employment with the Woodmen of the World, Simmons clearly recognized the Klan's membership as a captive audience for insurance sales.

The newly organized Klan formally named Simmons as its head—an office known as the Imperial Wizard—on July 4, 1916. As Wizard, his power over the affairs of the organization was near absolute. He had the right to appoint and remove officers, issue and rescind charters to klaverns, and generally manage the affairs of the organization in a way that would ensure his dominance of it—as well as his right to the potentially lucrative income from it. His dream now a reality, Simmons set out to recruit members.

For the first four and a half years of its existence, the new Invisible Empire was not especially successful. Although there were plans for a national organization, the Klan was initially active only in limited areas of Georgia and Alabama. Simmons, for all of his knowledge and interest in the details of fraternal orders, appears to have been poorly organized and unsystematic in his recruiting efforts. The organization struggled financially and was chronically short of money. Numerous accounts suggest he was quite fond of liquor, despite the Klan's avowed support of prohibition. The thing that made the Klan unique, however, was the call for positive action against society's perceived evils.

Initial public reaction to the Klan's efforts was described by one historian as "generally favorable." Supporting the war effort, the Klan took action in 1918 against a planned shipyard strike in Mobile. In Birmingham, potential strikers were intimidated and local hoodlums threatened. In Montgomery, "loose women" were warned to stay away from the soldiers at the local military base. Favorable publicity aside, recruiting efforts struggled. By 1920, estimates suggest the group had about 2,000 members, essentially all in Georgia and Alabama. More than four years after its founding, the Klan was failing; it had become "just another indolent southern fraternal group."

If credit is to be given for turning the reincarnated Klan into a true national organization, it must go to two individuals, Edward Young Clarke Jr. and his business partner, Elizabeth Tyler. Clarke, a former reporter for the *Atlanta Constitution*, and Tyler, a widow in her mid-thirties, had met during the war years and formed the Southern Publicity Association. They had successfully run campaigns for the Anti-Saloon League, the YMCA, the Theodore Roosevelt Memorial Fund, and the Salvation Army, among others. They were introduced to Simmons in 1920 through Tyler's son-in-law, a member of the Atlanta Klan. Tyler later described the organization as struggling financially and sorely in need of additional income.

After some negotiation, it was agreed that the Southern Publicity Association would be absorbed into the Klan, becoming the organization's Propagation Department. Clarke assumed the newly created office of Imperial Kleagle, charged expressly with increasing membership both in numbers and geographic reach. As women were not allowed to join the Klan, Tyler became his "first assistant," but was believed by many to be the driving force behind the organization's expansion drive. Clarke's contract, signed June 7, 1920, specified that of each $10 klectoken donated by new members, he was to retain $8, with Simmons and the Klan receiving the remaining $2. From his cut, Clarke agreed to pay all recruitment expenses. It was a harsh bargain, but Simmons was desperate.

A master of organization, Clarke soon had hordes of kleagles (recruiters) in the field, all employed on a pyramid-based commission scheme. Of his $8 cut, fifty cents went to district managers known as Grand Goblins, $1 to state managers called King Kleagles, with the recruiting kleagles retaining $4. This left $2.50 for Clarke, a sum that could total millions in an era when the average per capita income was just under $700 per year. By 1922, hundreds of kleagles were actively seeking members nationwide, a process informally known as "kluxing."

The ranks of kleagles were filled with men familiar with secret societies and fraternities, most notably Masons. The opportunity for membership was presented to potential recruits as an honor and privilege, with local Masonic lodges serving as rich sources of inductees. In a new area, Protestant ministers were frequently early targets for membership, with emphasis placed on the Klan's support of morality and sobriety. Oftentimes, as additional enticement, a minister would be offered the position of kludd (chaplain) within the organization of new klaverns, without having to pay the usual $10 "donation," of course.

Though the Klan's stated creed of upholding true American values was general and generic, each area targeted for membership had its own unique concerns. In the South, for example, support for law and order, clean government, and enforcement of prohibition ordinances played well. In northern Midwestern cities such as Detroit, anti-black, anti-immigrant stances appealed to men whose jobs might be threatened by those willing to work for less. Even in states with a relative homogenous population such as Oregon, the Klan did well as a social organization with an emphasis on morality and family values. Adapting to the challenge, kleagles were "told to sell the Klan in a way that most appealed to the community." By September 1921, some fifteen months after Clarke and Tyler began their recruiting drive, Klan membership had grown exponentially. Estimates ranged from as few as 100,000 to as many as half a million members. The latter figure, quoted by the *New York World*, was undoubtedly an exaggeration, but soon was to be wildly surpassed.

With its rapid expansion, it was evident that the Klan would soon attract national attention far beyond those eligible for membership. The organization from the beginning had stressed action to back up its rhetoric. Following the tradition of the original Klan of the 1860s, those deemed to have violated some legal or moral code and not otherwise brought to justice could fear a written warning or perhaps a visit from masked men in Klan robes. Those foolish enough to ignore these ultimatums were at risk of being kidnapped, flogged, tarred and feathered, or worse.

By mid-1921, persistent tales of Klan-related excesses led to an investigation by the Pulitzer-family-controlled *New York World*. The exposé, published in a series of twenty-one consecutive articles beginning September 6th of that year, shed light on a side of the Klan that many knew existed but few acknowledged. Sensational in their content and damning in their detail, the articles accused the Klan of greed, bigotry, fraud, and lawlessness. Worse, they exposed the ugly unspoken side of the organization, with a "detailed account of 152 Klan outrages, including four murders, forty-one floggings, and twenty-seven tar-and-featherings." The series of articles was picked up and reprinted by at least eighteen other newspapers throughout the country, leading to national discourse on the true nature of the Klan. The response from the headquarters of the Imperial Wizard in Atlanta was a threat of legal action for libel seeking millions of dollars in damages from the newspapers.

Paradoxically, the *World* articles resulted in a flood of new applications for membership in the Klan. It soon became evident that actions considered by some to be acts of extrajudicial vigilantism were construed by others as morally justifiable enforcement of a threatened society's morés. The controversy was heard in Washington, bringing calls for congressional investigation of the Klan. Sensing the potential value of publicity as well as the opportunity to present his organization in a positive way, Simmons telegraphed every member of the House of Representatives urging a positive vote on a bill that proposed hearings on the Klan's activities.

On October 11, 1921, the House Committee on Rules convened in the large caucus room of the House of Representatives. During the course of the following week, the committee probed into the workings of the Klan, hearing testimony with accusations of lawlessness and financial impropriety. The star witness was Imperial Wizard Simmons, whose multiday testimony dominated the hearing. Immaculately dressed in a vested suit with a high-collared shirt and a gold watch chain adorned with fraternal keys, he gave his testimony while reading through pince-nez glasses and appearing for all the world as the high-moraled Methodist minister he had portrayed earlier in his career. In measured words, he explained that the goal of the Klan was to promote Christian American ideals, with loyalty to God and country. It stressed positive values, not negative ones. No law-abiding citizen need fear the Klan. It was not racist. As to its rejection of blacks, Jews, Catholics, and others, Simmons pointed out that such groups as the Knights of Columbus were open only to those of the Catholic faith. The Klan, like many other existing organizations, had the right to limit its membership eligibility. In regard to the tales of violence documented by the *New York World*, Simmons explained that such actions were antithetical to the moral code of the Klan, therefore these excesses—if they indeed happened—were the responsibility of those seeking to damage the Klan's reputation or by renegade members acting on their own.

The proceedings were followed closely in the national press as well as in Washington. On the third day, Tom Watson, by then one of Georgia's senators, appeared at the hearing during Simmons's testimony, asserting that he was there to defend his constituent from "any unjust attacks from anybody." Watson, despite his overt support of Simmons, pointedly noted that he was not a member of the Klan.

The net result of the *World's* exposé and the congressional hearings was an explosion in Klan membership. The publicity, originally intended to reveal the true nature of the organization, had touched a previously unrecognized chord that appealed to American men of the era. Within three months, applications were being received at the rate of a thousand a day. Within a year, membership had surpassed one million.

While the Klan of the 1920s is often remembered for its vitriol and violence, it should also be recalled that it attracted an enormous following. Klan membership, by order of Imperial Wizard Simmons, was kept secret. Klavern records were often destroyed or hidden, and retrospective approximations of the number of members are extrapolated from fragmentary evidence. At the apex of its success in 1924 and 1925, estimates range from a low figure of two million to as many as five million-plus members. In 1920, the population of the United States was approximately 106 million persons. If one considers the fact that membership was open only to native-born white male Gentiles, it becomes evident that a staggering number of citizens chose to join. As such, it was—for a brief moment in time—one of the largest and most successful organizations in American history.

While current history often focuses on negative aspects of the Klan's existence, it must also be remembered that it had broad appeal as a social organization that stressed family and religious values. There were Klan picnics, outings, and excursions. There were Klan auxiliaries that welcomed women and the Junior Klan for the young. When a klansman or a member of his family was sick, there were flowers and remembrances. Should a member die, the Klan attended his funeral. Furthermore, in the first decade of its existence, the Klan attracted a broad range of members, from professionals to blue collar, often including a community's politicians and leaders.

If one asks why anyone would join an organization noted for its bigotry, it must be recalled that America of the post-War War I era had a different ethos. Consider *The Birth of a Nation*. By current standards, the movie is blatantly racist, yet it was a wildly popular film for years after its release. The Klan's deep suspicion of Catholicism may seem strange and inappropriate by today's standards, but many current Americans display deep distrust directed toward followers of Islam. In so many ways, the growth of the Ku Klux Klan in the 1920s was a product of the times, a concurrent—if not centrist—view of America.

Klan members were average folk drawn from a broad social background. In Athens, Georgia, for example, the typical member was a married man with children. He may have held some position of esteem in the community and may have been a member of other civic organizations such as the Kiwanis Club or the Masons. In Knoxville, Tennessee, roughly a third of the members were white-collar professionals while the rest held blue-collar jobs. More than three-quarters were Baptists or Methodists, with the remaining scattered among other Protestant denominations. In separate klaverns in

Chicago and Aurora, Illinois, more than 60 percent of members pursued professional occupations.

It surprises many to learn that at its peak, the Klan was primarily a Midwestern organization with a strong urban base. In 1924, more than 40 percent of all members resided in Indiana, Ohio, and Illinois. The states of the Southwest were home to an additional 25 percent, with fewer than one-sixth of its members residing in the entire South east of the Mississippi River. Chicago was estimated to have the largest number of Klansmen, followed by Indianapolis, Philadelphia, and Detroit.

The misdeeds that have become the legacy of the Klan of the 1920s grew from its self-anointed role of moral enforcer. Well-documented instances of intimidation, floggings, whippings, and even murder are too numerous to mention. The occurrence varied widely by region—Texas klaverns, for example, seemed more prone to violence. Contrary to popular thought, those persons who were recipients of Klan punishment were often from the same social and ethnic group as members. As one historian noted, "the Georgia Klan seldom directed its violence toward the Jew, Roman Catholic and Negro. They were objects of its semantics, but its direct action was visited primarily on its fellow, white, native-born Protestants."

Roger Hux's study of the Klan in Macon, Georgia, in the 1919 to 1925 period is typical. The occupational spectrum of members ran from physicians and attorneys to shopkeepers and policemen. The publicly reported actions of Klan violence most often involved victims accused of marital infidelity. A local podiatrist was kidnapped and flogged on two occasions. A physician who had abandoned his wife was ordered to leave town. Other interventions resulted from the "operation of an illicit house, bootlegging, and simple drunkenness." Despite indictments and "overwhelming" evidence against him, juries refused to convict a local dentist who was one of the leaders of the klavern.

The popular lore of Klan-led lynch mobs directed against blacks seems to be an exaggeration. Extrajudicial lynchings in the United States date from the early days of the Republic and were especially common in the South. The practice was reported to have reached its peak in the 1890s and was in decline by the post-World War I era. While Klan violence was all too common, "the national lynching toll actually declined" during the 1922 to 1924 period, "the most influential and active years of the second Klan."

As the Klan's membership grew in response to Edward Clarke's and Elizabeth Tyler's recruiting, a gaggle of other Klan officials helped attend to the day-to-day functioning of the organization from headquarters in Atlanta. Among them was Hiram Evans, a Dallas dentist and early Klan supporter who had been promoted to a management position after his success in his home state of Texas. Evans was given the position of Imperial Kligrapp, or national secretary. Imperial Wizard Simmons, meanwhile, showed little interest in the details of day-to-day management. He was said to be in declining health—attributed by many reports to excessive alcohol use. In June 1922, Simmons was convinced to take a six-month vacation, turning management completely over to the administrative staff. Clarke assumed the role of Imperial Wizard *pro tempore*.

With Simmons temporarily absent and Clarke in charge, a small group that included Hiram Evans was growing increasingly concerned about the direction the organization was taking under the existing management hierarchy. A seventh-anniversary Klonvokation, or national convention, was planned for November 1922. Evans, working with others, hatched a plan to "kick Simmons upstairs," giving him the largely ceremonial office of Emperor while assuming the position of Imperial Wizard himself. The conspirators sprang the idea on Simmons after awakening him from sleep between three and four in the morning prior to a leadership vote scheduled for later in the day at the convention. An agreement was quickly reached, with Simmons certain that his new position would allow him to retain all his previous power while freeing him from routine daily management duties. Evans was elected Imperial Wizard by acclamation.

Within days, Simmons discovered that he had been the victim of a well-managed coup. The powers that had been promised to the position of Emperor were not contained in the Klan's newly approved constitution, making him effectively little more than a figurehead. Evans now turned his attention to Clarke, who, as a Simmons's ally, stood to lose much with the change of leadership. Within months Clarke, too, had been ousted. A fierce legal battle for control of the Klan ensued. The national press, now focused on the goings-on in Atlanta, covered the struggle extensively.

A temporary agreement was reached that would reward Simmons with $1,000 a month for life. In early 1924, Evans removed any doubts about his dominion by banning both Simmons and Clarke from the Klan. In February, he reached a permanent settlement with Simmons, buying out any remaining interest he might have in the Klan for $145,000. Simmons promptly attempted to form a new but similar fraternal organization, "The Knights of the Flaming Sword." It failed soon after, and the founder of the second Ku Klux Klan spent the remainder of his life in relative obscurity.

As Imperial Wizard, Hiram Evans sought to change the direction and enhance the national power of the Klan while at the same time not altering its basic tenets. Realizing the toll that Klan-related violence was taking on the organization's reputation and its ability to recruit new members, he ordered the klaverns' assistance in suppressing such activity and in allowing law enforcement to punish offenders. Hoping to move the Klan more toward the mainstream, he urged a strengthening of its social and civic sides—the concepts of Klankraft and Klannishness. While Klan-backed candidates—some of whom were Klan members themselves—had been successful on a local and state level, Evans aspired to make the group a potent force in national politics.

In many ways, Evans's push for change was successful. Incidents of Klan-related violence seemed to wane but by no means ceased. There were public displays in support of Prohibition, often in conjunction with organizations such as the Women's Christian Temperance Union. There was support for state-run public schools, most often in parts of the nation where Catholic school systems were well established. Considering workers' rights movements to be antithetical to American ideals, the Klan took strong stands against Bolsheviks, communists, and the labor unions in general.

As the membership and power of the Klan grew, it increasingly became involved in politics. One of its early successes was achieved in Georgia, where Klan member and former attorney general Clifford Walker defeated Gov. Thomas W. Hardwick for reelection to the governorship in 1922. Hardwick had sponsored an anti-mask ordinance, which angered the Klan. They, in turn, handed him "one of the biggest electoral defeats in state history." Not only did the Klan hold sway in state government, during the same period the mayor and a number of elected officials in the city of Atlanta were Klan members.

On a national level, the Klan's influence was significant. The election of as many as sixteen United States senators was attributed directly to the group's support. A number of individuals who would later go on to play major roles in American political life were active Klan members at some point in their career. Most famously, perhaps, was Robert Byrd of Virginia, who served for nearly six decades in the House and Senate. In his earlier years he had held the positions of Kleagle and Exalted Cyclops in his local klavern. Hugo Black, later a United States Supreme Court justice, was a member of the Alabama Klan in the 1920s.

The Klan's most successful venture into political control—and later, one of the major factors in its decline—took place in the state of Indiana. Even though the vast majority of its citizens were white Protestants, the Klan's message played well there, in large part due to the organizing skills of David Curtiss Stephenson. Stephenson, a former salesman, had a unique bent for leadership and politics that enabled him to elevate the Klan to the practical level of a political party, recruiting approximately a quarter-million members over a few short years. One historian estimated that as many as one out of three eligible men in Indiana joined the organization in the early 1920s. With supportive officials in the governor's mansion, the statehouse, as well as at regional and local levels, the Klan's (and Stephenson's) power was immense.

Having supported Hiram Evans in his overthrow of Imperial Wizard Simmons, Stephenson was granted the title of Grand Dragon over twenty-three northern states, including Indiana. A consummate salesman and showman, he journeyed around the state in a private Klan airplane emblazoned with "KKK" and sponsored massive rallies attracting tens of thousands. He was said to have kept a bank of phones in his office, one of which was a fake hotline to the White House, often used to impress and intimidate visitors. Possessed with a mighty ego, Stephenson clashed frequently with others in the Klan hierarchy. In 1924, he was ejected from the organization, but continued to retain significant influence with its members and the politicians he and the Klan had helped elect.

Like many in leadership positions in the Ku Klux Klan of the 1920s, Stephenson had a dark side, and it was this that would be his undoing. Even though he was no longer a member of the Klan, in the public's mind he was remembered as one of its leaders, making the events that followed all the more ironic. In the spring of 1925, Stephenson took a fancy to twenty-seven-year-old Madge Oberholtzer, the head of a state-run antiliteracy program. Enticing her to join him at his house, he coerced her into drinking alcohol and later that evening savagely attacked and sexually assaulted her while on a train to Chicago (or so she would later avow from her deathbed). Distraught, she swallowed poison, dying several weeks later after giving testimony against Stephenson. A jury convicted him of second-degree murder and sentenced him to life in prison.

Stephenson was convinced that Indiana's governor, Ed Jackson, would find a way to free him. Jackson had been put in office by the state's Klan and owed its now-disgraced ex-leader. Months passed and nothing happened. Angry at what he considered his betrayal, Stephenson began to talk, not only to the press, but also to grand juries. The governor, as well as mayors, congressmen, police, and other local officials were implicated in a widespread scheme of corruption. Indictments and jail terms followed for many. Stephenson spent a total of thirty-one years in prison before his release in 1956.

In light of the scandal, the membership of the Indiana Klan dropped precipitously. Of greater importance, coverage of events by the national press, coupled with growing awareness of the lawless side of the Klan, combined to accelerate what would become a sharp decline in membership.

The events in Indiana aside, there was a growing national uneasiness about the role of the Klan in American life. With the exception of the *New York World* and a handful of other national newspapers that chose to carry its exposé, many local papers had either supported or chose not to oppose the Klan. A prominent exception was the *Columbus* (Georgia) *Enquirer-Sun*, edited by Julian Harris, son of the beloved Joel Chandler Harris. An early staunch opponent of the Klan, the *Enquirer-Sun* reprinted the *World*'s series while taking a firm stand on its own against the Klan and its excesses. As the true nature of the Klan's existence became more evident, the paper was awarded the 1926 Pulitzer Prize for Public Service for "its brave and energetic fight against the Ku Klux Klan."

Imperial Wizard Evans, sensing the reversal in the Klan's fortunes, arranged for a massive parade—and show of power—to be held in Washington, DC, on August 8, 1925. For nearly four hours, tens of thousands of white-clad Klan members marched down Pennsylvania Avenue led by Evans himself. A rally followed, only to be curtailed by a drenching rain. The national press was full of derisive commentary. Perhaps it was not evident to those present, but it was to be the last major national event for a now-weakening Klan.

As an additional nod to its hoped-for role in national debate, Evans decided to move his headquarters nearer the seat of power. The Klan had maintained a lobbying office in Washington, DC, since 1923. In late 1925, he shuttered the Atlanta offices, transferring his headquarters to Washington, away from the partisan bickering that had befallen the former central office.

Over the next five years, the fortunes of the Klan followed a sharp downward spiral. By 1930, the organization was a mere shadow of its former self. Most importantly, however, was the exodus of persons with power and influence. No longer would ministers and white-collar professionals eagerly accept a membership invitation; no longer would politicians seek the Klan's support and counsel. Evans remained in power as Imperial Wizard, using his remaining political influence in Georgia to reap monetary commissions in the 1930s from state expenditures for printing and asphalt purchases. He would later be sued by state attorney general Ellis Arnold and pay a hefty fine.

In 1939, Evans resigned as Imperial Wizard, turning the position over to a long-time associate. William J. Simmons's brainchild, the revived Ku Klux Klan, finally died a quiet and ignoble death when it was formally disbanded in 1944 in the wake of federal charges of income tax evasion.

From the moment it burst onto the national scene in the early 1920s, the second Ku Klux Klan has been the subject of interest, commentary, and analysis by pundits and academics alike. What was this strange group that seemingly saw no contradiction between its avowed Christian and pro-American philosophy and the use of violence against others whose moral code, origin, skin color, or nationality might be different? There is no simple answer. Viewed through the prism of history, one fact seems evident. There was a sharp dissymmetry between the goals and desires of the Klan's leaders and those of the ordinary Klansman. As a general statement, the leaders of the Klan, specifically Simmons, Clarke, and Evans, were more interested in the financial and political potential of the organization than the promotion of any specific philosophical agenda. Most who joined the Klan, however, were attracted to it for its mystery, stated creed, and penchant for action in an effort to right America's perceived wrongs. It was this basic disconnect that eventually lead to the Klan's demise. Stated succinctly, people eventually figured them out.

It is noteworthy, as well, that the rise of the Klan was temporally related to other, somewhat comparable, movements in other parts of the post-World War I Western world. The Fascist movement in Italy and the National Social movement in Germany bore many similarities to the Ku Klux Klan of the 1920s in the United States. All were *über*-nationalist, opposed to things foreign, anti-Semitic, anti-Communist, and willing to use intimidation and violence in pursuit of their goals. The Fascists and Nazis took control of their national governments through the electoral process. If the Klan's aspirations had succeeded, a Klansman (or at the least, someone friendly to the order) would have been elected president in the 1920s. In the end, the Klan failed, and history's timeline took another direction.

For many reasons, the name of the Ku Klux Klan is indelibly associated with bigotry, hatred, and violence. Yet for a few short years in America's history, it attracted massive numbers of members holding the apparently honest belief that as an organization it represented a positive way to enrich and enforce true "American" values, a path that could propel the nation to even greater success in the new century. Instead, through its own arrogance, intolerance, and corruption, the Klan squandered whatever good works or positive momentum that might have come out of such a mass movement. In the end, it was doomed by its own creed, so blinded by its own selfish agenda as to forget the fundamental truths on which the country it sought to "preserve" was founded.

Sources and Resources

This article, in a somewhat modified form, originally appeared in the winter 2012 issue of *Georgia Backroads* magazine. In vastly expanded form, it became the basis of a book of the same name, *The Second Coming of the Invisible Empire—The Ku Klux Klan of the 1920s*, published by Mercer University Press in 2016. While there are a number of excellent histories of the various Klans, this work represents the single most comprehensive account of William J. Simmons's fraternal order, The Knights of the Ku Klux Klan, Inc., between its founding in 1915 and its demise nearly three decades later. The account is drawn for the most part from original and contemporary sources, including perspective gleaned from newspapers and periodicals of the day. The Lost Cause movement and the rise of fraternalism in late nineteenth and early twentieth century America are given special attention as the backdrop for the formation of this "new" Klan in 1915. The book version follows closely the leaders of the Klan, focusing on the hooded order's rise and fall between 1915 and 1930.

Other works of interest include:

Chalmers, David M. *Hooded Americanism.* Durham, NC: Duke University Press, 1987. Originally published in 1965, with updated editions in 1968 and 1987, Chalmers's book has long been considered the "standard" history of the Ku Klux Klan from its earliest days in the 1860s through the 1970s. This is an excellent reference work, but it loses much in its attempt to be comprehensive. A good but wordy starting point for the interested reader.

Jackson, Kenneth T. *The Ku Klux Klan in the City 1915–1930.* New York: Oxford University Press, 1967. In this insightful and interesting look at the Klan of the 1920s, Jackson skillfully refutes the popular misconception that the order was primarily Southern and rural.

MacLean, Nancy. *Behind the Mask of Chivalry: The Making of the Second Ku Klux Klan.* New York : Oxford University Press, 1994. Based in large part on the surviving records of the 1920s Ku Klux Klan in Athens, Georgia, McLean provides important perspective on the Klan's place in the social and political issues of the day.

Wade, Wyn C. *The Fiery Cross.* New York: Oxford University Press, 1987. Wade's work is perhaps the best written of the major Klan histories. He tells the story from the 1860s through the mid-1980s in a most readable and interesting style.

The second of the organizations calling itself "The Ku Klux Klan" had nothing to do with the fabled "Klans" of the Reconstruction Era. It was a fraternal order, like hundreds of others of the day, founded in 1915 by William J. Simmons, a failed Methodist minister and fraternal organizer. Here Simmons is seen at the October 1921 Congressional hearings.

Library of Congress

Were it not for Edward Young Clarke (above), a skilled marketer, the second Klan founded in 1915 would have failed. By using new and innovative techniques to promote the hooded order, the Klan grew from perhaps 2,000 members in 1920, to as many as five million-plus by mid-decade. Below, Elizabeth Tyler, E. Y. Clarke's business associate and sometime lover, was said by some to be the true intellect behind the rapid spread of the Klan in the early 1920s. Wisely, she withdrew from Klan work in early 1922.

The World's Work, May 1923

The Klan's official newspaper, *The Imperial Night-Hawk*, bore a cover illustration copied directly from the movie poster for *The Birth of a Nation*. In fact, the Klan's regalia and the symbol of the burning cross were also copied directly from the movie. The Klans of the 1860s, on which Simmons's Klan was allegedly based, had no standard uniform. The burning cross was chosen by *The Birth of a Nation's* director as a leitmotif for the Klan, and as such was originally nothing more than a movie prop.

Public Domain

When Clarke and Tyler began their promotion of Simmons's Klan, the organization was near bankrupt. A year later, the Klan had acquired a huge mansion on Atlanta's Peachtree Road as its Imperial Palace, a measure of its success.

Public Domain

As a "secret fraternal order," Klan initiations were solemn events with near-religious rituals that incorporated the fiery cross, the Bible and the American flag. This photo depicts a ceremony that took place in Mississippi in 1923.

Library of Congress

In late 1922, W. J. Simmons was deposed as Imperial Wizard by Hiram W. Evans, a former Dallas, Texas, dentist. Evans would serve as Imperial Wizard until 1939. A far more efficient administrator, he worked to reduce the violence that had become associated with the Klan of the early 1920s, while maximizing its income potential and its political power. Here Evans (center) leads a massive Klan parade down Pennsylvania Avenue in Washington, DC in August 1925. The US Capitol can be seen in the background.

Library of Congress

By mid-decade of the 1920s, the Ku Klux Klan had become a politically powerful organization, electing Klansmen (and their supporters) to all levels of political office nationwide. In this photo from the Library of Congress taken in 1925 or 1926, robed Klansmen visit the US Capitol.

Library of Congress

CHAPTER 16

REIGN OF TERROR: THE KU KLUX KLAN OF THE 1920S IN MACON, GEORGIA

At approximately 8:30 P.M. on Friday evening, January 13, 1922, Dr. Robert F. Mills, a podiatrist, stood on the corner of Appleton Avenue and College Street in Macon, Georgia, not far from his residence. Earlier, he had received a telephone message requesting that he make a house call to see an ill patient. He was now waiting for a car that would pick him up and take him to the patient's house. Mills was accompanied by his twelve-year-old son, Francis, whom he had invited along on what was to be a routine home visit. The car arrived promptly, and Mills and his son climbed in. He apparently did not know either the driver or another male passenger. As the four headed toward a rural area on the Columbus Road, the passenger drew a gun and told Mills to raise his hands. Taken by surprise, the podiatrist initially refused but did so after being struck with the weapon.

They soon came to a secluded spot where another vehicle was parked by the edge of the dirt road, awaiting their arrival. Five or six masked men sat inside. His captors pulled Mills from the car, hurled him to the ground, and severely lashed him with a leather whip while his son was forced to watch. The assailants declared that Mills had earned the punishment because of his alleged marital infidelity. Afterwards, he was left to walk home in the dark while his son was taken back to town, given a dollar, and dropped off a block from his home at 245 Appleton Avenue. The terrified boy crawled to the house on all fours, too frightened to stand up. Even though Mills recognized several of his attackers, he did not report the matter to the police at the time. Thus began the Ku Klux Klan's reign of terror in Macon, a period characterized by violence attributed to the local branch of the secret order and culminating in a series of court trials that sought to bring justice to its victims.

As detailed in the previous chapter, the Ku Klux Klan of the 1920s was created by William J. Simmons as a "beneficial, fraternal order," not unlike hundreds of others of the day, including the Woodmen of the World, the Benevolent and Protective Order of the Elks, the Knights of Pythias, the Masonic Orders, and others. In its early days during the World War I era, the Klan morphed into a secret organization, in the process adopting the self-ordained activist role of moral enforcer. Warnings, followed by kidnappings, floggings, tar-and-featherings, and similar violence, were commonly aimed at those who had come to the Klan's attention, most often as a result of the perceived violation of some unwritten moral code. While officially denied by the order's hierarchy, such activity was at least tolerated, if not encouraged. As the home state and headquarters of the order, from the outset Georgia saw her share of Klan-related violence. This continued well into the 1930s and 1940s, long after the Klan had ceased to be a significant national force in American life and politics.

The actions of the Ku Klux Klan in Macon during the early 1920s offer a vivid example of the order's aggressive attempts to fulfill its role as an extralegal enforcer of public morals. While popular thought holds that the Klan's violence was directed primarily toward blacks, in Macon many of its victims were white, often prominent, and well-educated citizens. For nearly two years in 1922 and 1923, members of Macon's Ku Klux Klan terrorized and intimidated this small, middle Georgia city. Though perhaps supported initially by some, in the end it was the Klan's own violence and arrogance that brought an end to the spate of kidnappings and floggings.

Macon's Dixie Klan No. 33 was organized in August 1920 with "over forty" initial members receiving the provisional charter. The order grew rapidly. By November of that year, the local klavern (lodge) had some 125 members, a sufficient number to warrant a permanent charter. The klavern initially positioned itself as a positive force in the community. In March 1922, for example, two robed Klansmen silently "invaded" a luncheon of Community Chest workers to contribute $25 "to be distributed among the welfare organizations represented by the campaign." There were numerous other similar public examples of the Klan's largess, most often calculated to promote the beneficent side of the secret order. At its peak in mid-decade, the klavern was said to have some 1,700 active members. By 1929, at least two additional klaverns had been established in Bibb County.

The Macon Klan's public persona hid its private one. The Dixie Klan No. 33, like others, had a Vigilance Committee that received and responded to reports of legal and moral infractions. Many were sent by aggrieved spouses and lovers, others by those self-righteously reporting some perceived wrong. This committee, or members of it, issued warnings and often dispensed punishment to those deemed to have violated some tenet of the social order. Most commonly in Macon, the punishment came in the form of beating or flogging. Most victims had been accused of such behaviors as marital infidelity or drunkenness or of violating laxly enforced laws such as the distribution of illegal liquor. A warning from or action by the Klan induced extreme fear in its recipient, often hindering legitimate attempts by law enforcement to investigate the incidents.

The Klan's nighttime activities burst onto the public scene with the June 1922 kidnapping of Dr. Eugene Schreiber, a thirty-three-year-old physician who had recently moved to Macon from Boston. One evening, at approximately 10 P.M., he was lured to the street near his home on the corner of First and Oglethorpe streets in downtown Macon on the pretext of attending to a sick patient in "a big touring car." Sensing danger, Schreiber asked to go back to the house to get his instruments, but a gun was poked in his ribs and he was forced into the vehicle. Bound, gagged, and blindfolded, Schreiber was driven to an unknown location where he was severely lectured and told to leave the city. He was released, shaken but physically unharmed, and walked back to town. The kidnapping came to light because a servant reported the events to police, who were in the process of searching for him when he returned.

Schreiber had moved to Macon in 1921 in the company of his sister-in-law, Mrs. Vera Bergenheim, who also acted as his office nurse. Subsequent inquiries revealed that Dr. Schreiber was still married to his wife and had two minor children, all of whom were living in Boston. He had sued his wife for divorce in April 1921 on the grounds of denial of "conjugal rights." She, in turn, had charged him with abandonment and nonsupport. It turned out that Mrs. Bergenheim, whom the papers described as a "handsome, well-built woman," was neither Schreiber's sister-in-law nor a nurse; she was his mistress for whom he had left his wife. When Georgia governor Thomas Hardwick refused an attempt to extradite him to Boston to face his wife's charges, Schreiber left town.

Newspaper reports did not speculate as to the identity of Schreiber's kidnappers. The *Macon Telegraph*, which prior to the time had been cautiously neutral in its assessment of the Ku Klux Klan, ran an editorial condemning the concept of a citizen being "taken out by a band of masked men and mistreated," calling for state "regulation" and unmasking of the order. In response, J. P. Durkee, the local Klan's Kleagle (recruiter) and public spokesman, penned a long letter to the editor strenuously denying that Klan members ever participated in lawless acts. In his words, "A State law holding the Klan responsible for lawlessness done in its name would be a rank injustice to the order, as it would tend to lend itself to the order's enemies."

The issue of Klan-related kidnappings and floggings faded from the press for the next few months, although they apparently continued. Victims were too terrified to report them to the police and, as later events would reveal, the police showed no great eagerness in pursing the alleged offenders.

In early November 1922, the plight of Dr. Robert Mills made headlines after he was kidnapped a second time. Following his first abduction in January, the Klan let Mills and his wife know that he was being watched, going so far as to follow him on a trip to Florida and sending a note to his wife stating that if he failed to come home "you will know that we have gotten him." After months of fear and intimidation, Mills marshaled enough courage to have his attorney write a letter to Governor Hardwick appealing for his help and protection. Shortly thereafter, an "investigator" who identified himself as Detective Payne contacted Mills and arranged to meet with him. Flashing a badge under his jacket, Payne told Mills that he had been dispatched by the governor to address the problem. He reassured the doctor that the matter would be looked into and would have Hardwick's personal attention.

It was within days of his meeting with the "governor's investigator" that Mills was kidnapped a second time. As he drove down College Street with his twelve- and four-year-old sons on November 4th, a large Cadillac touring car with its registration plates removed forced him to the curb. Five men leapt out of the car as Mills, who had taken to carrying a pistol to protect himself, attempted to draw his gun. He was subdued before he could fire, handcuffed, and pistol-whipped with his own weapon. His son, Francis, and the younger four-year-old were abandoned in their father's car as Mills was carried away in the Cadillac. He was taken to a lonely spot near the Ocmulgee River, where a rope was placed around his neck in order to hang him. As Mills recounted later, his kidnappers changed their minds and beat him severely. Wounded and bleeding profusely, Mills made his way home and was attended to by a physician.

Over the next few days, the incident became a major subject of public interest. Mills openly blamed the Klan, claiming that "he recognized one of the floggers" and that at least one was a member of the sheriff's force. He said that over the months since his initial abduction, he and his wife had observed "policemen entering and coming out from the local Ku Klux Klan headquarters" on Poplar Street, declaring "half of the police force and half of the sheriff's force are members of the Ku Klux Klan."

The *Macon Telegraph* was quick to condemn the events. In response to the allegations, Klan spokesman Durkee stated, "The Knights of the Ku Klux Klan is a national patriotic, non-political, secret, Christian organization of the highest ideals and principles, unselfishly co-operating for the defense of our constitutional rights and privileges against the organized efforts of the un-American interests and foreign elements of this country and believing in just laws legally enforced by the constituted authorities." Mill's wife curtly dismissed the Klan's statement as "part of their propaganda scheme."

The episode became even more bizarre when Mills contacted Governor Hardwick to inquire about the ongoing investigation. The governor said that this was the first he had heard of the matter. He had not received any letter from Mills and neither had he dispatched an "investigator" to meet with him.

The Klan's vigilante-dispensed moral justice made front-page headlines again a few months later with the kidnapping of Lynwood Bright and his lover, the wealthy Mrs. Frederica Pace. Prior to the abduction, the couple were well known locally as the result of a sensational divorce case being fought out in the Macon courts. Bright and his wife had been living in New York when he became involved with the widowed Mrs. Pace, described by the *Macon Telegraph* as a "woman of refinement with a college education." Bright's estranged wife had sued Mrs. Pace in New York for alienation of affection, the matter being settled for a moderate cash payment. Mrs. Bright had also sought and obtained the indictment of her husband and Pace for "statutory offenses" as a result of the lovers' three days spent in Atlanta's Piedmont Hotel, where they had falsely registered as man and wife. On April 3, 1923, after a number of months of legal actions, Lynwood Bright was granted a divorce in the Bibb County courts.

The following day, Mrs. Pace observed the now-divorced Mrs. Bright in the company of "a tall man" on a downtown Macon street. Mrs. Bright was apparently pointing her rival (Mrs. Pace) out to the unnamed man, who was momentarily seen getting into a Cadillac. That afternoon, as Mrs. Pace drove about town, she noticed that she was being trailed by a Cadillac, apparently the same one she had seen earlier in the day. She had the presence of mind to record the tag number.

At approximately 10 P.M. that evening, Lynwood Bright and Mrs. Pace were driving near the corner of Second and Arch streets. Bright was at the wheel. Suddenly, their car was boxed in by a Cadillac and a Ford, forcing them to stop. A man standing on the Cadillac's running board thrust a gun in Bright's face and demanded that he raise his hands. The couple was pulled from Pace's Lincoln and forced into the Cadillac, Bright handcuffed, gagged, and hooded, and a blindfold placed over Mrs. Pace's face. They were driven to a spot about four miles from the city, where Bright was stripped and given some 200 lashes with a leather strap. Mrs. Pace was forced to watch as he was horsewhipped. She noted later that her lover clearly recognized some of the kidnappers, who this time did not bother to wear masks. The flogging was administered because of the circumstances surrounding the divorce, Bright was told. He was given twenty-four hours to leave town. The victims were then left to find their own way back into the city.

Alarmed bystanders had reported the abduction to police, who found the pair several hours later wandering down a dirt road, clearly lost. The incident made front-page headlines the next day. Mrs. Bright, contacted at a local hotel, seemed unsurprised by the events, stating, "I am very glad to know there are some men in the world anyway." The tag number of the Cadillac, which Mrs. Pace reported to police, appeared to have been stolen from another vehicle. Within days, Lynwood Bright deeded his residence in Macon to his children, and both he and Mrs. Pace left town for an unknown destination.

Despite the fact that the kidnappings and floggings were being openly attributed to the Ku Klux Klan, the group had no hesitation demonstrating its strength and apparent public support. In late May, Kleagle Durkee petitioned the Macon City Council to allow the Klan to parade in full regalia, i.e., masked, through the streets of the city prior to a "naturalization" ceremony for new initiates. Mayor Luther Williams opposed the idea, and no member of the Council was willing to make the motion. The matter was tabled. A week later, Durkee returned with a petition signed by a number of businessmen and prominent citizens asking for a reconsideration of the request. This time permission was given "in a spirit of fairness."

On June 19, 1923, "thousands" lined the sidewalks of Mulberry and Cherry streets, two of the city's main thoroughfares, to watch as several hundred uniformed Klansmen paraded to Central City Park to initiate more than 400 new members. The masked marchers carried banners reading "Duty without Reproach" and "We Are the Soldiers of the Cross, the New Militia of Christ." The Klansmen's auto tags were covered to prevent identification; lawmen present to direct the crowd did not object.

Within days of the event, local news reports confirmed that the Klan was likely to field a candidate to oppose Mayor Williams's reelection. Despite all that had transpired over the preceding year, it might appear to a casual observer that the Ku Klux Klan, and presumably its deeds, had garnered significant public support. The events of the following months would completely change this perception.

July and August 1923 brought a dramatic increase in kidnappings, floggings, and intimidation attributed to the Klan. On July 9, John H. Knight, an east Macon painter, was taken away by unmasked men and told to change his ways. He admitted the problem was his drinking and "family troubles." A week later, Third Street resident Ben Green was kidnapped and whipped, again by unmasked men. Admitting that "the morals of his home were not the best," he told a reporter that "they were right to give [me] a flogging." He was commanded to leave town.

On August 9, a band of twenty-five to thirty unmasked men threatened to storm the gates of the Georgia Training School for Boys at Milledgeville, demanding that two resident caretakers, a black husband and wife, be delivered up to them, presumably for lynching. It was rumored that the couple had somehow figured in the dismissal of a white man previously employed at the institution. A shotgun-wielding physician, who had been left in charge during the superintendent's absence, held off the mob. Reliable rumors held that the unruly group was composed of Klansmen from the Macon and Milledgeville klaverns. The superintendent, on her return, arranged to have a machine gun and "experienced operator" installed to prevent similar future events.

That same night, there were four reported kidnappings in Macon, as well as rumors of others that went unreported. R. E. Bobo of Turpin Street was taken and severely beaten because he had "talked rough to a white woman." Threatened with death, he departed within days for Key West, hoping to make it to Cuba. Ollie M. Perry, recently released from the Alto Sanitarium with a diagnosis of advanced tuberculosis, was taken and beaten by masked men. He was accused of trafficking in illegal whiskey. Those who saw his "wounds after the whipping said that the skin was broken open in many places, exposing the quivering muscles." In the days that followed, it was reported that Perry was expected to die as a result of the flogging.

Two other men, Gus Roberts and Jim Goodyear, were abducted and flogged during the long night. News reports indicated that these crimes appeared to be the work of the same gang. Despite the fact that some of the men may have recognized their captors, none were willing to cooperate with police. Ben Green's response to questioning was typical: He admitted that he knew some of the men who kidnapped him, but added, "The information will die with me."

With the spate of violence having reached crisis proportions and the victims unwilling to cooperate, Bibb County Sheriff J. R. Hicks concluded that the only way to break the impasse was to offer a substantial reward. The Sheriff's office put up $500, which was soon matched by the Macon City Council. Gov. Clifford Walker offered $1,000 on behalf of the state. In what was deemed by many to be a cynical gesture, the Dixie Klan No. 33 offered $100, bringing the total to $2,100, an amount equal to more than a year's income for many.

In an editorial, the *Macon Telegraph* promptly noted "the general impression was that the Ku Klux Klan was conducting these whippings," suggesting that "the offer of $100 could easily be a blind by which to lead suspicion away from that organization." As the ongoing events were clearly tarnishing the reputation of not only the local but the state Klan as well, Nathan Bedford Forrest II, the Grand Dragon of the Georgia Klan and grandson of the famed Confederate general, offered an additional $1,500 on behalf of the state organization.

On August 17, Sheriff Hicks announced the formation of a special motorcycle squad to aid in the apprehension of the whipping gangs. They were to be on call and ready for instant response, able to reach any section of Macon within five minutes and anywhere in Bibb County within ten. Meanwhile in Milledgeville, an arrest had been made in connection with the incidents at the Training School for Boys. A local judge, speaking at the time of the suspect's arraignment, commented that "these mobs are simply ruining the reputation of the Ku Klux Klan."

Shortly after midnight the next day, police and kidnappers engaged in a gun battle in front of Terminal Station in central Macon. At approximately 2:40 A.M., bystanders heard screams coming from a Ford car parked about fifty yards in front of the station. Several men were observed beating a white male in the rear of the vehicle as he cried, "Help! Police!" and "Murder!" A group of men responded, but were driven away by a volley of gunshots fired at them from the car. A policeman on duty rushed over but was also driven back by gunfire as the Ford sped away. The officer commandeered another car and gave chase but lost track as the kidnappers sped away firing a trail of bullets at their pursuer.

Word of the incident spread rapidly, and soon other officers had the suspects' vehicle bottled up in a dead-end street in east Macon. As law enforcement and a crowd of spectators gathered at the scene, the car suddenly sped through police lines, making a clean getaway. Shots fired at the escaping Ford apparently missed their mark. Nothing further was heard of the incident. No gunshot wounds were reported, and no victim ever came forward to report the crime.

Events were clearly spiraling out of control. Governor Walker ordered his adjutant general to Macon while threatening to send in National Guard troops and to declare martial law if the violence did not stop. In addition to the mob attempt to invade the Training School in Milledgeville, there were reports of "the lynching of two Macon negroes in Houston and Bleckley counties, both near Bibb." Unknown at the moment, a break in the case was near.

On the same evening of the day Governor Walker issued his threat, passers-by spotted several men struggling with a black man, trying to pull him out of a vehicle that had crashed into an embankment. Police were called and within minutes arrested three white men, brothers S. R. Hudson, C. F. Hudson, and J. C. Hudson. They were attempting to whip Emory Roberts, and minutes earlier had whipped another black man. Inside their two cars, sheriff's deputies found leather and cloth masks and a piece of heavy felt to be used as a gag. It would soon be revealed that the three were members of the Ku Klux Klan.

Days passed without further kidnappings. The *New York Times*, which had taken an active interest in the events of the distant Georgia city, reported that the Hudson gang was "being financed by an organization" that remained unnamed. Based on information obtained from the brothers, Sheriff Hicks announced that the police "were preparing to round up an organized band of floggers." Further arrests were said to be imminent. On August 29, Charles H. Hall, a prominent attorney, spoke to the weekly meeting of the Macon Kiwanis Club, "charging that lawlessness in Macon is an organized effort of the Ku Klux Klan" and that "a prominent Macon dentist" was the "whipping boss" of the organization.

The arrests began on August 31, 1923, when the authorities took into custody J. F. Alexander, cotton merchant and Klansman. On September 4, J. E. Patrick, an official of the Macon Municipal Court, W. F. Lamar, a salesman, and Dr. C. A. Yarborough, a well-known dentist, were arrested. Four days later, J. E. Bloodworth was arrested. The final arrest of the nine men charged was J. P. Durkee, the Kleagle and local Klan spokesman. All proclaimed their innocence.

Among those charged, the most prominent were Yarbrough and Durkee. Caesar Agustus Yarbrough, who preferred to be known as "C. A.," was a forty-three-year-old dentist, a 1912 graduate of the Southern Dental College. Tall and wearing horn-rimmed glasses, he had established a "lucrative" dental practice in the Citizens and Southern Bank Building. He lived "in one of the best homes in the city, a colonial mansion at 438 Vineville Avenue," and drove a Cadillac touring car.

Yarbrough had been under suspicion for some time. Earlier investigation had revealed the tag number of the Cadillac given to police by Mrs. Frederica Pace was similar to that of Yarbrough's vehicle, suggesting the possibility that instead of the tags having been substituted, as originally thought, the number had been misstated. Yarbrough's office was decorated with photos of men in Klan regalia. He shared his office space with Durkee, who often used Yarbrough's rooms for Klan initiations and the teaching of Klan doctrine. While Yarbrough had been described as "the whipping boss," Durkee was described as "the big man" behind the floggings.

Charles H. Garrett, solicitor general of the Bibb circuit, was unequivocal in his assessment of the Klan's involvement, stating: "The evidence in a vast majority of the cases indicates that those arrested are members of the Ku Klux Klan. There also is evidence of organized activity of members of this body. Apparently this is well understood by the people of this community."

News of the arrests could not be ignored by Klan headquarters in Atlanta. M. O. Dunning, chief of staff of the Klan's Realm of Georgia, arrived shortly after Yarbrough's arrest, bringing with him two Klan investigators whose ostensible duty was to work with local law enforcement in order to bring the guilty to justice.

The first of the trials of the accused was scheduled to start the week of September 10, but there were new revelations yet in store. Rhodes McPhail, a recent employee of the Klan's Imperial Palace and now an ex-Klansman, advised the *Telegraph* that the Klan's investigators were more bent on damage control than on assisting in punishing the alleged floggers. The most stunning of his allegations involved the fate of the letter that Dr. Robert Mills had sent to Governor Hardwick. Mills's attorney, it seems, was either close to or a member of the Klan. He advised the Klan of the letter, and the Imperial Palace in Atlanta arranged to have it stolen from the post office. Two mail distribution clerks and one postal inspector were "highly commended" for their "faithfulness to the Klan." Rather than being delivered to the governor, the letter had ended up in the possession of Dr. Yarbrough.

The dramatic turn of events caused an immediate panic among the Klan hierarchy. Chief of Staff Dunning called a member of the Klan's Klonсilium (the ruling council) in Atlanta and said, "Who is this fellow [Rhodes] McPhail and what have you got on him? For God's sake do something and have him arrested. If he talks any more he is liable to undo the whole thing down here." The conversation was duly reported to McPhail by his informant and appeared the following day on the front page of the *Telegraph*.

From among the several defendants, the state elected to bring Dr. C. A. Yarbrough to trial first, specifically for the kidnapping and assault of Dr. Robert Mills. Yarbrough faced seven charges in all, including rioting, assault and battery, and use of a firearm during a crime. The one charge on which he was initially to be tried was rioting, a catch-all term applied at the time to the kidnapping and flogging of the Klan's victims. As expected, Yarbrough pled innocent. State Solicitor Roy W. Moore acted as lead counsel for the prosecution, while Judge John Ross, an admitted member of the Klan, led the defense team.

Among the first witnesses for the state was Dr. Robert Mills. The podiatrist confidently pointed out Yarbrough as the man who had flogged him. The strange case of "Detective Payne" and the missing letter sent to Governor Hardwick was solved when Mills identified Kleagle J. P. Durkee as the man who had posed as the governor's investigator.

The connection between Yarbrough and the Lynwood Bright flogging was revealed by evidence that the dentist had stood the bail for the ex-Mrs. Bright when she had been sued by her husband for recovery of some marital property. Yarbrough was apparently the "tall man" with the Cadillac seen by Mrs. Frederica Pace on the day she and Bright were kidnapped.

As the trial progressed, the evidence against Yarbrough seemed overwhelming. The element of conspiracy was confirmed as a number of other flogging victims identified the dentist as the man who had whipped them. Yarbrough was found in possession of letters addressed to the Klan requesting punishment of individuals who had somehow offended the writers. A typewriter expert testified that unsigned threatening notes sent on behalf of the Klan were composed on Yarbrough's office typewriter.

Following the practice of the day, the defendant took the stand to make an unsworn statement to the jury. As reported by the press, Dr. Yarbrough's statement "was largely a history of his life in which he told of the hardships he has undergone to rise to the position in life he now occupies. Noticeable in the prepared statement, which he read from a notebook, was the absence of an alibi. He made no effort to explain his whereabouts at the time of the floggings."

The trial lasted five days. It took the jurors (whose names had been published in the paper for all to see) three hours and five minutes to find Dr. Yarbrough innocent of the charge of rioting. In a front-page editorial the next day, the *Macon Telegraph* opined,

> There are many speculations as to how the jury in the Yarbrough whipping case yesterday arrived at its verdict of not guilty and set the accused free on the charge of having participated in the flogging of Dr. Mills some time since. One of these suggested solutions is that the jury thought the people who had been whipped were so bad that they should have been whipped, and therefore the jury justified the lawlessness. Another is that the jurors were afraid of the Ku Klux Klan, and therefore would not take a chance on convicting a prominent member of that body. Another is that Yarbrough's character was of that high order as to make it impossible for a jury of self-respecting oath-bound men to believe that he would attend church in the day and go on flogging expeditions at night—and so on.

One juror told the paper that the charge of rioting as presented to the jury required the participation of more than one person. This juror said some on the panel were not "satisfied as to the proof of others accompanying Yarbrough." The paper noted he was still subject to be tried on six additional charges.

On September 24, 1923, Dr. Yarbrough went to trial a second time, now charged with the whipping of W. O. Barnett, a harness maker who was flogged by a band of men on February 17. Once again, the evidence presented against the accused was direct and specific. After a four-day trial and more than seventy hours of deliberation, the jury announced that they were hopelessly deadlocked. The judge declared a mistrial.

Meanwhile, Sheriff J. R. Hicks was determined to clear his office of Klan influence. Noting a "lack of cooperation" with the flogging inquiries, he admitted that "practically his entire force were, or had been members of the Ku Klux Klan." By early October most of the force had been fired or resigned, leaving only the sheriff and two deputies to patrol the county.

Solicitor Moore announced plans to next try J. F. Alexander on the charges of rioting and assault and battery in the flogging of Ollie M. Perry, one of the men abducted on August 9. Unfortunately, the star witness for the prosecution, a man named Melton Britt, had "mysteriously disappeared." Unable to proceed with the Alexander case, Moore opted to retry Dr. Yarbrough for the Barnett case, which had resulted in a mistrial a few weeks earlier. The trial got underway on October 22, with much of the same testimony as before. Once again, after some fifty hours of deliberation, the jury announced it was unable to reach a verdict. For a second time, a mistrial was declared.

After a delay of more than a month, Dr. Yarbrough's fourth trial began on December 3, 1923. After two mistrials, the prosecution sought to try him for a third time in the abduction and flogging of Barnett, the harness maker. By now, public interest in the cases had waned. After the arrests in August, the kidnappings and beatings had come to an abrupt halt. News reports simply repeated the testimony given at the previous three trials. This time, both prosecution and defense wrapped up their arguments in two days, sending the case to the jury on December 4. By the next afternoon, the jury had rendered its verdict: Yarborough was acquitted a second time.

The missing star witness having been found, the J. F. Alexander trial started immediately after the Yarbrough jury began its deliberation. As in the case of Dr. Yarbrough, the evidence against Alexander was damning. Alexander was known to be a member of the Klan, something he had acknowledged to one of the sheriff's deputies, also a Klansman. Ollie Perry, the victim, was "charged with selling whiskey to minors" and had been previously convicted of receiving stolen goods. Despite earlier reports predicting his death, he had survived and was able to show his scarred back to the jury, many of his wounds still unhealed nearly four months after his abduction and flogging. Perry testified of pleading with his kidnappers "not to whip me on account of my physical condition."

After a brief two-day trial and four hours and twenty minutes of deliberation, the jury found Alexander guilty. The judge sentenced him to six months on the chain gang, or, as an alternative, a month on the chain gang and the payment of approximately $700 in fines and court costs. Alexander's attorneys vowed to appeal.

Alexander's supporters, including Dr. Yarbrough, began a petition drive to have his conviction reversed as his lawyers appealed his case. Their efforts were initially unsuccessful. Unable to raise the necessary funds to shorten his sentence, Alexander began his six-month stint on the Bibb County chain gang in September 1924. In mid-November, Gov. Clifford Walker unexpectedly commuted Alexander's sentence to time served and reduced his fine to $200. It was a most unusual (though not unprecedented) action. Instead of going through or even consulting the state prison commission, Governor Walker simply issued an executive order releasing Alexander. Only weeks earlier, it had come to light that the governor not only had the support of the Georgia Ku Klux Klan, he had been a Klansmen himself for some four years, a fact that he had long sought to conceal from the voting public.

The other seven men who had been charged in the abductions and floggings of 1922 and 1923 were never brought to trial. The failure of four juries to convict Yarbrough despite what seemed to be clear evidence of his guilt was most likely the primary cause. Of equal importance, the outrages had stopped suddenly after the arrests of the Klansmen. While some of the accused might have escaped prosecution, the willingness of the state to pursue the matter served as a warning to those who might have considered similar crimes in the future.

His legal troubles behind him, Dr. C. A. Yarbrough continued his semi-public role as a "high official" of the Macon Ku Klux Klan. In February 1925, he met with Macon mayor Luther Williams in an effort to rescind the city's refusal to allow the Klan to use the City Hall Auditorium for a public lecture. The following month, Yarbrough and five other armed men personally raided a moonshine still in an Ocmulgee River swamp, resulting in four arrests. When a reporter for the *Telegraph* questioned his presence and motive for participating in the vigilante-style raid, the dentist replied, "Sure I was there, and it was a thriller, too. I went, first, because I was invited by Mr. Phillips [one of the other raiders]; second, because I believed it my duty and right, and third, because I like a thrill as well as the next one." Yarbrough would remain active in his fight against liquor through the end of Prohibition, and later in the 1930s as an organizer of the Laymen's Anti-Liquor League.

On March 12, 1927, front-page headlines of the *Macon Telegraph* read, "Dr. C. A. Yarbrough Arrested; Statutory Offense Is Charged as Result of River Road Ride." Two days earlier, Dr. Yarbrough had been apprehended "in the company of a woman" in an isolated part of the county about five miles from Macon. Three deputies claimed to have "discovered Dr. Yarbrough and the woman in the woods" while investigating local residents' complaints of loitering, joy-riding, and "petting parties" in the area. Yarbrough and the woman agreed to follow the deputies back to town to be formally charged, but instead he "stepped on the gas and speeded around them in his Cadillac car, leaving them far behind in his rear." When Yarbrough did not appear at the sheriff's office the next day, warrants were taken out charging "a statutory offense because of alleged acts involving a woman" and speeding.

Given the prominent reporting of the events, it is clear that the irony of the situation was not lost on the editors of the local paper. Yarbrough was formally indicted by a county grand jury in May; the eventual outcome of the charges is unknown.

Beginning in the mid-1920s, Ku Klux Klan membership began to fall rapidly, not only in the order's home state of Georgia, but also nationally. The causes were many, not the least of which was the Klan's lawlessness and its attempts to amass political power. The Macon Klan's course followed that of many others. In August 1929, the Dixie Klan No. 33 formally surrendered its charter. Its remaining members—estimated at the time at about 800—were to join Bibb County's two other remaining klaverns. The cause of the failure of the klavern was not revealed, but was rumored to be "internal dissention." Dr. Yarbrough, now described as the "recognized leader of the Klan," refused comment.

The following month, the Klan's meeting hall, a large frame building at 658 Arch Street in downtown Macon, was gutted by a midnight fire, said to be "of undetermined origin." The gas and electrical connections to the building had been severed. A caretaker who had lived in the building had been dismissed only a few days earlier by Dr. Yarbrough, rumored to be the owner of the building. When asked about the ownership of the structure, Yarbrough replied, "I don't care to say anything about it or the origin of the fire."

Some six months later, Yarbrough penned a long letter to the editor of the *Macon Telegraph.* Admitting he was no longer a member of the Ku Klux Klan, he defended its ideals and bemoaned the ordeals to which he felt he had been subjected. "The reason of prosecution, persecution, and embarrassment of me and my family was due to my activity against the liquor traffic and my being known to be a Klansman," he stated. "There have been many falsehoods sworn against me, spoken against me, written against me, and even my life has been threatened.... I am not complaining. I know there is still a God in heaven and I can number my friends by the hundreds." As to the Klan, he concluded his letter by saying, "While I am not a member of the Klan, I stand for those principles, and some day when the organization adopts a more democratic form of government, etc., I believe it will then grow to be the greatest organized force for good in America except the Protestant church."

Dr. Yarbrough went on to lead a long and successful life. Among his many accomplishments, he served as president of the Georgia Dental Association for several years in the 1940s. In contrast, this second incarnation of the Ku Klux Klan dwindled to a shadow of its former self, in the process becoming nearly universally reviled before its final disbandment in 1944.

Sources and Resources

The kidnappings and floggings in Macon during the early 1920s were widely covered by both the local and national press. Quoted material is drawn primarily from news articles appearing in the *Macon Telegraph*, the *Atlanta Constitution*, and the *New York Times*.

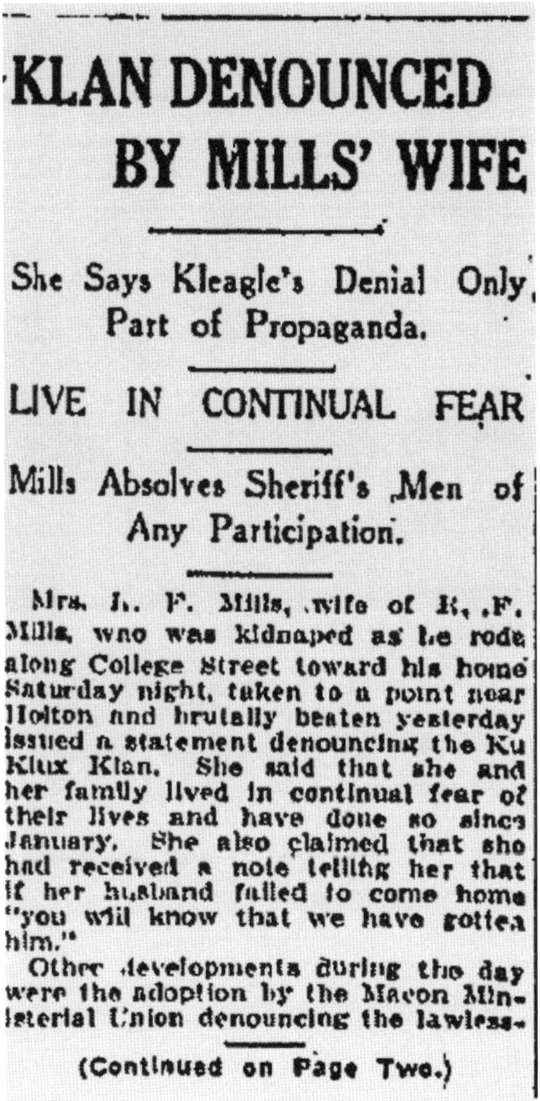

KLAN DENOUNCED BY MILLS' WIFE

She Says Kleagle's Denial Only Part of Propaganda.

LIVE IN CONTINUAL FEAR

Mills Absolves Sheriff's Men of Any Participation.

Mrs. R. F. Mills, wife of R. F. Mills, who was kidnaped as he rode along College Street toward his home Saturday night, taken to a point near Holton and brutally beaten yesterday issued a statement denouncing the Ku Klux Klan. She said that she and her family lived in continual fear of their lives and have done so since January. She also claimed that she had received a note telling her that if her husband failed to come home "you will know that we have gotten him."

Other developments during the day were the adoption by the Macon Ministerial Union denouncing the lawless-

(Continued on Page Two.)

Macon, Georgia's Ku Klux Klan terrorized the city with kidnappings, floggings and intimidation for much of 1922 and 1923. The editors of the *Telegraph*, the city's paper, took a strong stand against the hooded order once it became clear that the crimes were Klan-related. This clipping from November 7, 1922 is typical of the fear generated by the Klan's bold lawlessness.

Macon Telegraph, 7 November 1922

Victims of Kidnaping in Macon Last Night

KIDNAPED COUPLE

Mrs. Fredericka Pace, of New York City, and Lynwood L. Bright, son of the late Green L. Bright, of Macon, who were kidnaped here last night at 10:30 o'clock by a band of unmasked men. Bright was flogged, but Mrs. Pace was not harmed.

The divorce case of Lynwood Bright and his involvement with the wealthy Mrs. Frederica Pace had made headlines in Macon prior to the couple's kidnapping by the Klan. Mrs. Pace was accused by Bright's wife of being "the other woman."

Macon Telegraph, 5 April 1923

NOTICE OF REWARD

It has come to my attention that the law of the State of Georgia has been flagrantly violated in the Counties of Bibb and Baldwin in the instances of the recent outrages in these counties. The Ku Klux Klan stands for law and order. It has dedicated its every power and influence to the suppression of crime through the regularly constituted officers of the law and in building a sentiment for the strict enforcement of our laws. Representing the Knights of the Ku Klux Klan, the undersigned hereby gives notice that he is increasing the rewards already offered by the Governor of this State for the arrest and conviction of the guilty parties in the sum of Fifteen Hundred ($1,500.00) Dollars in each county.

NATHAN BEDFORD FORREST,

Grand Dragon of the Knights of the Ku Klux Klan for the State of Georgia.

Atlanta, Ga.
August 20th, 1923.

In what appeared to be a clearly cynical gesture, the state Klan organization offered a reward for the arrest and conviction of those involved in the "outrages" in Bibb and Baldwin Counties, despite strong evidence of local Klan involvement.

Macon Telegraph, 20 August 1923

Dr. C. A. Yarbrough, a prominent and successful Macon dentist, is seen here in a senior photo from his 1912 dental school annual. He was implicated as the "whipping boss" in several of the floggings that took place during the Klan's "reign of terror" in Macon.

1912 *Sodecoan*, the annual of Atlanta's Southern Dental College

EPILOGUE

We so often think of history as something dull, a tedious litany of marginally useful facts with little or no pertinence to our daily lives. I now know that nothing could be further from the truth. Like many of us, I suffered through high school and college history courses, cramming just enough information into my head to assure a passing grade on the next exam. In *my* world—at the time at least—I felt perfectly secure in my belief that events long past, while mildly interesting, had little to do with *my* reality or the future course of *my* life. At some point, though, I grew up. Perhaps it was when one of my daughters suggested that events occurring during my teenage years represented "ancient history," while in my mind I considered them as current events.

Gradually, ever so gradually, I came to realize the truth contained in the old French epigram "*Plus ça change, plus c'est la même chose.*"[90] Yes, the names, the places, and the dates may be worlds apart, but there is an amazing commonality in the human condition. The concerns of both the common man and great nations, reduced to their basic themes, have remained the same over thousands of years of recorded history. Random quirks of fate, the power of nature, and the vagaries of human quests for wealth, power, sex, and religion have, over the centuries, joined in varying ways to yield a kaleidoscopic montage of events spanning the spectrum from happiness to horror.

If, indeed, the past repeats itself, our only hope is to learn from it, doing the best that we can to avoid the mistakes of our forebears. In this light, history, and the study of it, becomes an ongoing source of warning, instruction, and inspiration. I trust that the readers of this book have found a bit of these in the stories presented.

To avoid closing with a dour note, I present the following brief account of a country parson named Wray and his fateful interaction with a blue jay one Sunday morning the better part of a century ago.

---

[90] Roughly translated, "The more things change, the more they remain the same." Generally attributed to Jean-Baptiste Alphonse Karr (1808–1890), a Parisian journalist and novelist.

On Sunday, June 8, 1919, the Rev. William A. Wray, pastor of the Sandersville Baptist Church, produced a shotgun during the morning services and used it to kill an annoying blue jay that had become trapped in the sanctuary. This episode earned him national derision and the sobriquet "Jay-Bird Wray."

Author's Collection

THE JAYBIRD WRAY EPISODE

The June 11, 1919, edition of the *Sandersville Progress* carried a front-page headline reading "Shot Bird in Church Sunday." The incident took place at the Sandersville Baptist Church, which formerly occupied the corner of West Church and South Harris streets, now the location of a national chain pharmacy. During the morning services the preceding Sunday, June 8th, the minister, the Reverend William A. Wray, had produced a shotgun and killed a bird in the sanctuary.

The weather being hot at the time, the doors and windows of the church were open and a blue jay had flown in. According to the paper's account, the bird had been flying about near the ceiling "occasionally uttering the cry, 'Jay,' which is probably because of the name it bears." Reverend Wray stated, "If the bird uttered the cry again he would get a gun and kill it." The bird once again said "Jay." The minister procured a small gun "and fired at the bird which fell dead. The services were resumed as if nothing had happened."

The incident was the talk of the town and apparently made it to the national news wires, heaping a bit of not-undeserved ridicule on the local church. In the next week's paper, Mr. A. L. Evans, chairman of the Board of Deacons, felt obligated to issue a statement to correct certain "erroneous reports" found "in the press throughout America." It seems that the bird had appeared during "Sabbath School," and efforts were made to get it out of the sanctuary before the main service. When this was unsuccessful, "a small gun was sent for" during the intermission and placed in an anteroom to be ready just in case the annoying bird resumed its squawking. Evans was careful to note that "the gun shoots a cartridge the size of one's little finger, loaded with mustard shot," in case any readers might think this would lessen the severity of the act.

The statement went on: "The bird continued to squawk as the Pastor endeavored to read the Scripture. It was then fully realized that the service must either be dismissed, or the bird shot. The Pastor then stated that if the bird continued to shriek he would have to shoot him though he hated to do so." With that, he shot the bird, which was removed by a deacon.

In an apparent attempt to downplay the incident, Evans reported, "There was no smoke from the gun, and very little noise, compared to a shotgun." And as if to illustrate the relative normality of such events, he noted, "The Pastor afterwards made his regular announcements, preached and took a large collection for Mercer University." It is unclear from the record what influence the presence of a shotgun-wielding minister may have had on the size of the collection offering. The following Sunday, June 15th, the entire church voted unanimously that "the action of the pastor in the entire proceedings was correct and essential for the good of the cause."

But memory of the incident did not so quickly fade. Some twenty months later, on February 23, 1921, a front-page *Progress* headline again reported "Jaybird Parson Shoots a Hen." The article took the form of a letter to the editor signed only by "Citizen." The correspondent reported the Reverend Wray "has made another bid for the lime light by shooting up the Widow Walden's setting hen." He stated, "About 3 o'clock last Friday afternoon [the] neighborhood was startled by the report of a gun discharged in the immediate vicinity of where Willie dispenses the gospel to a fashionable congregation at $2,500 per annum with no charge for extra thrills."

Reverend Wray seems to have found the hen annoying in that it occasionally wandered into his unfenced yard. He had applied to the police for permission "to use all force necessary to repel the trespasser." Rather than contact the hen's owner, the minister simply shot it. "Citizen" opined that "more peaceable means of settlement did not appeal to [Wray's] sense of the spectacular."

With regard to the preacher's involvement in the whole incident, the letter writer said,

> There may be a few old fashioned people who think that a very poor substitute for the dignity, not to say piety, that is usually expected in his sacred profession. But you can't please everyone. Or it may have been that the good lady who owned the hen (and not much else) had neglected to send him any toothsome delicacies since last hog killing time, as was her custom. But be all that as it may, Mrs. Walden has had her little "cry," and been duly sympathized with by indignant friends, and the parson has once more vindicated his valiant manhood to an admiring populace, and all is well.

"Citizen" also noted that Reverend Wray's free-ranging pet goat had been using "the Walden front porch for a bed-chamber," often leaving "a more substantial remembrance," all without protest from the good widow.

Wray apparently chose not to reply. For whatever positive contributions he may have made during his tenure in Sandersville, he is to this day remembered by older members of the Baptist congregation as "Jaybird Wray."

APPENDIX

EXPLORING OUR PAST:
A SHORT, PRACTICAL GUIDE TO
HISTORICAL RESEARCH FOR WRITERS

One of the most common queries I receive from readers is, "How do you discover all of those interesting things you write about?" It's a good question. Writing is neither an art nor a science, but instead a craft, a little bit of both. If one chooses to write fiction, the plot and its details are whatever the author wants them to be. For nonfiction, however, facts are paramount. The key to finding the necessary facts to turn otherwise dry "history" into a living tale of past events is often related to one's research skills. This section, which is based on a number of presentations I've given on the topic, is designed to help the novice writer and/or researcher explore the myriad sources of historical fact. Although I have directed my comments toward those interested in historical nonfiction writing, the concepts apply equally well to writers seeking accuracy when penning historically based works of fiction.

Why Write Nonfiction?

I recall reading somewhere that roughly 90 percent of aspiring authors start out wanting to create works of fiction. I did. Like many who later take up the craft as a vocation or avocation, I grew up being read to as a child, later becoming a voracious reader on my own. Most of the vacations I took from my high school years onward are remembered for the connection between the places I visited with what I read while there. I associate George Orwell's *1984* with the summer spent backpacking around Europe with my then-girlfriend. The works of Gabriel Garcia Marquez and Mario Vargas Llosa bring to mind long vacations in Venezuela and Ecuador. I love fiction for its beauty, its mystery, and its romance. I still do.

As beginning writers, many of us harbor the notion that all we need do is simply get our manuscripts into print (or online, as the case may be). We fantasize that once folks read our words, we will immediately be recognized for our skill and intelligence, inevitably leading to a prominent slot on national best-seller lists. It happens, but rarely—probably about as often as people buy lottery tickets and win the grand prize. I was once asked to serve as a judge for an "Author of the Year" competition involving a certain genre of fiction. I ended up having to read—over a four-month period—nearly fifty works by authors of all stripes. At one extreme were first books of unknowns, at the other the latest works by "*New York Times* Best-Selling Authors." The great epiphany I took away from the experience was that commercial success seemed to have little correlation with the author's skill of writing. Some of the unknowns were outstanding; some of the established and successful authors were tiringly trite. I realized that commercial "success" is more often related to the size of the advertising budget than it is to basic writing skills.

If we measure success by sales, any aspiring author should remember the adage, "Write for the market." The fiction market is crowded and fickle. Well over a million new titles hit the market every year, the majority of which are self-published. Today's successful genre fiction is the source of the pile in tomorrow's remainder bins. Which brings up the question, "Why not write nonfiction?" I started out writing fiction, and by most standards was successful at it. Yet as my knowledge of the craft of writing grew, my interests turned toward nonfiction. I began first with magazine articles, soon switching to full-length manuscripts. Let me explain why.

The market is less crowded: According to data collected over the past few years, the two single largest subject groups brought to market by traditional publishers are works of fiction and books aimed at juveniles, comprising together more than a quarter of all titles. The rest are divided into more than two dozen nonfiction groups. Categories of nonfiction are smaller and often better defined. In writing nonfiction, it is far easier to assess and understand potentially competing works in the marketplace.

One can write for a specific audience: In writing suspense or women's fiction, for example, an author is potentially in completion with a host of other similar books. Yes, you may be the best writer of the twenty-first century, but absent your Madison Avenue publicist and million-dollar ad budget, it's easy to get lost in the crowd. With nonfiction, however, you can often know your exact reading audience, gauge potential sales, and find ready (and low-cost) ways to advertise. To illustrate, if one chooses to write about some pivotal event of the Civil War, finding individuals and groups of potential readers is quite easy. This opens doors for speaking engagements to historical societies and Civil War remembrance groups, an inexpensive and cost-effective way of author-driven marketing.

Nonfiction has a much longer "shelf life": One of the things that struck me as a new writer was how quickly interest faded in my latest releases. Yes, they sold well and were popular with readers, but one of the more common comments I received was, "I loved your latest book; when's the next one going to be out?" There are lasting masterpieces of fiction prose, of course. For most of us, however, a work of fiction is something to be enjoyed and passed on. An author may spend a year or more working on a manuscript only to discover that by six months or so after the book's release, sales have fallen to near nil. Nonfiction works, however, often stay in print for decades, continuing to sell steadily based on the timeless nature of their topic. In writing my last book, a new history of the Ku Klux Klan of the 1920s, I noted that one of the most widely quoted "standard" references was David Chalmers's *Hooded Americanism*, first published in 1965 and still in print in its third edition from 1987. A press run of more than half a century is nothing to be scoffed at.

Nonfiction works can establish your niche and your career as a writer: If you, as an author, are able to establish yourself as an expert on a given subject via your writing, you often become the go-to person for others interested in the topic. This opens doors to many opportunities, including speaking invitations and consulting prospects. A number of "experts" I've known over the years have been advanced in their careers via writing in their field of expertise.

My Philosophy of Writing

Any way you look at it, writing is hard work. It involves days spent hunched over a keyboard and frustrating hours spent staring at a computer screen while you struggle to find the perfect words for a single sentence. Writing works of nonfiction can be even more demanding. You are dealing with facts, and you have to get things right. Given these factors, one needs to be committed to the task at hand, hoping the physical and mental stress of the short term will lead to greater rewards in the future. Here are my thoughts on how I approach the task.

You want to do good work; theoretically, it will be here long after you are: As I noted above, most works of fiction are consumed like a good meal: tasty, interesting, and memorable until it's time to eat again. On the other hand, nonfiction is read not only for enjoyment, but also for education, instruction, and enlightenment. Such works can become records of our shared knowledge, remaining valuable resources for decades. Errors, sloppiness, and shortcuts can and do influence the author's reputation.

Good writing is good writing, whether fiction, nonfiction, or anything in between: I can fully understand how nonfiction is often assumed to come in one flavor: boring. In doing the research for the chapters in this book, I had to force myself to wade through some incredibly tedious works of history, many written by well-meaning academics bent on writing textbook-like tomes in their fields of specialization. They were factually correct but from the standpoint of this reader, often a monotonous litany of facts. Other works on the same subject, however, were enjoyable, laying out the train of events in the manner of an unfolding story, missing nothing in the process. This leads to the next point, below.

A "plot" is necessary; otherwise you simply have a list of facts: Think about this: if I were to tell the story of a friend who had something most interesting happen to him, I might start out with the background—who the fellow was, how he got in his peculiar situation, etc.—then move on to the events of the story, and finally tell you how it all affected him. That's simple, right? Historical writing is no different. For most subjects one writes about, there is a beginning, a middle, and an end. Readers expect closure, which can take the form of events, conclusions, or opinions. Remember, there are few things more boring than raw facts.

Good nonfiction writing is difficult and demanding. Fiction is infinitely easier: In creating works of fiction, an author is free to create the world in which his characters exist. With nonfiction, the world is already there. It becomes your job to describe it in a manner that is appealing to the reader. We all remember that Columbus "discovered" American in 1492, but what do we know about the man, his life, the times in which he lived, the reasons behind his voyages, and the personal obstacles he was forced to overcome? It's the latter that make this story interesting, not the mere event. This brings up the issue of the accessibility of information regarding things of the past, in other words, facts.

Facts are facts. You can work with them but you can't change them: Several years ago, I was told a fascinating tale of murder and revenge that took place in the chaotic turmoil following Sherman's march through Georgia in 1864. The basic story was well known; it had become part of local folklore. I was able to confirm the details from a number of unrelated sources, all of whom had heard them from their elders. It would have made a great Civil War magazine piece except for one thing—the total absence of confirmable facts. There was no objective record of what happened. All I had to go on were memories passed down over a century and a half and subject to change and exaggeration. So, without verifiable details, I had nothing to write about, at least from a nonfiction standpoint. As writers of nonfiction, we are often limited by what we can know. To approach it any other way pushes your work toward the realm of fiction.

The Problems of Writing Historical Nonfiction

Attempting to write respectable works of history presents its own special set of problems. The ones that follow have been among the most troubling to me. Oftentimes, the decision to write about a particular topic is the result of a winnowing process, allowing practical considerations to help choose what can be turned into written history.

The search for Goldilocks: In striving to write good historical accounts, we are constantly searching for the "Goldilocks zone," enough facts to accurately write the story but not so many as to overwhelm us. It is here that the "wheat versus chaff" analogy is particularly important. The real skill of the nonfiction writer is the ability to work with what is available, spinning an interesting and coherent tale from the information we have. Sometimes it is difficult or impossible to accomplish in a satisfactory manner. Speculation and assumption are allowed but must be labeled as such. To create dialogue and situations based on inference moves the work to the category of "creative nonfiction," often introducing the author's biases at the expense of historical truth.

Oftentimes, everybody's dead: For anything that happened a century or more ago, it is safe to assume there are no living witnesses. The hunt for facts must turn elsewhere. As a researcher and author, there are primary sources to be found in the form of newspapers, magazines, and other ephemera. One productive source for me has been interviews with the relatives and associates of individuals who figure in the story I'm trying to write.

Sometimes folks don't really want you going there: The story that I told in my first nonfiction book, *A Killing on Ring Jaw Bluff*, was a controversial one. At least two previous attempts had been made to write about it. Both times, the potential authors received threats and discouragement. I think my success in telling the story was related to the fact that by the time I began my investigation, the key characters were all dead, thinking they'd taken their secrets to the grave with them.

No matter what you think you know, you really don't...: Accounts of past events evolve. The tired adage holding that "history is written by the winners" is entirely true. The basic accounts of events long past were often penned by those who had an interest in telling the "proper" version of the story. Witness the subtle rewriting of Southern history under the influence of the Lost Cause movement. Objectivity and the willingness to change one's preconceived notions are necessary when writing about historical events.

It's all connected: One of the more amazing realizations I've gleaned from writing on historical subjects is the intertwined nature of events. Rarely can one outcome be traced to a single cause; more commonly it's a chain of events that, when followed backwards, lead in the strangest directions. While chasing down these connections through historical research is often difficult, it's one of the most interesting and rewarding parts of the process.

Getting Started

Here is a bit of generic advice about the process of writing works of nonfiction and especially about historical events: you cannot simply sit down in front of the computer and decide you want to write about a subject. That occurs much further into the process. Here is how I have approached it:

Understand fully what you want to write: Over the years, I have often come across topics that seem perfectly suited as the subject of a newspaper or magazine piece, an essay, or even a full-length book. Almost as often, my perceptions have been dashed once I looked at the subject in more detail. The various reasons for my disappointment have little in common. Sometimes the story loses its luster once I read about it in more detail. At other times, another talented author has told the tale as well or better than I might. Or perhaps it is a lack of facts. Once you identify a topic that might be appealing, you must understand fully what attracted *your* interest and why it might be of interest to readers. You must have a general idea of where the story will lead, the eventual conclusions you will reach, and why this tale is important.

Do preliminary research to see if it is possible to write it. Take notes! There are some incredibly appealing stories that simply cannot be written, from a factual standpoint, anyway. An example is the Civil War-era murder I mentioned above. In this case, there was no hard evidence to support the story, just oral history. At other times, the facts are so incomplete or contradictory that what you may hope to write becomes speculation. As long as you label it as such, that's acceptable, but it cannot be presented as true without a high level of certainty. Sometimes you find the exact piece you want to write can't be done, but a variant on it is possible. You must be certain that you've got something to write about before you invest a lot of time and energy into the project. Always take notes. When you're done and trying to put your thoughts in order, written notations become invaluable.

Sketch an outline of where you think you want to go with the story: Once again, written history without a logical "plot" of sorts becomes simply a list of facts. Based on my personal experience in writing both fiction and nonfiction, one writes toward a goal, a conclusion, or a logical ending. To keep the narrative flowing, what you write in the first chapter should have a bearing on the last, and what comes in between should lead to the points that you want to make in the end. An outline, even if you change it multiple times during the writing process, helps keep you on track.

Get organized: One of the most problematic aspects of crafting a long work of nonfiction is the amount of reference material you accumulate, not only in physical form, but also in digital downloads and what you've garnered from reading. I start with a hard-bound notebook, leaving the first several pages for an index. As I read, I devote a single page to important points to be revisited later when writing. As you'll soon discover, your mind often becomes overrun with information, impossible to retrieve unless you've taken good notes. For reference material such as newspaper or magazine articles, I set up a filing system to allow easy retrieval. Depending on the topic, sometimes I do this by date of the article, and at other times by topic. The same applies to material downloaded from the Internet. A good, branching electronic filing system saves countless minutes spent searching one's memory drives. Everyone works a bit differently; the best system is whatever seems best for the individual.

Starting the Search: Sources and Resources

As a matter of definition, "sources" are where you find the facts on which you base your writing. "Resources" are where you find the sources. In this regard, a library collection of historical manuscripts is a resource; the manuscripts themselves become sources. You may be asking yourself at this point why I have not said more about the Internet. The Internet can be both a resource and a source, but you must be constantly aware of two very important things:

The Internet is your friend.

The Internet is your enemy.

One of the beautiful things about life (as well as doing historical research) in the digital age is the ready availability of information. How often do we interrupt a conversation to look up some point of discussion on our smartphones? How often do we rely on electronic resources as the prime source of our knowledge about almost every new thing? On a certain level, we have come to accept the near-infallibility of Google search results. That may work well for baseball stats or the latest news, but not so for the historical past. Here is a fundamental truth: the Internet is a source of unfiltered information. What you find may be true, or false, or propaganda, or some or all of the above.

Items of questionable veracity are often found in relation to controversial subjects. Anyone holding an opinion can post their own viewpoint as if it were an absolute certainty. This extends even to what are rapidly becoming "standard" digital resources, such as Wikipedia. To get an overview and the big picture, a simple Google search will often suffice. However, to take for granted what you read online is one of the best ways to embarrass yourself as an author.

With this said, Internet availability opens provides access to many *resources*, where one can often find primary *sources* generated in the historical era of interest. For example, most university libraries have online catalogues, and some allow access to digital copies of important documents. Knowing what is available for further investigation dramatically speeds the research process. The best advice I can give is this: unless you are quoting a primary source, never reference anything you discover online when doing research. Unreliable sources only serve to cast doubt on everything else you may write.

Finding Resources to Begin Your Search

Once again, I use the term "resources" to describe the sites where one finds "sources" from which one gleans facts. If the distinction seems somewhat artificial, it is a concept that has become quite useful to me over the years that I have been doing historical research. The main consideration here is one of efficiency. Your time is limited and valuable. The time you spend traveling or online takes away from time that could be better spent writing. The more information you can find from one single source, the more efficiently you can use your time. Researching historical topics can often be compared to solving a mystery. You find a clue that leads to another clue, and that to yet another, and so on. The more "sources" you can find under the umbrella of one resource site (be it physical or electronic) the quicker you can complete your work. Here is my listing of top general digital and physical resource sites pertaining to historical research:

- The Library of Congress (www.loc.gov): Potentially one of the best overall depositories of material related to American history. The Library of Congress has a well-designed website with extensive search functions. For assistance, there is the "Ask a Librarian" resource (www.loc.gov/rr/askalib/), which often saves much searching. In addition to extensive printed and digital resources, the photo collection of the library is quite extensive.
- The National Archives (www.archives.gov): Holds an extensive collection of historic records of the United States government, including reports of Congress. For those interested in Southern history, the archives have a branch facility near Atlanta (www.archives.gov/atlanta/) that includes important records of the region, many of which are on microfilm.
- State Archives: Every state has an archives division, with varying degrees of public access. For Georgia, the State Archives (www.georgiaarchives.org) are located adjacent to the regional branch of the National Archives, a depository for many of the state's historical documents in physical, digital, and photographic formats.
- The Digital Public Library of America (https://dp.la/): The DPLA is a site of sites, a centrally collected series of links to other websites for archives, libraries, and museums. As of early 2016, the DPLA boasted of

links to more than thirteen million items in American collections, including books, manuscripts, photographs, ephemera, etc. It is an excellent site from which to begin an electronic search.

- Local Courthouses: An incredibly valuable source of local history, including deeds, probate records, court records, and old newspapers.
- Local and Specialty Museums: For specific locations or topics, these can be invaluable. In Washington County, for example, where I live, there is a collection of Civil War items focusing on Sherman's March to the Sea, a genealogy museum, and an exhibit devoted to the famous Georgia architect Charles E. Choate.
- Genealogy Resources: There are many Internet-based sites, e.g., www.ancestry.com, www.genealogybank.com, as well as local and regional museums. An Internet search will often lead you in the correct direction.
- Photographic Collections: These are frequently a part of national, state, university, or local archives. For example, the Vanishing Georgia Collection (http://dlg.galileo.usg.edu/vanga/) is administered by the University of Georgia.
- University Collections: Many colleges and universities maintain archival collections. Some are quite extensive, such as those of Emory University's Rose Collection (http://rose.library.emory.edu/) or the University of Georgia's Hargrett Library (http://www.libs.uga.edu/hargrett/). I have found it often takes a bit of digging to find the hidden treasures. Even smaller institutions may have a special collection given by or based on the life of a famous alumnus/a.
- Local Visits: For memorable events in history, it is often worthwhile to try to visit locations of importance in the narrative. The Ku Klux Klan of the 1860s, the namesake forerunner of subsequent "Klans," was founded in Pulaski, Tennessee. As I was working on my last book, I visited the buildings where the first meetings were alleged to have taken place, learning in the process far more than I could from any written record.

There are other types of resources, but this list should give the aspiring researcher somewhere to start his or her investigations.

Sources: My "Value List"

When it comes to direct sources that you may rely on for information and may quote in the footnotes and bibliography of your text, some carry more reliability than others. You may hear the terms "primary sources" and "secondary sources." The former term (also known as "original sources") generally refers to eyewitness accounts or written or recorded material that dates from the time of the event in question. The closer the source, the more valuable it may be. For example, if you were writing on the Battle of the Bulge in 1944 during World War II, the memoirs of a veteran who was there would presumably be more accurate than a contemporaneous newspaper account, although both would be primary sources. Further removed, a book on the history of World War II written at a later date would be considered a secondary source. The list that follows is my personal ranking of the value of sources in descending order.

1. Eyewitnesses: There are some who might argue that persons observing an event can at times give the most unreliable accounts but, as a general rule, I have found the opposite. Such minor items as the exact time of day, the prevailing weather, and the hopes and fears of the participants bring past happenings to life. Often, individual accounts may be incomplete, but the more witnesses that you interview, the clearer picture you can draw of the event.

2. Photographs: A photo may indeed be worth a thousand words, and for the last century and a half, many of the world's pivotal events have been captured on film or by electronic media. If you plan to submit your work for publication in popular magazines, photos are not only helpful, they are necessary. Recall that many times images are copyrighted and cannot be reproduced in other works without permission. Also, images submitted for publication in printed material need to have a minimal level of resolution (generally 300 dpi). Two useful resource sites include the Vanishing Georgia Collection (cited above) and the Library of Congress (www.loc.gov/pictures/). For a very long list of images resources in the public domain, [91] the following link to Wikipedia may be helpful: https://en.wikipedia.org/wiki/Wikipedia:Public_domain_image_resources.

[91] The term "public domain" used in this sense means that, generally speaking, the images may be reproduced without charge in other publications in both print

3. Newspapers: Living in the digital age, it is sometimes difficult to remember that prior to the 1920s, the printed word was just about the only steady source of news of the outside world. It was only in the early twenty-first century that print newspaper circulation began to fall dramatically based on the shift to electronically based information sources. As the modern-era print newspaper business began to wane, a host of resources featuring the content of past newspapers began to come available on the Internet. As strange as it may sound, much of the news and routine business of cities a century ago can be assessed almost as easily as that of the same places today. Old newspaper archives can be accessed via a number of websites. The ones with the greatest amount of content require a subscription. Among my favorites is Genealogy Bank (www.genealogybank.com), nominally an ancestry site but with a superb collection of newspapers and an accurate search engine. Others include Newspaper Archive (www.newspaperarchive.com), Newspapers.com (www.newspapers.com), and Google (www.news.google.com/newspapers). The first two are paid sites, but Google's site is free. A number of major national and regional newspapers maintain their own archives, including the *New York Times* and, in Georgia, the *Atlanta Journal-Constitution* and the *Augusta Chronicle*.

4. Magazines: One of the best sources for commentary and opinion is old magazines. Rather than simply reporting the news of the day, their writers often delved more deeply into a wide range of issues, delivering both fact and measured commentary. Perhaps the best single source for old magazines from the late nineteenth through the twentieth century is UNZ.org (www.unz.org). The site's header says it all: "*Many Millions of Pages of Readable, Searchable Content at Your Fingertips*," and the content is free. Other magazines, for example, *Time*, maintain their own archives with access available for a fee.

5. Ephemera: The term refers to things that have a short, useful existence, such as handbills, memorabilia, political posters, and the like. In practice, I've found these minor items of importance in understanding an event or era. For example, in 1925, one might ask if the Ku Klux Klan was still considered part of the mainstream of life in Atlanta. The answer comes from a "Klan Day" poster from the Southeastern Fair in October 1925. The event

---

and digital form. Depending on the source, there may be certain requirements, including the designation of source credit.

included a “Klan Parade,” “Klan Fireworks,” and an “Address by the Imperial Wizard.” The original of the poster is in the Archives of the Atlanta History Center.

6. Theses, Dissertations, and Academic Journals: Important historical events attract academic interest. Every year, thousands of master’s theses and doctoral dissertations are written on a wide range of subjects. Though secondary sources per se, their underlying research usually relies on primary sources and as such they can be a rich source of information. The greatest problem is identifying and accessing these documents. Although there is no central registry, some universities maintain an online index and provide access to copies. Other services, often for a fee, will conduct searches. As to academic journals, far and away the best resource is JSTOR.org (www.jstor.org), a website that provides full access to the contents of some 2,000 academic journals that in some cases date back for decades. Though some articles can be read for free, downloads require payment based on usage.

7. Books: Even though many books are written long after the events that make up their pages, they provide excellent background reading and oftentimes valuable opinion from their authors. *With exceptions*, publications copyrighted before 1923 are free of current copyright and may be available online. One robust source of out-of-copyright books (and other publications) is Google Books (https://books.google.com). The Internet Archive (www.archive.org) and Project Gutenberg (https://www.gutenberg.org) are two other, among many, resource sites.

Putting It All Together

No person can tell another exactly what and how to write. Finding the story among the facts and rendering it in a fashion that is both appealing and informative for readers is not easy. It requires practice, the willingness to make mistakes, and the willingness to accept and learn from constructive criticism. I hope this section will make the job of research a bit easier. The rest is up to you.

CHAPTER NOTES

Introduction: Several of the chapters that make up this book were originally published in *Georgia Backroads* magazine between 2009 and 2016. These include "The Great Yazoo Fraud," "The Strange Journey of the Confederate Constitution," "The Freedman's Land Insurrection of 1875," "Gutzon Borglum and the Lost Stone Mountain Confederate Memorial," "The Drum Returns Home," "A Vast Pool of Oil," "A Killing on Ring Jaw Bluff," "The Myth of the Boll Weevil," "The Second Coming of the Invisible Empire," and "Reign of Terror." All have been modified as they appear in the current work. Some have been completely rewritten while others changed only minimally. Chapter 4, "The Saga of the Lost Confederate Treasure" is based on an expanded version of lectures I have presented over the past decade. "The Jaybird Wray Episode" was previously published in the *Sandersville Progress*, a local weekly newspaper in my hometown of Sandersville, Georgia. Two of the chapters, "A Killing on Ring Jaw Bluff" and "The Second Coming of the Invisible Empire," were later expanded into full-length books of the same name, published in 2013 and 2016, respectively, by Mercer University Press.

Chapter 4: In the spring of 1865, President Jefferson Davis's party, fleeing Federal troops, passed within a few miles of what is now my home. I knew that they had camped near the settlement of Warthen, a few miles north of Sandersville, and that they were rumored to have been carrying a large quantity of gold and silver. I grew up hearing rumors of this Confederate treasure, something that fueled my boyhood imagination. During my high school years, using Korean War-era military surplus mine detectors, we spent many weekends searching for hidden treasure around old house sites and in places where we thought someone might have buried something of worth. We found a few coins and a number of rusty plowshares, but little or nothing of any real value.

The thought never really faded from my memory. Later, when I took up writing, it occurred to me that this would be a great plot for a novel. What if there had been some hidden Confederate gold, a lot of it, and what if the protagonist of my proposed novel found it? I had my plot, and it became my second novel, *The Rutherford Cipher*.

The book was well received. Hardly a week went by that I was not asked to speak to some civic or historical group. It was optioned for a movie, only to lose out to another movie with a similar plot that was already in pre-production. The novel's protagonist went on to appear in two subsequent books. I received emails and letters from readers who swore they knew almost exactly where the missing gold was hidden. Each had a different but plausible explanation as to why they'd not yet retrieved it. But I had made everything up. From all I had read, there was no Confederate treasure, just rumors and legends. At that point, I didn't really care; my book was selling well.

One sunny October morning I was at a local festival where I had set up my table to sell books. An older gentleman approached me, saying that he had read the new book and thought it was quite good. He appeared to be in his late seventies, perhaps older. I had never met him personally, but I knew his name and several of his family members. He had moved away when I was a child. He said, "You know, we used to own a farm right close to where Jefferson Davis's party camped for the night when they were running from the Yankees." I replied that I didn't, and he continued, "Most folks think those stories about buried treasure are just a bunch of fairy tales, but they are not. Let me show you something."

He reached in his pocket and pulled out a well-used leather wallet. Fishing around inside he extracted a worn but legible Mexican Peso dating from the 1850s. "See this," he said, "I think that's part of the Confederate treasure." I was stunned. The old man went on to tell me how in the 1940s he had been out with a logging crew cutting timber. While clearing a path into the forest, they pushed over an old dead tree trunk. As its roots emerged from the ground a mass of dark metal objects were thrown up with them. These turned out to be a horde of Mexican silver coins. "We split 'em up," he said. "Everybody got a few. I've carried this one in my wallet ever since. Good luck, you know. Had to be some of the Confederates that buried 'em there." I never saw the gentleman again. He's been dead now for a number of years. Subsequently, I have been shown a ten-dollar gold piece owned by a family that traces its roots to Lincoln County, Georgia. I was told quite reliably that it was part of the Richmond bank gold that traveled south with Jefferson Davis's party, which was looted from Federal troops in May 1865. Sometimes what we believe to be fiction is based on truth.

Chapter 6: The following chart presents a numerical picture of the effects of the negation of the "Three-Fifths Clause" (Article 1, Section 2, Paragraph 3) of the United States Constitution by the Thirteenth Amendment.

Chart Comparing the Effect of Freed Slaves in Calculating

CONGRESSIONAL REPRESENTATION IN THE ELEVEN STATES OF THE FORMER CONFEDERACY

State	1860 Census: Total Population Free and Enslaved	Slaves	Slaves as Percent of Total Population	Population for Congressional Apportionment Prior to 13th Amendment	Percent Increase with Freed Slaves Counted After 13th & 14th Amendments
Alabama	964,201	435,080	45.12	790,169	22.02
Arkansas	435,450	111,115	25.51	391,004	11.37
Florida	140,424	61,745	43.97	115,726	21.34
Georgia	1,057,286	462,198	43.72	872,406	21.19
Louisiana	708,002	331,726	46.85	575,311	23.06
Mississippi	791,305	436,631	55.18	616,652	28.32
North Carolina	992,622	331,059	33.35	860,198	15.39
South Carolina	703,708	402,406	57.18	542,745	29.66
Tennessee	1,109,801	275,719	24.84	999,513	11.03
Texas	604,215	182,566	30.22	531,188	13.75
Virginia	1,219,630	472,494	38.74	1,030,632	18.34
Totals	**8,726,644**	**3,502,739**	**40.14**	**7,325,548**	**19.13**

Ref: http://en.wikipedia.org/wiki/List_of_U.S._states_by_historical_population

Chapter 13: The authorship of works of history requires a strict observance of the facts. Speculation and conjecture are permitted but must be acknowledged as such. As noted in the overview for "The Golden Age of Cotton and Its Aftermath," the chapter titled "A Killing on Ring Jaw Bluff" originally appeared as a magazine article prior to its expanded metamorphosis into a full-length book of the same name. In the book version, I go into far more detail about the life and times of Charlie Rawlings, including his run-in with the Ku Klux Klan. Succinctly put, Charlie was not only a philanderer, he was someone whose tastes crossed racial lines. For this apparent reason he was waylaid and castrated by the Ku Klux Klan, probably in 1921.

In writing both the article and subsequently the book, I had at my disposal a complete transcript of one of the murder trials. In reading it in detail, one cannot help but be convinced of the almost certain fact that Noah Covington was a liar and that the judge showed a significant bias against the defense. For reasons of academic honesty, I could not and did not state this so bluntly in either the article or the book. There is little doubt in my mind that Charlie Rawlings was innocent of the crime for which he was convicted, a conclusion that seems most obvious based on the available facts. This raises one simple question: why?

As an author, one treads on dangerous ground when writing about family members, especially those accused of crimes or other malfeasance. I recall one friend, on hearing that I was writing a book on Uncle Charlie, accusing me of the dreaded sin of "ancestor rehabilitation," an attempt to absolve one's forebears of some sin or crime. This was not my intention. As far as I was initially concerned, the man was guilty. The fascination the story initially held for me was the tale of a wealthy but flawed man's fall from grace.

At the time Charlie was brought to trial, the Ku Klux Klan was at its peak. It was then, and for years remained, a prominent force in Johnson County. Charlie had angered the Klan. As has been adequately demonstrated in other situations, a Klan-dominated (or influenced) jury was often responsible for verdicts that seemed to fly in the face of evidence and facts. (See, for example, chapter 16, "Reign of Terror.") The Klan wanted him out of the way, and this was a good way to accomplish it. I suspect, without any documentation, that the jury was made up of Klan members or sympathizers, and perhaps the same can be said about the judge. Among the various possible explanations of the events of the summer of 1925, this explanation seems most reasonable. It is, needless to say, speculation on my part. I want to make that clear. The truth will never be known.

ACKNOWLEDGMENTS

Any published work is a joint effort of numerous individuals, among whom the author is only one. First and foremost, I must thank Dan Roper, publisher of *Georgia Backroads* magazine, for his encouragement and support over the past few years, not to mention his willingness to publish my articles. There are many others to whom I am most appreciative, including (in no particular order) my assistant Brandi Taylor, my office nurse Jessica Heldreth, and Kayla Jackson, who has always been willing to help with research and proofreading. My family has been supportive in their willingness to allow me the tremendous amount of time necessary to pursue research, read, and put the results on paper. The staffs of the rare book and manuscript libraries at both Emory University in Atlanta and the University of Georgia in Athens provided invaluable assistance in research. This book is my third work published by Mercer University Press. The staff there have been a pleasure to work with, making the sometimes technical and confusing process of editing and publication all the easier for me. And, as always, I owe an eternal debt of gratitude to the lovely Laura Ashley, my muse and confidant.

SOURCES AND FURTHER READING

The following is a cumulative listing of sources and resources provided at the end of the various sections of the text. The citations include not only those used as references, but also others of a topical nature related to individual chapters or eras.

Books, Pamphlets, and Related:

Balinski, Michel L. and H. Peyton Young. *Fair Representation: Meeting the Ideal of One Man, One Vote.* New Haven, CT: Yale University Press, 1982.

Beckert, Sven. *Empire of Cotton—A Global History*. New York: Alfred A. Knopf, 2014.

Bragg, William H. *De Renne: Three Generations of a Georgia Family*. Athens: University of Georgia Press, 1999.

Cadle, Farris W. *Georgia Land Surveying History and Law.* Athens: University of Georgia Press, 1991.

Casey, Robert J. and Mary Borglum. *Give the Man Room*. New York: Bobbs-Merrill Company, 1952.

Chalmers, David M. *Hooded Americanism.* Durham, NC: Duke University Press, 1987.

Chappell, Absalom H. *Miscellanies of Georgia, Historical, Biographical, Descriptive, Etc.* Part II. Atlanta: James F. Meegan, 1874.

Clark, Helen. *The Yazoo Land Fraud*. Louisville, GA: The Jefferson County Historical Society, 2009.

Coulter, E. Merton. *The South During Reconstruction 1865–1877*. Volume VIII of *A History of the South*. Baton Rouge: Louisiana State University Press, 1947.

Dattel, Gene. *Cotton and Race in the Making of America*. Chicago: Ivan R. Dee, 2009.

Davis, William C. *An Honorable Defeat: The Last Days of the Confederate Government.* New York: Harcourt, Inc., 2001.

Foner, Eric. *Reconstruction: America's Unfinished Revolution 1863–1877*. New York: Harper & Row, 1988.

Foster, Gaines M. *Ghosts of the Confederacy.* New York: Oxford University Press, 1987.

Freeman, David B. *Carved in Stone: The History of Stone Mountain.* Macon, GA: Mercer University Press, 1997.

Hanna, Alfred J. *Fight into Oblivion*. Baton Rouge: Louisiana State University Press, 1999.

Harnden, Henry. *The Capture of Jefferson Davis*. Madison, WI: Tracy, Gibbs & Co, 1898.

Howard, Sidney. *GWTW—The Screenplay*. Edited by Richard Harwell. New York: Collier Books, 1980.

Jackson, Kenneth T. *The Ku Klux Klan in the City 1915–1930.* New York: Oxford University Press, 1967.

MacLean, Nancy. *Behind the Mask of Chivalry: The Making of the Second Ku Klux Klan.* New York: Oxford University Press, 1994.

McLendon, Samuel G. *History of the Public Domain of Georgia.* Atlanta: Foote & Davies Co., 1924.

McPherson, James M. *Ordeal by Fire: The Civil War and Reconstruction.* New York: Alfred M. Knopf, 1982.

Mirsky, Jeannette and Allan Nevins. *The World of Eli Whitney.* New York: The MacMillan Company, 1952.

The Myth of the Lost Cause and Civil War History. Edited by Gary W. Gallagher and Alan T. Nolan. Bloomington, IN: Indiana University Press, 2000.

Polakoff, Keith I. *The Politics of Inertia: The Election of 1876 and the End of Reconstruction.* Baton Rouge: Louisiana State University Press, 1973.

Porcher, Richard D. and Sarah Fick. *The Story of Sea Island Cotton.* Layton, UT: Gibbs Smith, 2005.

Rawlings, William. *A Killing on Ring Jaw Bluff.* Macon, GA: Mercer University Press, 2013.

———. *The Second Coming of the Invisible Empire.* Macon, GA: Mercer University Press, 2016.

Shaff, Howard and Audrey K. Shaff. *Six Wars at a Time.* Freeman, SD: Pine Hill Press, 1985.

Stevens, William B. *A History of Georgia.* Vol. II. Philadelphia: E. H. Butler & Co., 1859.

Wade, Wyn C. *The Fiery Cross.* New York: Oxford University Press, 1987.

Wilson, Charles R. *Baptized in Blood: The Religion of the Lost Cause 1865–1920.* Athens, GA: University of Georgia Press, 2009.

Wilson, Steve. *The Making of Gone with the Wind.* Austin: University of Texas Press, 2014.

Woodward, C. Vann. *Reunion and Reaction: The Compromise of 1877 and the End of Reconstruction.* Boston: Little, Brown and Company, 1951.

Yafa, Stephen. *Cotton.* New York: Penguin Books, 2005.

Journals, Magazines, and Related Periodicals:

The American Historical Review. "Correspondence of Eli Whitney Relative to the Invention of the Cotton Gin." 3 (1897): 90–127.

Bell, Karen B. "The Ogeechee Troubles: Federal land Restoration and the 'Lived Realities' of Temporary Proprietors." *The Georgia Historical Quarterly.* 85 (2001): 375–97.

Borglum, Gutzon. "Engineering Problems to Be Met in Mountain Sculpture." *The Black Hills Engineer* (November 1930): 306–34.

Cason, Roberta F. "The Loyal League in Georgia." *The Georgia Historical Quarterly* 20 (1936): 125–53.

Coulter, E. Merton. "Cudjo Fye's Insurrection." *The Georgia Historical Quarterly* 38 (1954): 213–25.

Davis, Robert S. "The Georgia Odyssey of the Confederate Gold." *Georgia Historical Quarterly* 86 (2002): 569–86.

Elsmere, Jane. "The Notorious Yazoo Land Fraud Case" *The Georgia Historical Quarterly* 51 (1967): 425–42.

Formwalt, Lee W. "The Camilla Massacre of 1868: Racial Violence as Political Propaganda." *The Georgia Historical Quarterly* 71 (1987): 399–426.

The Gray Book. The Gray Book Committee, Sons of Confederate Veterans. Privately printed pamphlet, 1920.

Hayt, James A. "The Confederate Archives and Felix G. De Fontaine." *The South Carolina Historical Magazine* 57 (1956): 199–203.

Heath, William E. "The Yazoo Land Fraud." *The Georgia Historical Quarterly* 16 (1932): 274–91.

Irvine, Dallas D. "The Fate of the Confederate Archives." *The American Historical Review*. 44 (1939): 823–41.

Mackaye, Milton. "The Birth of a Nation." *Scribner's Magazine* 102 (1937): 40–46, 69.

Pell, Robert L. *The Lands Belonging to Robert L. Pell in the State of Georgia*. New York: Privately printed pamphlet, 1865.

INDEX

59th Georgia Regiment, CSA, 151-155
Adams, John Quincy, 26
Akerman, Amos T., 118
bank closures in Georgia between 1916 and 1925, 211
Beach, W. Roger. *See* oil well scams in Georgia.
Bealer, Alex W., 56
Birth of a Nation, The, 127, 137, 157-165, 223-224, 229
Bitzer, Billy, 161. See also *The Birth of a Nation*.
Black Codes, 95
boll weevil, 181, 190, 205-6, 210-213
Borglum, John Gutzon de la Mothe, 131-149; as a Klan member, 137-142, 145; early years, 133; fired by SMCMA, 146-147; plans for Stone Mountain Confederate Memorial, 134-135
Bourbon County, Georgia, 19
Breckinridge, John C., 61
Buchanan, James, 61n
Bulloch, Rufus, 110, 121
Children's Founders Roll. *See* Borglum, John Gutzon.
Chisholm vs. Georgia, 25
Clansman, The, 161, 223. *See also* Thomas F. Dixon, Jr.
commoditization of cotton in the World War I era, 208
Compromise of 1877, 103-104
Confederate gold. *See* Confederate Treasure
Confederate treasure, 47-53, 275-276; estimates of value, 48-49, 51; stolen by raiders, 51-52
Constitution of Confederate States of America (1861), 75-83; comparison to Constitution of US, 76; offered for sale (1883), 78-81; purchase by De Renne family, 82; purchase by University of Georgia, 83
Constitution of United States (1787/1789), 75; Fifteenth Amendment, 99, 105, 111; Fourteenth Amendment, 96, 99, 105, 111; Thirteenth Amendment, 92, 99-101, 105, 108, 277
Cook, Philip, 33, 39
cotton gin: social, political and economic significance 7, 14-15, 44, 206; and slavery, 7, 14-15, 44
cotton: varieties, 8
counties of modern Georgia: Baldwin 32n, 121, 122; Banks 32n; Barrow 31n; Bryan 35; Bulloch 35; Burke 30, 35, 107, 110, 111, 112, 115, 117, 120, 121; Camden 30, 35; Chatham 23, 30, 35; Clarke 32n; Columbia 35; Effingham 30, 35; Elbert 30; Emanuel 32n, 38n; Franklin 31, 32, 33, 35, 36; Glynn 30, 35; Greene 32n, 35, 115; Gwinnett 32n; Habersham 32n; Hall 32n; Hancock 32n, 35, 111; Hart 32n; Jackson 31n, 35; Jeff Davis 180, 182, 183; Jefferson 32n, 35, 110, 111, 114, 115, 175; Laurens 32n, 38, 58, 66, 115, 188, 189; Liberty 30, 31, 35; Lincoln 35, 52, 276; Madison 32; McIntosh 35; Montgomery 32n, 35, 36, 38, 64; Oconee 32n; Oglethorpe 32n, 35; Richmond 30, 35, 115; Screven 35; Stephens 32n; Tattnall 32n; Warren 35, 111; Washington 24, 30, 31-33, 35-36, 38, 108, 110-117, 120, 128, 151, 152, 155, 171, 174,

176, 178, 180, 182, 183, 186, 200, 211; Wilkes 30, 35, 38
Covington, Noah, 194-203
Danburg Crossroads, 52
Davis, Jefferson: details of capture, 55-73; disguised as female, 57, 67, 73; flight from Richmond, Virginia, 47-53; imprisoned after capture, 64n
Davis, Varina, 55-73
De Fontaine, Felix, 81-82
De Renne family, 82-83
deflation, economic, in the early 1920s. *See* Great Recession of 1920-1921.
Dixon, Thomas F., Jr., 161, 223. See also *The Clansman.*
Dred Scott vs. Sandford, 95, 96
Edward Young Clarke, 139, 142. *See also* Ku Klux Klan.
Edwards, Harry S., 144
Evans, Hiram W. *See* Ku Klux Klan.
Farrow, Henry P., 120-121.
Federal Farm Loan Act of 1916, 209-210
Fifteenth Amendment. *See* Constitution of the United States.
Fletcher vs. Peck, 25-26
Florida, purchase by United States (1819), 18n
Fortress Monroe, 64, 66
forty acres and a mule, 119
Fourteenth Amendment. *See* Constitution of the United States.
Frank, Leo Max, 222-223
Freedman's Land Insurrection, 108-122
Freedmen's Bureau, 87-88, 95-96
Goebbels, Josef, 158, 165
Golden Age of Cotton, 127, 128, 170
Gone With the Wind, 128, 128, 157-165
Grand Army of the Republic (GAR), 125, 126n, 159
Great Migration, 212
Great Recession of 1920-1921, 171, 181, 182, 210, 212
Greene, Catharine, 9, 14, 15
Griffith, David W., 161-162, 223. See also *The Birth of a Nation.*
Gunn, James, 21, 23
Hammond, James Henry, 44, 206
Hammond, Nathaniel J., 118
Hampton, Wade, 21
Handley, George, 32
Harris, Cordy. *See* Freedman's Land Insurrection.
Hayes, Rutherford B., 102-104
Head Right counties: actual land area vs. registered land area, 35
Henry, Patrick, 19
Industrial Revolution in England, 11
inflation, economic, in 1915-1920 era, 143, 170, 181, 209, 211-213
insurrections in Reconstruction Era, 109-110. *See also* Freedman's Land Insurrection.
Irwin, Jared, 24
Jackson, James, 23, 24
Jefferson, Thomas, 12, 20, 142n
Johnson, Andrew, 61n; ascension to presidency 93; conflicts with Congress, 93-97; Presidential Reconstruction, 94-97
Johnson, Herschel V., 114, 117-118
Jones, Charles C., Jr., 34n
kaolin in Georgia, 179,183, 202
Kilpatrick, Hugh J., 79
Knights of Mary Phagan. *See* Ku Klux Klan.
Ku Klux Klan, 211-254; Congressional hearings (1871), 223; Congressional hearings (1921), 228; David Curtiss Stephenson, 233-234; demographics of Klansmen, 229-230; Edward Young Clarke, 225-235; Elizabeth Tyler, 225-227, 231; first, second and third iterations, 219-221; Hiram Wesley Evans, 141, 231-235; Knights of the Ku Klux Klan Inc., 219-236; in Macon, Georgia in 1920s, 239-254; membership estimates at peak, 228-229; New York World exposé,

227-228; politicians as Klansmen, 232-233; propagation of the Klan, 226-227; similarity to fascism and Nazism in Europe of the same era, 235-236; source of name, 219; terminology and iconography, 224; William Joseph Simmons, 221-232
Ku Klux Movement, 88. *See also* Ku Klux Klan.
Land Grants: buying and selling of 32; corruption in obtaining 32-36; process of obtaining 30-31; "shingling" of 35-36
Land Lottery Act (1803), 36
Lincoln, Abraham, plans for national reconciliation post-Civil War, 93
Lost Cause, 57; background and definition, 125-128, 160-161; *See also* Borglum, John Gutzon.
Loyal League(s). *See* Union League(s)
Lukeman, Augustus, 147-148
Marshall Plan, 89
Mathews, George, 22-24, 34
Middle Georgia Oil & Gas Company. *See* oil well scams in Georgia.
Miller, Phineas, 9, 10-15
Mitchell, Margaret, 163
Morris, Joseph ("Joe"). *See* Freedman's Land Insurrection.
Morris, Robert, 21, 37
Mount Rushmore, 131, 147, 149
National Association for the Advancement of Colored People (NAACP), 162
Newsom, Solomon, 91
North American Land Company, 37-38.
O'Fallon, James, 20-21
oil exploration in Georgia, 175, 183
oil well scams in Georgia, 173-183
Pell, Robert E., 38-39
Personne, *See* De Fontaine, Felix
Phagan, Mary, murder of, 222
Pine Barrens Speculation, 29-40
Plane, Helen, 132-134, 136, 138, 143, 148
population settlement patterns in early post-colonial period, 3-4, 17-18, 30
presidential election of 1876, 102-104
Presidential Reconstruction, 94-97. *See also* Johnson, Andrew.
Radical Reconstruction, 97-104. *See also* Reconstruction Era.
Radical Republicans. *See* Reconstruction Era.
Randolph, Hollins N., 142-149
Rawlings, Charles G. ("Charlie"), 185-203; accused of murder, 192; early years and business success, 185-187; murder trials, 196-202
Reagan, John H., 59, 60, 62, 72
reapportionment, Congressional, in response to Thirteenth Amendment, 99-101
Reconstruction Amendments. *See* Constitution of the United States.
Reconstruction Era, 87-122; conditions in South during, 87, 101-102. *See also* Freedman's Land Insurrection.
Rescinding Act of 1796. *See* Yazoo Fraud
Riefenstahl, Leni, 157-159, 165
Rivers, Prince. *See* Freedman's Land Insurrection.
Sandersville, Georgia, 30, 56, 61, 62, 112-117, 120, 151, 154, 173, 178, 182, 184-203, 257-259
Scillius. *See* Jackson, James.
Selznick, David O., 163-164. See also *Gone with the Wind.*
Seward, William H., 91
sharecropping. *See* tenant farming.
Simmons, William J. *See* Ku Klux Klan.
Smith, James M., 114, 115, 116, 118, 122
Sons of Confederate Veterans (SCV), 126, 132, 159
Sparks, Thomas H., 151-155
Stephens, Alexander H., 76
Stephens Pottery, 121

Stephenson, David C. *See* Ku Klux Klan.
Stone Mountain Confederate Monumental Association (SMCMA). *See* Borglum, John Gutzon
Stone Mountain half-dollar, 144-145, 148-149
Stone Mountain: as a Lost Cause monument, 131-132, 135; relationship to Ku Klux Klan, 134, 137-138, 223. *See also* Borglum, John Gutzon.
Tanner, J. J., 191-202
Tarbutton, George A. ("Gus"), 185-203
Tarbutton, Herschel, 188-189
Telfair, Edward, 20
Ten Percent Plan, 93, 94
tenant farming, 114, 207
Terrell, Joseph M., 189
Terrell, William H., 132
The Birth of a Nation. See *Birth of a Nation, The.*
The Clansman. See *Clansman, The.*
Thirteenth Amendment. *See* Constitution of the United States.
Three-Fifths Compromise, 99, 277. *See also* Constitution of the United States.
Tilden, Samuel J., 102-104
Toombs, Robert A., 58
Treaty of Paris (1783), 18, 30
Treaty of San Lorenzo (1795), 20
Turner, Nat, 89
Tyler, Elizabeth. *See* Ku Klux Klan.
Union League(s), 88, 97, 98, 107, 109, 110, 115, 116, 117, 121
United Confederate Veterans (UCV), 126, 153, 159
United Daughters of the Confederacy (UDC), 65, 65, 126, 127, 131-138, 144, 146, 147, 159
United States Warehouse Act of 1916, 208
Venable, Samuel, 134, 138, 141, 142, 147
voting rights in Reconstruction Era, 97-100
Walker, Clifford, 147, 232, 246, 247, 252
Washington, George, 20
Watson, Thomas E. ("Tom"), 222, 228
Whitney, Eli, 4, 7-16, 43; association with Phineas Miller 12-14; early life 8-9; invention of the cotton gin 10-12; at Mulberry Grove 9-10
Wilkinson, James, 20
Wilson, James, 23
Wray, William A. ("Jaybird Wray"), 257-259
Yarbrough, Caesar Agustus ("C. A."), 248-254. *See also* Ku Klux Klan in Macon, Georgia in 1920s.
Yazoo Act of 1795. *See* Yazoo Fraud
Yazoo Fraud, 17-27; federal government bailout of deed-holders, 16, 26; loss of Georgia's western territory as a result, 26; Yazoo lands sale of 1789, 19-21; Yazoo lands sale of 1795, 21-26